Personalized Learning

Preparing High School Students to Create Their Futures

Edited by
Joseph DiMartino, John Clarke,
and Denise Wolk

A SCARECROWEDUCATION BOOK

The Scarecrow Press, Inc.
Lanham, Maryland, and Oxford
2003

A SCARECROWEDUCATION BOOK

Published in the United States of America
by Scarecrow Press, Inc.
A Member of the Rowman & Littlefield Publishing Group
4720 Boston Way, Lanham, Maryland 20706
www.scarecroweducation.com

PO Box 317
Oxford
OX2 9RU, UK

British Library Cataloging in Publication Information Available

Library of Congress Cataloging-in-Publication Data

Personalized learning : preparing high school students to create their
futures / edited by Joseph DiMartino, John Clarke, and Denise Wolk.
    p.   cm.
   "A ScarecrowEducation book."
   Includes bibliographical references.
   ISBN 0-8108-4530-X (cloth : alk. paper)—ISBN 0-8108-4531-8
(pbk. : alk. paper)
   1. Individualized instruction—United States—Case studies. 2.
High school teaching—United States—Case studies. 3. Educa-
tional change—United States—Case studies. I. DiMartino, Joseph.
II. Clarke, John H., 1943– III. Wolk, Denise, 1959–
LB1031 .P373 2003
371.39′4—dc21   2002010515

⊗ ™The paper used in this publication meets the minimum
requirements of American National Standard for Information
Sciences—Permanence of Paper for Printed Library Materials, ANSI/
NISO Z39.48-1992. Manufactured in the United States of America.

Contents

Editors' Foreword

This book represents the combined knowledge and experience of more than two dozen teachers, administrators, and researchers in the pursuit of creating a more personalized environment for high school students.

We have pulled together many pieces of a puzzle to create a complete picture of what personalized learning can be in high schools. Some chapters are written in the first person by classroom teachers and veteran administrators, while others are presented from the objective view of researchers. Most chapters offer a resource guide to consult for further information in its subject area. What we all have in mind are realistic ways to improve teaching and learning environments so high school students have the best possible atmosphere in which to learn and grow.

There is a growing body of evidence to support the notion that smaller, more personalized schools are better for both students and teachers. In a recent speech given to the National Alliance on the American High School in Providence, R.I., veteran school reformer Ted Sizer said there are three central changes all schools must make in order to improve student outcomes.

First, students must be known *exceedingly well* by adults in the school. There must be stability of assignment, and students should stay with the same group of peers and adults for the duration of their high school experience. School schedules must allow no more than 50 students to be in a group, and those students must have one-on-one adult interaction. Further, there must be a "ruthless focus" that will require choices to be made. Schools must simplify without cheapening what kids do.

Second, graduation and promotion must be based on demonstration of knowledge, not just testing. Sizer believes that students must demonstrate a real mastery of the subject. We must give students realistic targets to shoot for, and objectives and standards must be in language that students can understand. He says that faculty has to rethink how to get students from point A to point B with real knowledge. This is the most difficult intellectual challenge that teachers face.

Finally, he says that collaboration in schools must be intense. All members of a school community must interact and share with one another in order to serve kids well. Time must be allotted for professional development and planning, and we must consider what will hook kids to give them intellectual power and freedom to think for themselves.

In collaborating on *Personalized Learning: Preparing High School Students to Create Their Future,* we have designed a road map for educators who are embarking on the journey of changes that Sizer calls for.

Introduction

Honors Night

JOSEPH DIMARTINO
Education Alliance at Brown University

I sat alone at the Honors Night celebration on that June evening in 1995—mortified that my wife, Pat, had stormed out of the high school rather than suffer through another minute of hypocrisy. At that ceremony, we were lavished with praise for being outstanding parents. I sat alone through it all because Pat had the courage to express her indignation publicly by leaving. Maybe I should have joined her protest, but, as I sheepishly asked others for a ride home after the dinner was complete, I reflected on the events that prompted her to abandon the celebration of her parenthood in the middle of the principal's speech. Pat had launched her public demonstration against a school environment that had failed all of our children. She had seen better than I that perhaps all of the children who attend the American High School of the 20th century are being shortchanged in unnecessary ways. Her departure from the honors ceremony fueled my own quest for high schools that serve all students, a quest that now includes my part in developing this book with educators from across the Northeast.

FAILING EACH IN THE NAME OF ALL

To appreciate what precipitated Pat's demonstration, you will need some background on our family, our commitment to public education, and the events that led up to the emotions of "Honors Night." Having graduated from the schools in the same town, where both Pat and I had strong family roots, I was convinced that our children would benefit from exposure to diverse learners and ethnic populations who fill our high school. After all, the high school had worked well enough for me and for all my siblings. Our family had developed the belief that it is the public's obligation to provide a high quality education for all—the foundation of a democratic society. So, we were unprepared for the inequities and shortfalls that we would discover as our children advanced through public schools.

In the fall of 1985, Pat and I made a life-changing decision to complete our family by adopting two older boys from Guatemala. Mauricio was twelve years old at the time and Erick was six, making a family of six children, all approaching high school age. Tom, a biological son and our oldest, was twelve years old that summer. Mick, who was adopted from Korea in 1981, was ten. Gina, adopted from Korea as an infant in 1976, was also ten. And Lisa, a biological daughter, was eight. It was that fall when we began to despair for the fate of public education in America. Clustered from age eight to twelve, our children began to prepare for high school in the '90s.

In 1981, when Mick was adopted, we had been totally oblivious of the needs of children from a different culture that spoke a different language. We enrolled Mick in a regular kindergarten program and waited while everyone assured us that it would take a year for him to be fully fluent in English. When he began to fall behind in the first grade and was referred for special education services, we were thankful for what we perceived to be the knowledge and caring that would address Mick's specific "learning disability." Five years later, Mauricio and Erick came to this country speaking only Spanish. We also were aware that their schooling in Guatemala had been woefully inadequate. It was obvious to us that the boys, especially Mauricio in the fifth grade, would need more than a year's kindergarten to catch up to their peers in their command of the English language.

Although we requested that Mauricio and Erick be placed in the elementary school that our other four children had attended, we were informed that the only way they could get English as a Second Language (ESL) services was to be bused to an elementary school several miles away. At Mauricio's and Erick's school open house that fall, we discovered that the boys had been placed in basement classrooms which had been a wood storage closet and a locker room when I had attended junior high in that very same building. We were firsthand witnesses to the "services gap" that is the precursor of the achievement gap in high school that so often occurs for children of different cultural backgrounds. The dark basement setting where our boys were first exposed to the "promise" of an American education was a despairing place indeed!

As we began to understand how the ESL program worked, we also came to the realization that we had already failed Mick, our Korean son, who had been tagged as a special education student in his elementary years. His only "learning disability" was that he spoke a different language and experienced his formative years in a cultural setting that is unfamiliar to us here in America. Rather than receiving special education remediation, he needed to be taught English as a second language. During the next several years as we advocated for better educational conditions for all immigrant children, we saw that our problems were not unique. In school after school, we encountered the same low expectations, poor facilities, and highly impersonal programs.

Mauricio is an outstanding athlete with a winning personality who tries hard to please. In high school, he wasn't any trouble in his classes. In fact, he had a calming influence on those around him. He was careful to turn in all his homework assignments, so he got through high school with reasonably good grades. But, as we so rudely discovered, he was nowhere near possessing the minimal skills needed to succeed in college. In Mauricio's high school classes, virtually every teacher counted the completion of homework as 25 to 30 percent of the final grade. Also, in every one of those classes, the homework was not examined to determine whether it was done properly. Mauricio's desire to please resulted in his always turning in his homework. (Amazingly, it didn't seem curious at the time that he seemed to always have a girlfriend who was in all of the same classes that he was.) So, Mauricio, by merely turning in all of his homework and by getting the additional 25 percent of the grade that accompanied good behavior in class, started out with fifty points toward his term grade. He could bring that up to a solid "C" average without knowing much of anything at all!

When faced with 130 sets of homework papers daily, a cursory two-minute examination of each of them would require more than four hours of a teacher's time! Besides, the teachers had no way of knowing whether any individual student had actually done the homework alone, or whether it was merely copied from a friend's copy. In 1916, Professor Eugene C. Brooks, a North Carolina professor, concluded that because of homework, schools either "consciously or unconsciously" reproduce social inequality. Unfortunately, we discovered this too late.

During that fateful second semester in 1995, Erick began running from school, the first of what would turn out to be Erick's three years as a high school freshman. Erick repeated the ninth grade three times because he hadn't earned enough credits to advance to sophomore standing. He absolutely hated being at the school. We spent much of the semester doing all that we could to get Erick to go to school. We would drag him to the front entrance kicking and screaming. At the first opportunity, he would escape out a back door. At that time, the consequence for leaving school without permission was a three-day suspension—four free days for the price of one.

While he wouldn't admit it at the time, we are certain that Erick felt incapable of doing the work at the school. Not being seen as stupid by his peers was very important to him. In the culture that existed in the high school with his friends, it was okay for him to be delinquent but it was decidedly not cool to be dumb! During that semester, his English teacher called for a disciplinary meeting because of his failure to attend her class—a memorable meeting with the assistant principal. In fact, on days when Erick was actually in school, he would often sneak up to the library rather than attend this particular class. I asked if she could just tell us about something she had done that might make Erick want to be in her class. She stuttered and made it very clear to us that she had made no attempt to make her class appealing to students. "After all, this is high school and high schools don't do such things as make learning interesting or entertaining." Unfortunately, the whole high school day leaves little room for student interests or aspirations to be considered as integral to their learning.

Mick's first semester grades included a grade in meteorology that was so low that passing the course was an impossibility. Although he had accumulated enough total credits, Mick would not be able to graduate with his class because failing in May would leave him one credit short of the science requirement. In a flurry of meetings at the school, we sought ways to allow Mick to meet the science requirement in an alternative way. School policy allowed students who failed a course to be tutored for thirty hours on the same content, giving the student a grade for the tutoring to be averaged in with the class grade. After suggesting this course of action, we were informed that the policy existed only for students who had actually failed a course. Mick had not yet failed the course and would not be allowed to utilize the tutoring option until he did.

Still struggling to get Mick through high school, we discovered that the local community college offered a course that he could take that would allow him to meet the science requirement. When we asked about that possibility, we were informed that the courses at the community college were semester courses. Even though the content covered in the course was comparable to the high school course, it did not include enough seat time to earn the one Carnegie Unit necessary to meet the graduation requirement. Again, the rules prevailed over common sense.

As the year was drawing to a close, Pat and I had come to be seen by both teachers and administrators alike as the most annoying and irresponsible parents in the town. Teachers and administrators at the school made it clear that they believed a lack of appropriate parental guidance was behind the failure of Mauricio, Mick, and Erick. During the same semester, Tom, who had always been motivated for good grades but never became truly engaged in learning, was getting by but clearly not excelling as a junior at Drew. Gina, a strong student in high school, was struggling as a freshman at Wheaton College. With the receipt of her first semester grades, we discovered that Gina was totally unprepared to deal with the quantity of research and writing that was required at a competitive college. We also received Mauricio's first semester grades at Salve Regina College. It was only then that we realized that he had somehow managed to get through high school without learning anything. Their college malaise brought us to a rude awakening. High school had failed to prepare all our children, even those who seemed successful.

HONORING THE FEW WHO FIT

It was against this backdrop that we attended honors night. Lisa was graduating in the top 5 percent of her class and was receiving recognition for that accomplishment. At honors night, we were being praised as outstanding parents—all because Lisa happened to be the kind of student who could do well in that high school setting. After a certain amount of praise from the podium, Pat tapped me on the shoulder and whispered, "What do you think was harder, getting Mick to miss graduation by one credit or getting Lisa to make honors?" A few minutes passed and Pat poked me again. "Look around the room. Do you think any of these parents could have gotten Mick to graduate with his class?" Another few minutes and more praise for the parents in the room and I got another poke. By this time the pokes were stronger. "How much harder was it for us to get Mauricio, Erick, and Mick an adequate education through high school than it was for Gina, Lisa, and Tom?" Her face was getting red. The final poke came from a rigid finger with a sharp fingernail and caused some serious pain. "Don't you think that Lisa could have learned just as much if she had been given the course syllabi and a library card?"

I knew the answer to these questions. We believed that Lisa, Tom, and Gina would have learned just as much with the syllabi and library card as from fitting into the four-year high school system. We also knew that for every hour we spent supporting, monitoring, or advocating for Lisa, Tom, or Gina, we spent at least *one hundred hours* doing the same for Mauricio, Mick, or Erick. The school had made no effort to gain from the vast knowledge and experiences our children brought to school. So as the principal congratulated us again for Lisa's school achievement, Pat staged her lonely protest and stormed out of the room. I wished I had joined her.

PERSONALIZED LEARNING FOR EACH STUDENT

Although our children have moved on, we have continued to push the school district to seek ways to reach all of the students who attend the high school. During the next school year, I discovered that the State Department of Education reported that the dropout rate in our high school had soared from 17 percent to 46 percent! When I reported this publicly at a school board meeting, the board attempted to deny the veracity of the numbers. After much discussion, the superintendent in our district decided to form a committee to look into the cause and suggest strategies to address the dropout problem. Naturally, I volunteered to be part of the effort. And, since we had new administrative leadership in the district, someone who truly cared about making school a success for all students, I was asked to serve! I immediately accepted.

When I took a new position as director for Student Centered Learning of the Northeast and Islands Regional Educational Laboratory at Brown University, the LAB joined my town to conduct a survey of dropouts. This study, which included open-ended interviews of dropouts, documented a deep sense of alienation and anger that these former students had for their high school. When asked why they dropped out of school, virtually all of the respondents began by taking all of the blame on themselves. When we asked why other students quit school, the tone of our conversations changed, and the students began to identify problems that they had with the school. Their own sense of disenfranchisement became very apparent.

Nearly all of the students felt that the high school didn't care about "kids like me." They stated that teachers, and particularly administrators, cared about some other group or groups of students much more than their group. The identified groups were not always the same. It might have been the college prep students, the special education students, or the athletes, but it was always a group other than the respondent's group. Higher achieving students felt that the school favored athletes and special needs students. The athletes thought that the high achievers were favored. The special needs students thought that the school favored athletes. And, the immigrants felt particularly disenfranchised, believing that all were favored over them.

All those students who had chosen to drop out of school felt that the school didn't care about them. Their emotions are best illustrated by the student who said, "Teachers only care about smart kids." Interestingly, one respondent recognized his own favor in the school: "Teachers favor a lot of people, and have problems with others. I was one of the favored ones." A majority of the respondents' comments included statements that expressed disenfranchisement, such as "teachers (and/or administrators) don't care about me." Furthermore, an even greater majority commented that boredom was a significant factor in the decision to drop out. One student, when asked if he felt working too many hours outside of school was a contributing factor stated, "The real issue is at school. Not work."

Many of our interviewees mentioned the guidance they received at the school. In some instances students reported that guidance-related problems profoundly affected them. In one case a student discovered halfway through his senior year that an art class he had taken at a neighboring school could not be counted toward graduation credit because he had taken a similar course in his ninth grade year at a private high school. In another case a student discovered that he would be unable to graduate with his class without incurring substantial tutoring expenses in order to make up for a lost credit. He chose to take the GED instead. Another student contended that guidance had made a mistake in calculating his credits. He, too, found out late in his senior year that an error had been made and he wouldn't be able to graduate. Another student, responding to uncaring attitudes, simply said, "Guidance there stinks."

Our dropout study also included interviews with the parents of dropouts. Even though the families were more likely to allocate a good portion of the blame to their children, they expressed strong feelings of bitterness towards the high school. Most mentioned that their children were disenfranchised by the schools. Their perception was that the school didn't care to have their son or daughter in attendance. One mother stated, "Teachers have no patience for anything." Another alleged that she witnessed a guidance counselor tell her son, "You might just as well quit school." The parent's perception was that the statement was intended to urge her son to drop out. Another mother complained, "It wasn't cool to ask for help. Teachers should know to offer help in a quiet way." Yet another mother offered, "Public school teachers don't care as much as parochial teachers do."

The families agreed that guidance offered by the school did not benefit, and sometimes hurt, their children. They saw the guidance counselors as the implementers of the "Space Takers" contracts. These contracts were a creation of the school's administration. The contracts were aimed at any student over age sixteen who was not attending at least 75 percent of classes and who had a history of failing several subjects or who was considered a troublemaker. One of the conditions of these contracts was that if a student missed more than ten days of school in a quarter, he or she would be dismissed from school. One mother stridently complained about the contract, saying, "The contract takes control away from the parents. It tells the student if you don't go you'll get thrown out. It rewards the kids [who are dismissed] because they don't want to be there anyway."

During this time, I was acting as an educational surrogate parent for a number of adolescents who had special education needs and who were wards of the state. Many of these youths were in alternative educational settings. All had Individualized Education Plans. In many cases these IEPs worked extremely well in engaging the student in his or her own education, allowing them to have a strong role in establishing personalized learning goals and evidence of the achievement of those goals. The IEP could also provide a variety of methods for measuring progress toward goals. In short, the IEP planning and monitoring could become a positive tool for improving engagement and learning for students, if parents and caring adults were included. However, in schools where the meetings were more like contract negotiations between a special education administrator and parent or guardian without including all the adults that had contact with the student, there was less likelihood of success. If an IEP process could succeed in linking learning to an individual's goals, why not develop IEPs with all students, using their parents and teachers as guides and mentors for the special journey each must take to assume control over their own lives—and improve life in their communities?

AIMING REFORM AT PERSONALIZED LEARNING

Beginning in the spring of 1996, I began to see positive interest developing in personalized learning. At its annual meeting, the National Association of Secondary School Principals (NASSP) published *Breaking Ranks: Changing an American Institution,* which had been developed with support from the Carnegie Foundation for Teaching. In it, NASSP, which up until that time had been considered the staunchest promoter of the status quo, publicly acknowledged that our high schools needed to make radical changes in order to succeed with all students. *Breaking Ranks* delivered the message that "the high school of the 21st Century must be much more student-centered and above all much more personalized in programs, services and intellectual rigor."

In this book, we highlight current initiatives that aim to personalize learning for each high school student. The first section focuses on Personalized Learning Plans that tie learning to the talents and aspirations of each person. The second section focuses on classroom teaching that allows individuals to gain knowledge while pursuing their own interests. The third section describes high school designs that engage students in democratic processes. The fourth describes systemic changes that must accompany and support personalized learning for all students. The book is organized to provide a different entry point for people who are beginning to imagine high school learning based on personal engagement working at any level of school organization. Our writers are practitioners with practical interest in moving high schools toward personalization. Each of us is writing about what we have learned from experience and examined through research. A completely personalized high school may not yet exist, but its potential exists in the stories and thoughts you will encounter here.

I believe that the ideas described in these chapters would certainly have improved the high school experience for each of my very different children. If Tom had participated in some learning experiences outside the school walls, such as the internships at Montpelier High School, he might very well have developed a love of learning that he would be able to carry with him throughout his adult life. Perhaps Gina would have been better prepared for her college experience if she had had the opportunity to complete a yearlong senior project requiring substantial amounts of research, writing, and performance exhibitions, as is required at Souhegan High School in Amherst, New Hampshire. I suspect that Mauricio would have learned much more and been much better prepared for higher education if he had attended a high school like East Side High in Manhattan, where student work is the subject of study. Personal profiles and performance graduation requirements would not have allowed him to graduate without the skills necessary to be successful in college. I am convinced that if Mick had been allowed to pursue study in his own interest, as is done at the Met school in Providence, Rhode Island, he would have become more engaged in learning in many areas. Thus, he would not only have graduated with his class; he would know and be able to do much more than he currently does, with added self-confidence gained from hands-on experience. Lisa, who is civic-minded and caring toward others, would certainly have benefited from attending a high school with a strong emphasis on service at the heart of learning. A program such as Side by Side (highlighted in Chapter 7) would have made Lisa's high school experience much more enjoyable and meaningful for her. And, if Erick had the connection to an adult advisor and a personalized learning plan in the school such as exists at Montpelier or Mount Abraham Union High Schools, he would not have been alienated as he was, running from the school at every opportunity.

High school reform has had a disappointing history in American education because most reform initiatives overlook a defining attribute of young adult learners—their drive to establish an independent identity in their community. To date, the effort to change high schools has consisted largely of setting standards for all high school students, an approach that seeks uniformity of achievement among high school graduates—clearly a worthwhile goal. However, standards-based reform can be implemented in ways that prove unsuccessful because they fail to address a major condition of adolescence and young adulthood: burgeoning individuality, often manifested as rebellious determination not to be treated as members of any category as youths are striving for independence and responsibility.

The standards movement has already shown how imposing a single set of expectations on young adults may modestly improve test scores but fail to engage their minds. Throughout the high school years, students are growing increasingly determined to explore their uniqueness and assert an independent pathway into adult life. Young adults are driven to create and express a personal role in the adult world around them. Facing adult challenges in a highly complex society, high school students respond actively to learning opportunities in high school when they can assume increasing responsibility for plotting their own course. Changing high schools so every student meets common standards while designing and pursuing a unique pathway toward adult roles is the purpose of personalized learning—and this book.

Ruth Simmons, the newly named president of Brown University, has described her own experience with emotions that Pat and I were feeling at Honors Night in 1995. Phyllis Wheatley High School, where she had graduated, is no longer the place she remembers from her youth. When she visits Wheatley now, she senses a sadness there, a lack of excitement:

> A school ought to be a magical place where you are queen or king, and where what you get to do is to focus on your intellect, and on what you can accomplish as a human being, and you come to understand what your life can be. That's what school should be for children. Not a place where you go to study for a standardized test. Not a place where you go where you hear every day about the problems that you are. Not a place where you go where people tell you that you are under-performing. Not a place where you go where people tell you that you are part of some pathology.
>
> That's not what a school is supposed to be. School is supposed to be full of hope, and it's a place where you go to find out how magical your mind is and how terrific it will be when you develop your mind to its full potential. (*Washington Post*, March 21, 2001)

Personalized Learning: Preparing High School Students to Create Their Futures presents a rationale and best methods for adapting the high school experience to fit the talents and inclinations of students who grow increasingly more unique as they approach their graduation. Written by seasoned educators who have developed, studied, and practiced ways to institute "personalized learning" in the often impersonal machinery of the comprehensive high school, this book constitutes a general guide to reform-oriented educators throughout the United States. Personalized Learning Plans, community-based learning, project-based teaching, standards-based portfolios, and transcripts certifying high performance constitute a comprehensive reform strategy for high school learning that permits individual students to develop and demonstrate their unique talents and interests. Data-informed school development strategies that celebrate the growth of individual performance are proving to be powerful methods for engaging a high school faculty in reforming its own practice. This book presents personalized learning as the proper focus for high school reform, grounded in the concrete experience of writer-educators who have been working at all levels of high school organization throughout the country.

When Learning Matters

Using Learning Plans to Educate One Student at a Time

ELLIOT WASHOR
The Metropolitan Career and Technical Center,
Providence, Rhode Island

One hundred years ago in *Atlantic Monthly*, William James wrote, "In children we observe a ripening of impulses and interests in a certain determinate order. Creeping, walking, climbing, imitating, vocal sounds, constructing, drawing, calculating, possess the child in succession. Of course, the proper pedagogic moment to work in skill and to clinch the useful habit is when the native impulse is most acutely present. Crowd on the athletic opportunities, the mental arithmetic, the verse-learning, the drawing, the botany, or what not, the moment you have reason to think the hour is ripe."

James' thoughts make me believe that when learning matters, schools are student-centered. They are places that encourage, generate, and sustain the abilities and talents of every child. Our schools need to be places where learning matters, but instead most of the time they are places where only what is being taught matters. From early on the content starts to matter more than learning it. This includes at what grade material is taught, rather than what students are learning.

Ian Kelly, a first grade student living in Ireland, recently presented me with a telling riddle to ponder that went like this:

*Question: Who's still talking when everyone has stopped listening?
Answer: The teacher.*

This riddle lets us in on the secret that every child knows—that in school, teaching matters more than learning.

This chapter will focus on the importance of creating student-centered learning environments using Personalized Learning Plans (PLPs) to engage students in their own learning experiences. I discuss my own experience with the difference between the PLPs used at the Met and the Individualized Education Plans (IEPs) that are commonly used for students with special needs. The importance of creating a supportive link between the student, their family, advisor, and mentors in creating a challenging and personalized educational plan for every student is crucial, and examples of how the process works at the Met are presented here. By allowing students the opportunity to learn using hands-on experience they are able to demonstrate proficiency through a variety of nontraditional methods. In the end, we have found that students with PLPs are able to utilize the experience they've gained to determine their future goals for college and beyond.

THE MET

The Metropolitan Regional Career and Technical Center (the Met) is a six-year-old Rhode Island public high school with a mission to rethink and revamp the entire delivery of secondary school education. As researcher Adria Steinberg puts it, the Met "turns education on its head" by starting with the student instead of with a preset curriculum and classroom structured learning. The Met is a school that uses real-world experiences to build skills and knowledge, one student at a time. By engaging its students in real projects with working adults, the Met prepares them for college, work, and citizenship. It demonstrates how effective a school can be when the entire community is a resource for education.

All Met students have their own Personalized Learning Plan based on their particular interests, which are continually updated by the student and her teacher, parents, and mentors. Met students are intrinsically motivated to learn, because they have a say in choosing the work they do.

To carry out their learning plans, Met students establish a unique intern relationship called Learning Through Internship (LTI) with a mentor in the community. The LTI is based on the premise that adolescents need to learn in real-world settings and interact effectively with adults. The primary function of the school is to provide the infrastructure that supports experimental learning. The student works on learning goals and develops a portfolio of work as evidence of achieving those goals. The mentor is a role model, content expert, and learning resource.

Over the years, we have enhanced our work around learning plans so they have changed and evolved as we have changed. We have connected them and acculturated them into the Met as we grew from using them with incoming ninth graders to translating learning plans into a driving force for our students' entry into Senior Institute in the eleventh grade and as a resource for our innovative college transcript. The Met's evolution of the learning plan is a statement of what educators can do to make a community accountable for learning and engage families in learning if educators have students and families in mind.

All schools are mandated to use learning plans for children with special needs, but does this ensure that learning is personalized? Mandates do not ensure that learning plans are student-centered and that learning really matters. A student-centered environment is key to the success of learning plans that allow for accountability, flexibility, and family engagement.

MICHAEL'S STORY: IEP VERSUS PLP

The following story is my own account of my son Michael's Individualized Education Plan (IEP) meeting from a school he attended. Here I'm in the role of parent.

In his middle grades my son Michael was diagnosed with a language/reading disability. I will share here what transpired at a learning plan (Individualized Education Plan) meeting at his middle school. These meetings are mandatory for any child who is diagnosed as Special Needs.

As I went into the room you could see some of the testers talking with each other but keeping their distance from me. There were eight or ten people assembled in a circle. The group included the guidance counselor, special education teacher, school psychologist, two school testers, the assistant principal, and two of Michael's teachers. There were eight staff members from the school, and myself as a parent. It was quite intimidating.

The guidance counselor started the meeting. She introduced everyone and then asked the school psychologist to present and analyze the results of their test and observational data. It seems that their data showed Michael was easily distracted, tended to daydream, did a lot of drawing but was not a discipline problem. One tester said he fit into the average range of intelligence, showing some deficits and confusion when it came to putting details together. Another said his issues in learning to write are that his fine motor coordination is below par. One by one, each person talked about Michael through their data either from formalized tests or his grades in school. As the meeting went on one or two more of his teachers came in late and joined us around the circle. Each one pointed out Michael's deficits. It was a very uncomfortable feeling for everyone sitting around the table. I didn't know anyone there.

As they presented their evaluations and remediations, it was also clear that some were uncomfortable talking, some even broke out in hives, and others were displaying their discomfort through their body language.

From my perspective, it was uncomfortable as a parent to hear qualified educational experts talk about my child using test data and a smattering of observations. The intent is to somehow use scientific instruments that give a profile of a child but nothing can be further from the truth. I can't believe the original intent of any law was to mandate testing over really knowing a child well.

All the while I sat there listening, and I must confess I was doodling a bit to deal with my uneasiness. Finally, the guidance counselor said in summation, "So it seems everything is going along well. Michael is receiving some extra support in reading and language development. We are working on his writing. Thanks for coming. Do you have any questions?"

Now, no one in the room knew me, and they only learned that I was a principal because I told them that during our introductions. I said, "I have some things to say. First, all of you talked about Michael through your findings but do you really know my son? Do any of you know he is a protégé jazz guitarist who practices three hours a night? Do you realize the tremendous intellectual focus, concentration and dexterity it takes to play an instrument at that level? Do you know that athletically he is the fastest student in the school? (So much for his fine or gross motor coordination issues.) And do you know that he is well liked and respected by other students and seems to get along well with all the teachers in the building? People on both sides of his family have been musicians and artists for generations. This may account for his doodling but maybe not. Maybe he is not connected to what he is doing in school. You said, he is easily distracted, and doodles. Do his doodles look anything like this?" I turned the paper I was doodling on around so all could see. I smiled and everyone was a bit relieved. I did this in a way that was not casting blame but opening up a conversation about looking at the strengths and weaknesses. As my friend Bill Ayers from Chicago says, "our primary responsibility as teachers is to give hope."

After my comments we really started talking about Michael. It was apparent that these folks really do care about children, but there is no way in this system for people to really care. There was no way for these educators to really look at the whole child, their strengths and weaknesses, and build learning environments that will use strengths to get at a weakness.

Like most systems there is a distrust of parents as part of the educational planning, where they could be used as a resource. The work of student learning is relegated to what has been mandated either as remedial plans or standards-based reform. These mandates take all the craft, art, and in many cases, even the technical components out of teaching and learning. It is exactly the idea Dewey warned us about when he stated, "All reforms which rest simply upon the enactment of law, or the threatening of certain penalties, or upon changes in mechanical or outward arrangements, are transitory or futile."

Michael is now in his junior year at the Met. It is the third year he has had a learning plan where he, his parents, advisors/teachers and mentors have been involved in his learning, and we all know one another well. Everyone is encouraged to sit in on his learning plan meetings. His learning has evolved over the years to a place where things in Michael's life make sense for the person he is, where he wants to go, and what he wants to learn.

THE IMPORTANCE OF FAMILY ENGAGEMENT

My voice is that of a parent and an educator when I agree with Cremin's (1975) statement "the real message of the Coleman and Jencks studies of equal educational opportunities: not that the school is powerless but that the family is powerful." Family engagement at the Met is very different than most schools, and our learning plan meetings are a major part of the difference. The average family comes to the Met to learning plan meetings and exhibitions seven times a year. In the past, these families rarely went into their children's schools. In my own experience, I went to my son's school only for parent night, one or two events, and an IEP meeting. It was not that I didn't want to go to the school; it was that there was nothing for me to go to. As a matter of fact, one time I wanted to see the principal and the secretary told me I would have to wait three weeks for an appointment. The tipping point that gets families engaged at the Met is that families are used as a resource at learning plan meetings and are an important part of the learning process.

Families are not only participants in learning plans but at times are the topic of a project. A Met graduate who is now attending college in Rhode Island did a project on fibromyalgia, a condition with which her mom was diagnosed. This project illustrates the depth of the work that can be accomplished through an LTI, and how Met learning goals are woven into the academic needs of a student and agreed on at a learning plan meeting.

When Priscilla Santana came back to school in the fall of tenth grade, she had a new interest. Her mother had had carpal tunnel surgery over the summer and was doing physical therapy as part of her recovery. Priscilla's interest was awakened to physical therapy, and she decided that she wanted to learn more, both for herself and to help her mother. After searching, interviewing, and job shadowing, she started an LTI with a mentor in a physical therapy clinic. At a learning plan meeting, Priscilla, her mentor, her parents, and her advisor, Rachel, identified a product that the clinic needed, and it became Priscilla's responsibility and the basis for her project.

The following is an excerpt from Priscilla's learning plan on the project proposal:

Product:

An informational pamphlet for patients recently diagnosed with the condition fibromyalgia.

Investigation:

First try: Why do there seem to be more cases of fibromyalgia diagnosed in Rhode Island than in Florida as my mentor thinks from talking to another physical therapist down there? Is it doctor diagnosis and referral to physical therapy? Is it weather-related? Are there more retirees in Florida and therefore it's work-related? What accounts for the difference?

Second try: A thorough understanding of fibromyalgia, its causes, manifestations and various treatment options. Learn the "tender points" used to diagnose patients. Understand the physics of torque for biomechanics and how this translates to lifting objects.

Reflection:
(Synopsis of student's journal writing and student narrative.)

The first investigation didn't work because fibromyalgia is a recently developed diagnosis and even the Center for Disease Control had no information. I planned to survey doctors but when I tried to set up an interview with a doctor to look at my survey, he didn't respond. I had no idea that this kind of information might not be available yet and that it would be so hard to get doctors. This was frustrating and made me nervous because I was worried my project wouldn't be good. But then Rachel (my advisor) helped me see that it just meant sometimes projects don't go the way you plan and you have to be on top of it and make a change when you need to. So that's when we changed to the second investigation and I did all the research.

I was so surprised that I could read a lot of the medical journals and get the information I needed. My mentor also helped me by answering my questions to understand what I was reading about. I learned a lot of new terms like pressure points and bone names and what it meant that there might be a disease. I was also surprised to learn about how torque is measured in lifting objects. And when I had to put it all together, I learned how to use PageMaker to put it on a computer layout.

I learned so much in this project, not just about this syndrome, but also about myself and how I learn and how I do a project.

The concept of LTIs goes hand in hand with developing learning plans and portfolios for post–high school goals, whether it's college, vocational school, and apprenticeships or directly to work. From working on their learning plans, each student will have a portfolio that allows him or her to customize all of their experiences for application to each college or work situation.

Throughout this project Priscilla's parents, her mentor, and her teacher were all in agreement about her learning. Priscilla is now pursuing a college education. Her parents have been part of her education at the Met from her beginning enrollment. They have watched her develop interests in writing, poetry, and nursing. They have questioned her on her learning journey as well as got to know her teacher, Rachel; her mentors; and her principals. The learning plan meeting is one of the key places where this forum takes place and everyone can be accountable.

LEARNING PLANS AND ACCOUNTABILITY

The notion of high stakes accountability has been thrust on schools from the many varied constituencies that want schools to show what children are learning, and to be more precise, to see if what is being taught is being learned, and why it is not. Being accountable is one of those ideas that everyone agrees on, for surely students, schools, teachers, and parents must account for learning. For the most part, accountability has been measured by whether a child achieves a given content or skill standard by passing a test on a certain amount of information.

On the other hand, learning plans offer a way to account for student learning one student at a time, by literally bringing everyone to the table to agree upon what the goals for learning are in a given amount of time, and over an extended period of time. This is what happens at the Met. Our students demonstrate proficiency in what they have learned during student exhibitions that are held at least four times per year. Each student presents work and evidence of learning before a public panel of teachers, parents, mentors, students, and other community members who know him well or bring relevant field expertise. Panelists evaluate the student's work and presentation skills against criteria predetermined by the teacher and student, and against the standards of their own field. Through these exhibitions, students demonstrate mastery of skills and knowledge. Because a student's work at the Met is not quantified by the use of traditional courses or credits, other methods are needed to document what is accomplished. One of these methods is the creation of a portfolio, a comprehensive collection of artifacts of student work. The contents vary among students, but they typically include final papers and drafts, photos of products, notes, videotape of exhibitions, artwork, narrative reports and other assessments, and a student-authored journal. In the end, Met students prove what they learned through a comprehensive demonstration of skills, not just by fielding questions on a standardized test.

A learning plan meeting is not always easy to facilitate or to participate in. Parents, students, and teachers may disagree, but in order to connect everyone to learning, our teachers learn to facilitate and negotiate learning plans starting from student interest and the skills and knowledge a student has. Then, they develop a way to bring that student toward reaching his/her goals. Learning plans have become part of our culture at the Met. Our accountability to our students, their families, and ourselves is to ensure that our students graduate and are prepared to move on to forms of higher education and the workforce. After four years of learning plan meetings and LTIs, the Met's first graduating class had every student accepted to a postsecondary institute. Students, their families, their mentors, and teachers were involved through learning plan meetings every step of the way where education was planned one student at a time.

HOW LTIs HELP STUDENTS SHAPE THEIR OWN FUTURE

We have students such as John who have amassed experiences in a wide variety of LTI situations. For the Met, John's family, and for John, this is fine. John was born in New York City and came to Providence while he was in middle school. When he came to the Met in ninth grade, at his first learning plan meeting he expressed an interest in animation. His first year LTI was at a local graphic design studio, a start-up organization that is contracted by other businesses to do animation and multimedia presentations. He worked alongside programmers and business managers alike and developed a flipbook of cartoons and a Claymation video. Simultaneously, he took a short acting class at a local theatre company and discovered he had an interest in theater. His interest led him to a summer job as the sound manager for a local theater group's production of "Fame."

When John returned to school in the fall of his tenth grade year, he found out about internship opportunities with the state judicial system. Just a little over a year before, he had been involved with the legislative hearings for the opening of the Met and had testified before the House Finance Committee. This new opportunity interested him. At his tenth grade learning plan meeting everyone agreed on an LTI at the Supreme and Superior Court of Rhode Island, where he honed in on the juvenile justice system and conducted an opinion survey of people in the court system about why juveniles commit crimes. At the end of tenth grade, John earned a Summer Search scholarship and spent six weeks in Colorado in a wilderness-training course and was certified as a lifeguard as well as a CPR instructor. This New York-born teen, in his own words, had trouble getting his feet back on city ground when he returned to Providence.

In eleventh grade, John had an LTI with a dance choreographer/educator in the dance department in a local middle school. He worked on the technical aspects of performance and was the stage manager for a production of "Milan." Simultaneously, he, another student, and a Met teacher rehearsed for a three-person play written by a local playwright entitled "Slow Dance on the Killing Ground," scheduled to go on stage in the spring.

John already had a Summer Search scholarship lined up for the end of his eleventh grade year, and had to decide between a performing arts program in London or a language program in Spain to help him develop better literacy in his family's first language, Spanish. The sum of all these experiences was a prelude to his senior year, when he began the process of selecting colleges.

John now attends a college near Worcester, Massachusetts, is majoring in criminal justice, and is still performing in school productions. He was recently on a TV show talking about his first year of college and how an innovative high school prepared him for his college experience.

There have been a few movies made in recent years about learning. One movie, *Billy Elliot,* is the story of a boy with an amazing gift as a dancer. The school he attended never recognized or cared about his interests and passions. In *October Sky,* another student has a passion for rockets and one teacher supports his interests in the face of family and school obstacles. What would it have been like for these children to have had learning plans that allowed them to pursue their interests at their schools? I think we all know the answer. It is too scary to think, what if they don't?

RESOURCES

Cotton, K. (1994). *School Size, Climate, and Student Performance.* Portland OR: Northwest Regional Laboratory, U.S. Dept. of Education.

Cremin, L. (1961). "The Transformation of the School." *Progressivism in American Education, 1876–1957.* New York: Alfred A. Knopf.

Cremin, L. (1975). *Public Education.* New York: Basic Books.

Cremin, L. (1988). *American Education: The Metropolitan Experience, 1876–1980.* New York: Harper & Row.

Csikszentmihalyi, M. (1988). "Motivation and Creativity: Toward a Synthesis of Structural and Energistic Approaches to Cognition." *New Ideas in Psychology 6* (2): 159–76.

Csikszentmihalyi, M. (1988). *Optimal Experience.* New York: Cambridge University Press.

Csikszentmihalyi, M. (1990). *Flow.* New York: Harper & Row.

Dewey, J. (1916). *Democracy in Education.* New York: Macmillan.

Dewey, J. (1933). *How We Think* (Second Revised Edition). New York: D.C. Heath & Co.

Hillman, J. (1996). *The Soul's Code.* New York: Random House.

James, W. (1958). *Talks to Teachers on Psychology and to Students on Some of Life's Ideals.* New York: W.W. Norton & Co.; originally published in 1899.

Klonsky, M., & Ford, P. (1994, May). "One Urban Solution: Small Schools." *Educational Leadership,* 64–66.

Levine, Eliot B. (2001). *One Kid at a Time: A Visionary High School Transforms Education.* New York: Teacher's College Press.

Littkey, Dennis, & Allen, Farrel. (1999, September). "Whole-School Person-alization, One Student at a Time." *Educational Leadership*.

Meier, D. (1995). *The Power of Their Ideas: Lessons for America from a Small School in Harlem*. Boston: Beacon Press.

Montessori, M. (1966). *The Secret of Childhood*. New York: Ballantine Books.

Sarason, S. (1990). *The Predictable Failure of School Reform*. San Francisco: Jossey-Bass.

Schank, R. (2000). *Coloring outside the Lines: Raising a Smarter Kid by Breaking All the Rules*. New York: HarperCollins.

Steinberg, A. (1996). *Real Learning, Real Work*. New York: Routledge.

Wilson, F. R. (1998). *The Hand: How Its Use Shapes the Brain, Language, and Human Culture*. New York: Pantheon Books.

CHAPTER 1 APPENDIX

Los Latidos de mi Corazón: The Metropolitan Regional Career and Technical Center
by Priscilla Santana

I was ready to go to Alan Shawn Feinstein High School when my best friend at the time, told me that she had changed her mind. She found a better school to go to, one with no textbooks or classes where you could learn what you wanted. I had already gone to the required summer work-shop at Feinstein and was only two days away from the first day of school when she informed me of her decision. In a way I felt betrayed because we had already planned to go to the same school and do every-thing together. But I knew there had to be a way to fix that whole mess. Even before I started racking my brain for a solution, she invited me to the opening night of this friend-splitting so-called, Met School to see if the principal would take me in as a new student. I went. After the white-bearded man wearing a funny hat finished giving his speech about the kind of education and learning environment kids need my friend and I approached him. She said to him, "This is my friend Priscilla, she just found out about this school, she really likes it and was wondering if she could be a student here." I was certain he was going to say no, since school started the very next day and they had already exceeded their limit of 50 students. But instead of saying no, he asked, "Why do you want to come to this school?" All I was able to say was, "I was impressed by what you said up there." Then he told me something that shocked me. "I'll tell you what, if you can come tomorrow morning ready for school at 8:00 a.m. and be interviewed, then we will see what we can do."

I don't know if he meant what he said or not but at 8:00 a.m. the next morning I entered a room with my mom ready to be interviewed by a lady named, Leigh-Ann. They asked me questions like, "what made you decide in coming to the Met? What school did I attend before? What is your Interest and passion? Etc. . . . It was decided I was to be placed in Rachel's Advisory, hmm . . . advisory, I guess it was something like a longer homeroom. Right after saying goodbye to my mom and reminding her to pick me up exactly at 2:30, I was taken to room #316 and was introduced to my new teacher, Rachel. I could not differentiate her from the rest of the other students. She was the skinniest person I had ever seen with long black hair, a pointy nose, and a large smile on her face. I noticed she was dressed completely in black and I immediately thought she was a witch who managed to get a teaching job just to ruin the life of adolescents.

After discussing our agenda for the day, we introduced ourselves. Laura, Raysa, Lea, Dimitriy, Jeff, Kyle, Jimmy, Omar, and Joslyn were my classmates. I was familiarized with Raysa from the Kingdom Hall but I didn't really know her well. It took some time to adjust to my advisory, the smallness of the school, the guy who was always filming or taking pictures, get used to taking the public bus, some thing I had never done before. As I got to know Rachel, I realized what a great sense of humor she had and her great concern to make me and her other advisorinos feel at ease.

This was the very beginning of a great journey. I soon managed to understand the school's philosophy and got well adjusted to the LTI idea. Because my biggest interest at the time was to be a secretary, I got an internship with Melissa Ambrosia at Women and Infants' (the CHAD program). She was a research nurse and a study coordinator. From her I learned most of the steps involved in coordinating a study on very premature infants. I also spent time with the secretary, Geidy Nolasco. She showed most of the things I needed to know to run the office. She even showed me how to make power point presentations, which are very useful for me now. That was a great year. I learned a lot from the entire experience. It even made me realize how much I did not really want to become a secretary.

That summer while I was pondering on what would be my next interest, my mother underwent surgery on her hand for carpel tunnel syndrome. When I saw how physical therapy was implemented in making her hand return to normal, this immediately sparked a new interest. I wanted to become a physical therapist. My tenth and eleventh grade internships were with physical therapists. One of the things I learned a lot of in one was about Fibromyalgia Syndrome. I learned so much of it, I developed a pamphlet to distribute to the patients. Something I learned from my other internship was about Watsu; a form aquatic therapy much like shiatsu done under water. My mentor was the only person in Rhode Island licensed to practice Watsu, which I thought, was pretty neat.

As for my senior year internship, I decided that broadening my options to general medicine would be more beneficial than if I decided to study physical therapy for the rest of my life. This is why I got an internship a Hasbro Children's Hospital in the Emergency room. Although I did not spend a huge amount of time there, I was indeed able to see many cool things such sutures and very deep wounds. In one occasion I witnessed how a patient's fibula was pointing out through the skin and how an orthopedic doctor, placed it neatly back inside like it once laid.

In the midst of being in and getting new internships, I did take many college courses. These include: Introduction to Physical Therapist Assistant, human anatomy, human physiology, composition, general psychology, oral communications and algebra for technology various times. What I learned from those classes I don't think I will forget any time soon. It wasn't really the good or bad teaching but the experience derived from attending those classes. Meeting new people, speaking about our assignments, the professors, what would we do after class, what would we do before class, whose house would we study next and of course the question never failed to ask, when is the last day for this class?

One big Met experience that I know will never be expunged out of my mind is the advisory's first ninth grade camping trip. Oh . . . the canoeing!! I had never been camping in my entire life, never mind having to canoe 40 miles, which is why I decided to go. My parents did not like the idea at all. But with a teaspoon of the "Rachel convincing" they conceded. We were on our way to the Saco River. . . .

I wasn't afraid until I saw the river. The thought of getting into a canoe which ultimately would float on water had not yet cross my mind. I wanted to go home right then and there. Bob was my canoeing partner. I had no other choice than to follow whatever one else was doing and start rowing. It was fun, but at the same time gave me butterflies in my stomach. Although I had a life jacket on, my biggest fear was falling into the water. I guess that is due to the fact that I can't swim. Setting up our tents and eating by the fire was a completely new experience for me, never mind having to pee in back of a bush. Funny is the word. I remember one time that Raysa, Lea and I got up from our tents early in the morning to pee. We were all looking for the perfect spot except for Raysa. She was just going to pee anywhere. But when she noticed that we had left her alone, she got up from her peeing action and exclaimed, "Hey, you guys!" flashing all of us. This incident has been retold till this day.

Speaking of Raysa and Lea, my fellow advisees, I feel very fortunate for having the advisory that I do. They have always been there to make me laugh, help me with my projects, edit my papers, and speak to, but most importantly, they have made feel comfortable. Coming from schools leaded by structure to one without any structure was not easy. But what made the transition easier was my advisory. I knew that I could talk to them about anything and they would understand. And even if they didn't understand, it was o.k. The advisory has helped me learned to apply the goal understanding diverse perspectives to the best extent. I am thankful for having them.

I am also very thankful to my advisor Rachel, who led us all. I can only imagine how hard it must have been for her to deal with 14-knuckle heads, all with different opinions. The arguments, the too much laughter, the unwanted silence, the I don't want to talk to you right now Rachel, the hassling, the disciplining, the students copious worrying absences, the 6 million Rachel can you help me voices, the I don't want to do this Rachel, the I failed or I passed my college class Rachel, the are you going out with so and so Rachel?, the forget it I am going to Central Rachel, the staple throwing wall punching vivid cursing episodes, the sorry we gave you an ulcer Rachel!, the don'ts, and whys, the give me that that's mine, and because of this. . . . We not only love you but we will miss you Rachel!

They say that the time spent in college are the best years of one's life but I am sorry, I disagree, the best years of my life I have already lived . . . here at the Metropolitan Regional Career and Technical center.

CHAPTER 2

Assessing to Engage

Developing Personal Profiles for Each Student

ELIZABETH CUSHMAN BRANDJES
East Side Community High School, New York

THE CREATION OF A PORTFOLIO CULTURE

In 1997, after a year off from teaching in suburban and rural schools in Massachusetts, I reentered the classroom as the first twelfth-grade English teacher at East Side Community High School in Manhattan. East Side, founded in 1992 by Jill Herman, a former teacher at Central Park East Secondary School, is a small school with only five hundred students, grades seven through twelve. It is a neighborhood school, primarily serving the students of the Lower East Side, but several students travel from each of the five boroughs to attend. They have chosen this school, as students are allowed to pick which high school they would like to attend when they are in the eighth grade. Some NYC high schools control who attends through entrance exams. East Side takes its students on a first come, first served basis. The conviction that all students can learn and deserve an opportunity to do so is the foundation of the school.

Many of our students came to East Side in the seventh grade from neighborhood elementary schools. Therefore, the majority of the ninth grade is made up of students already familiar with the workings and the philosophy of the school. New students are rarely admitted past the tenth grade. This enables us to live up to our name as a "community" high school. The teachers, administration, and students have worked together to create the school, and students become accustomed to the expectations the school holds for them very early on in their experience here. Consistency of expectations aids in the transfer of power to the students, in terms of helping them develop a sense of responsibility and commitment to themselves, their education, and their school.

East Side is part of the Coalition of Essential Schools and was formed with the Coalition principles in mind. Curriculum is designed around essential questions, and content is studied in depth rather than for broad coverage. Over the past nine years of the school's existence, East Side has moved from scattered experimentation with course-based portfolios to a school in the process of designing and implementing contiguous, consistent portfolio experiences for our students in math, science, literature, history, community-based organizing, and the arts.

I was hired to teach the school's first graduating class and to design a graduation portfolio for my English course. In previous years, students had kept portfolios that resembled work folders. Some teachers required final exhibitions, projects that would guide students in looking back on the year's work and synthesizing what they had learned. Most of the teachers, however, were not using portfolios. What the portfolios could contain, how students and teachers would use them, and how the portfolios would be shared with others were questions the staff had not thought of collectively until after the end of 1997–98 school year.

Today, there are twelve humanities teachers, all of who teach interdisciplinary English and social studies courses, except in the twelfth grade where the humanities course is split between an English teacher (myself) and a history teacher. In the 1997–98 school year, the twelfth grade social studies teacher, Lori Chajet, and I experienced great success with portfolios and roundtable presentations. The portfolios gave students the power to express their learning in our courses in a variety of ways, and the roundtables enabled them to share that learning with many readers and responders, not just their teachers.

In addition to history and literature portfolios and roundtables, each student wrote a research paper on a self-selected topic and defended it to a committee of adults. Science and math courses in the senior year also required portfolios as well as research experiments designed by the students and presented to a committee of adults. The roundtables and the committees provided the teachers and students an opportunity to invite community members, parents, educators from other high schools and colleges, and each other into the process. This community of learners worked together, questioning, probing, pushing, and celebrating the work of that year and the growth of each student over his/ her entire time at East Side. Although an immense orchestration of people, the process successfully individualized learning for each child.

Many of the students in the first graduating class had entered East Side in the seventh grade. As they worked throughout the year, revising and editing their work for their senior portfolios and finally presenting them in May, they felt they had really accomplished something. They knew that they were able to meet these high expectations because all of their teachers over the years at East Side had prepared them. Students each created something slightly different, a thumbprint of their own learning, a collection of work that communicated their point of view on the material they had interacted with over the course of the year, and, indeed, over several years. This initial success, along with several other factors, prompted schoolwide discussion, implementation and a creation of a "portfolio culture" at East Side. We now had some evidence of the learning that had taken place for these students, and we could rethink what was happening at each grade level. Also, the portfolio experience had been so powerful for the students that most of the teachers decided to try to replicate it at their own grade levels.

Several factors influenced the swift development of a portfolio culture at East Side. After taking part in the twelfth grade history and English roundtables in May of 1997, many of the teachers became interested in the process. Debates began (and continue today) about whether the portfolio should contain similar works each year, whether they should be presented more than once a year, and how to involve the students more in driving the curriculum and therefore the content of the portfolios. Portfolios compliment the "less is more" curriculum and the emphasis on the Habits of Mind endorsed by the Coalition of Essential Schools. In his book, *Horace's School: Redesigning the American High School* (1992), Theodore Sizer envisioned places where student learning was organized around these five Habits of Mind: Viewpoint, Evidence, Connections, Relevance, and Supposition. Examining all learning through these lenses can, ideally, make the learning experience richer and less superficial. The portfolio asks students to engage in critical self-reflection and analysis of their own learning, and provides them with a body of knowledge that they have constructed throughout a year, or four to six years. We have discovered that the portfolios also provide evidence of the teaching and learning occurring at East Side, and are useful tools for growing literacy, critical thinking, community involvement, and individual accomplishment. Through their creation and presentation, portfolios build students' engagement and investment in their own learning, serve as a tool of true acquisition of knowledge, and provide teachers and students evidence of their learning.

Individual teachers also strongly influenced the spread of portfolio use at East Side. The twelfth grade teachers were all using the portfolio. Then, Kiran Chaudhri, a veteran teacher and user of portfolios from University Heights High School in the Bronx, joined our staff as a ninth grade humanities teacher in September 1998. Kiran's influence would stretch to grades seven, eight, and ten, just as the influence of the grade twelve portfolios strongly encouraged grade eleven. During the 1998–99 school year, parents, community members, and teachers were invited to participate in ninth grade roundtables at least three times. The twelfth grade invited the public in only once, at the end of the year. After attending ninth grade roundtables, it was clear to me that there are many possibilities for the process.

Kiran also prompted using the portfolios in a new way when humanities portfolios began to be used by the vertical team (the humanities teachers collectively, grades 7–12) to share curriculum and to look closely at student work. As the staff became aware of what students and teachers were doing in grades 7–12, we were able to redesign curriculum and discuss how we engage students in research, reading, and the writing process. Thus, the portfolios became a powerful tool for internal professional development, which further inspired all teachers to begin collecting and analyzing student work. At a full staff retreat in the spring of 2000, the humanities team brought samples of student work and looked closely at areas we had agreed to teach or which we had defined as important the previous year. These areas were defined as research paper writing, essay writing, independent reading, reading response, and creative writing. We met in small groups around these different types of work and described what the students had done. From these descriptions we were able to generate dialogue about what we value in the teaching of reading and writing in our humanities classes and begin making choices at each grade level about the content of the portfolios.

The staff retreats are taken twice a year, and all staff members are mandated to attend at least one of them. The success of the work at the retreats is due in part to the monthly work done at East Side's faculty meetings every Monday. These meetings take three different forms: whole staff, grade, or vertical. Whole-staff meetings are reserved for discussion of schoolwide issues and for communicating across the disciplines. Grade meetings are also used for communicating across the disciplines, but within each grade level. Grade meetings may be used to discuss math, science, and humanities curriculum planning, field trips, advisory curriculum, and individual student progress. The third type, the vertical meeting, groups the humanities teachers together and the math/science teachers together across the grades. Approximately once per month, sometimes twice, the 7th–12th grade vertical teams meet. It is here that East Side's humanities teachers have created the vision for the school's use of portfolios. Two of the science teachers have dedicated themselves to using portfolios, and their influence has helped to spread knowledge and techniques for using portfolios to the math and science team, which heretofore has only created portfolios in the tenth and twelfth grades. This year, the students will create portfolios in all subjects in all grades.

Though the staff has made a commitment to work toward school-wide implementation, it is important to note that external as well as internal factors have motivated our work with portfolios. Pressure from the state of New York has begun to require students to take Regents Exams in all academic areas to graduate from high school. East Side and approximately forty other schools in New York State have aligned themselves to develop some continuity in the portfolio systems used at each school, so as to speak with a unified voice about the value for students and schools of portfolio use. This group, known as the New York Performance Based Assessment Consortium, is a grassroots movement fighting for a variance from the Regents Exams. It is hoped that the rigorous systems of assessment used in our schools will be accepted as an alternative to the Regents Exams. Although each school has developed slightly different methods of portfolio use, we have agreed upon certain portfolio and performance requirements that meet the New York State Standards and the New Standards, which the Regents Exams have, theoretically, been designed to test.

This push to "beat the deadline" of statewide implementation of standardized testing has served as a motivating factor in East Side's overall use of portfolios. Just as students need voice in their own learning, schools need local control over how they will assess that learning. Since assessment is such a crucial element of curriculum design, as a faculty we believe we must be allowed to maintain and develop methods that match the instructional pedagogies and community involvement of our school. If standardized testing takes hold in the alternative schools, the entire structure of the schools (two-hour classes, team-planned interdisciplinary curriculum, and smaller class sizes) will be affected, as we will be forced to reorganize resources and begin teaching to the test. Such a scenario will disempower teachers, and many will leave.

THE CONTENT OF THE GRADE TWELVE PORTFOLIOS

In my previous teaching placements in Massachusetts, the schools and the curricula had been quite traditional, with little or no room for input from teachers or students. I was basically handed a curriculum and textbooks and told to "get through" as much as possible. These schools were interested in using portfolios, but mostly for collecting student work and keeping it on file as evidence of what had been taught, not what had been learned. They also considered the folders a deterrent to cheating, as tests and quizzes would not be in circulation after they were handed back. This "lock and key" approach to keeping portfolios resulted in little or no reflection done on the part of the students, or the teachers, and the portfolios sat in boxes in the corner of my room year after year. So, when I came to East Side, I was determined to create a system by which the students would become more invested in the curriculum, even creating a large portion of it individually. I was also interested in using the portfolios throughout the year and postgraduation to foster dialogue among students and faculty about what and how we were teaching the humanities, what standards were being met, and how students were growing over the years.

Although I gave the students a list of portfolio requirements at the beginning of the year, this list could be negotiated or altered if students felt they needed to express their learning in alternate ways. The first two years, the portfolio I asked students to complete included the following pieces: a book review, a new ending or additional chapter, a character analysis essay, an essay analyzing literary techniques, an essay informed by and incorporating literary criticism, a self-selected piece written in any genre, and a visual project. The students also wrote a culminating piece, called the cover letter, in which they reflected upon their growth as readers and writers and commented on the pieces in their final portfolio. The personalization of the learning process via the portfolio is evidenced in the reflective cover letters students wrote for their portfolios at the end of the year. The cover letter is a final paper in which students rank their reading and writing and reflect upon their processes and learning. In it, they write about themselves as readers and writers, and, in so doing, they inevitably write about the impact of the portfolios.

On the surface, this content-restricted portfolio may not seem to offer much student input; however, students were free to choose when and why they would write in these forms, the idea being they would repeat several forms throughout the year and then choose the best, representative piece in each form to include in their final portfolio. This allowed students to assess for themselves which form could best communicate their learning about a reading we had done as a class or one they had completed independently. It also made due dates more interesting for me, as the work collected could include ten visual pieces, fifteen literary essays, two character analyses, five new chapters, and so on. It was a new experience for me to read writing done by students who had decided on their own how to show their learning. It was also a very new experience for the students.

One interesting point is that there was little student resistance to the portfolio. They understood that completing the portfolio and presenting it to a group of adults from outside of the school was an East Side graduation requirement. Linking the portfolio to graduation was a huge motivator, but the students were also very engaged in planning out their work. The process invited them to think about the types of writing that they had not yet mastered and those with which they were comfortable.

Students often chose to write in their "comfortable" forms when a book they had read was particularly difficult for them. If the book was easier, they might choose to write in a form that needed practice. It was amazing to see them tailor the portfolio to suit their own learning needs. Just the act of being aware of what one knows how to do well and not so well is important, and the portfolios provided a structured way for the students to discover themselves as thinkers, readers, and writers. The choices they needed to make also fostered dialogue between my students and me. One student writes in her cover letter:

> The one thing that has helped me the most with my writing is completing numerous drafts. Several of my papers start off one way and by the time the last draft is due, it is an entirely different paper. Sometimes my topic/ thesis will not even be the same. I think that is because I write many drafts and my way of thinking changes from one draft to the next. For example, when I started to write my paper for *I Know Why the Caged Bird Sings*, I started writing about racism. But after I gave the first draft to Liz, I realized that I did not want to write about that topic. In fact, I did not want to write anything near that topic. I talked to Liz, and she said since I disliked the book so much I should write a book review.

We often had great conversations during writing conferences about why and how to write in certain forms. Additionally, because other students had probably already experimented in some of the forms they were considering, I could use the portfolios to find models of peer writing for reference. Often, I would create folders containing different types of papers for students to look at for ideas. So, not only was the course constructed by the students throughout the year, but also students in future years have built upon what their predecessors accomplished. In this manner, the students have driven the reform and development of the curriculum and portfolios each year.

The students quickly got used to not being assigned to respond in a particular way to the books they read. Instead, they were asked to choose from the list of portfolio requirements, repeating as many forms as possible throughout the year. The portfolio required they include one of each of the required pieces, though students often included more than one example of each genre. Additionally, they were asked to submit writings about their independent reading books. At East Side, independent reading has been emphasized at every grade level. Students are required to read twenty-five books independently in the seventh, eighth, and ninth grades, and ten books a year in grades ten, eleven, and twelve. In my class, papers written in reaction to independent reading carry equal significance in the portfolio to pieces written about assigned, whole-class readings. This further diversified the final portfolios, because not only did the students choose various forms of expression, they read a diverse range of self-selected books as well.

Several students commented on the impact certain independent reading books had on their lives, and on their writing. Often, students were motivated to read daily because that reading would be validated in school. Many students, even at the college level, do not read for their own enjoyment or edification because they see no concrete opportunity to use the reading for "credit" or grades. In this class, the fact that students could use writings about books of their own choosing in their portfolios led to increased independent reading. Often, they were able to make connections between their independent reading and the texts we were studying as a class. One student writes, "My independent reading is now connected to my writing. In previous school years, I used to write papers not connecting them to anything in my life. Now, if I see a quote in a book, I'll write it down and sometimes even reflect on it. Many times, the quotes I have picked have become the central focus of my papers." Many students wrote about how they specifically used the books they read to learn something or to create their portfolio pieces. For example, "I kept a journal this year for every book that I've read [so] I can reflect back on [it] to see if I ever wrote an entry that I may want to write a paper on."

Independent reading offered students a "safety valve," or an opportunity to construct their own path in the literature class if they felt disengaged with the common texts we were studying. After six years of being required to read independently, one student developed the following philosophy of reading, which he expressed in his cover letter:

When I was young, even though I had great joy while reading a book, especially if it was adventurous, I still would not pick up a book on my own time. Now I read everyday; it is a must. If I have spare time, I wonder to myself, what should I read, because now I want to know it all. I also know now that in order to expand my knowledge, one of the most effective ways is to read. The other single most important thing about reading is that it can take you to places that you have never been, and some places that you can never get to. It can take you through time periods that were before you, and it can even let you speculate what it would be like after you. Reading is a pathway to unlimited capabilities, boundless ideas, endless mysteries, and infinite knowledge. That is literature.

The independent reading requirement not only fostered a love and appreciation for literature. Through independent reading, the students began to understand themselves better as readers and writers. When asked to comment about themselves as readers and writers in their cover letters, it became evident that the reading requirement had allowed many of them to discover themselves in relation to the larger world and to reflect upon their own role in their learning. The following statement shows a young mind coming to realize the power of individualized learning: "This class was basically about reading books and incorporating them into something that connects to me. I have read a lot of books this year, and some have made connections [to me] while others have not. Every book connects to somebody and this is because people read books and go through similar things. An important thing I learned this year is that the way people perceive things is essential to how people learn." He went on to write, "Reading became a part of my daily routine this year, and going into college, I hear it will become a bigger part of my life. So this class prepared me well for what is to come. If this is my future, I am ready."

Independent reading became a powerful part of the self-designed portfolio process. The students had several genres to choose from whenever they finished reading, but not all of the writing was connected to literature. One of the requirements for the portfolio, the self-selected piece, asked students to write a piece that was not necessarily connected to literature. This piece could take any form. Ideas I suggested included a short story, a collection of poetry, a play, an article, an autobiographical piece, etc. Evidence from the cover letters shows that this was most often the students' favorite assignment. Several wrote about the power of their self-selected pieces, and time and again they ranked the self-selected piece as their best piece of writing. They wrote of the personal impact these pieces had on their lives, their learning and their process as writers.

In the following excerpt, one female student, now a sophomore at Western Maryland College, captures both the personal and intellectual significance of the poems she wrote for the self-selected piece. She also mentions that the freedom from a highly teacher-structured writing assignment allowed her to enjoy the assignment and to take it where she desired, thus creating what she deems to be a higher quality of work. She writes:

> I ranked these collections of poems first because they are pieces of work that were inspired by real life issues. These poems represent my feelings about my immediate family, and everything expressed through them comes from my heart. I enjoyed doing this type of writing because it was a task I assigned to myself. Assignments can be more enjoyable when they are not so much structured by the instructor of the class.
>
> These poems are different from other pieces of work in my portfolio because they connected school life to home life. I read books this year that led me to evaluate my current situation with my parents. Two of these books were *Like Water for Chocolate* and *The Bluest Eye*. Although these two books had different plots, they both focused some part of the book on parent and child relationships.
>
> The purpose and goal of my poems is to allow children who have problems with their parents to know that they are not alone and to inform parents of the emotions their children may be feeling.

This student mentions that her poems can help others to understand that they are not alone in the world. It is clear that her experience with *The Bluest Eye* and *Like Water for Chocolate* helped her to understand the power of literature. These two books were whole-class texts that I assigned. Her reference to them in relation to her own writing is evidence of how portfolios are constructed within parameters set up by the teacher. It also shows how portfolios allow for individualized focus and meaning making. It is very exciting to see a student think of her own writing and acclaimed literature as possibly having the same kind of impact on readers.

Other students also wrote about the significance of the unstructured assignment. Even though I had set up the portfolio requirements, students had a sense of freedom in selecting their own topics and genres for this self-selected piece. The following excerpt shows a student celebrating his opportunity to write what he knew most about: himself, his friends, and his environment. For this student, and many others, this sense of freedom was liberating and built tremendous confidence and validity in himself, his voice, and what he had to say in his writing.

One of the papers that I enjoyed writing most was the paper that I did based on my journal writing. In my journal, I found myself writing about how kids grow up in the inner city and the problems they go through growing up. When I had the chance to write a paper of my choice, I decided to write a short story based on the life of a kid living in the inner city called "The Hard Knock Life." This is the paper that I enjoyed writing the most. This short story was so motivating for me to write because I got to write about a topic that I knew a lot about. Since I am from the inner city, I wrote about things that happened to me and things that happened to people that grew up with me. I was free to write about whatever that I wanted to write. That is why this paper was most enjoyable, I was free, I did not have to follow a certain topic.

This paper was different from others because I did not have to read a book or research anything to get information on the topic. Everything I wrote came from my heart . . . this short story came to be my favorite piece of writing. I think I did a good job on this paper. In writing this paper I challenged my imagination and what I can do when not told to write about a specific topic.

Other students had a different experience with the self-selected piece. These were students who had always relied on the teacher to "tell them what to do." They preferred essay form because it was certain, finite. One student wrote: "I always like writing critical or analytical pieces. I have never enjoyed writing anything that needed me to be more creative. For some reason I would rather write a twenty page research paper instead of a three page short story." Essay writing is a genre we have reinforced each year at East Side. The students feel comfortable and confident writing in this form. As the vertical team has continued to analyze the strengths and weaknesses of our student writers, and the impact certain pieces have had on them, creative writing has become a more popular form in all grades. At the time these cover letters were written, only some of the seniors had been asked to write this way in the past. The student quoted above wrote a series of "Dear Abby" letters to the characters from *Wuthering Heights*, one of her independent reading books. Despite her confidence in her essay and research paper writing abilities, she still ranked this self-selected piece as the second best piece of writing in her portfolio.

Many struggled with the self-discovery creative writing brought, but overall they still ranked these pieces at the top of their portfolios. Laura, now a sophomore at Le Moyne University, wrote:

> My third most effective paper is the Creative Writing Piece. My creative piece was a mixture of poems and simple lines that express my feelings throughout different phases I have gone through, or will go through. I basically wrote about myself. Personal writing is not easy. I have never enjoyed talking about my feelings nor had I even tried. Because I learned different types of writing I also learned a new way of communication. Writing became my way of communication. I now write what I feel in and out of class based on the literary techniques I know.
>
> My creative piece is a collection of writing that I would have liked to eventually turn into a story. I felt that this was difficult because some of the lines in my poems say so much. I did not want to change them because these are my different feelings as I felt them. My creative piece did not end with this assignment. I try to write as often as possible. My objective is to continue writing and eventually create something like a memoir; a self-created piece about myself.

The most fascinating part of Laura's comments is the fact that she plans to continue working on this type of writing. These portfolios were presented in May, and the students were graduating in June. The idea that she sees writing as a process that will continue for her own purposes is similar to the testimony about independent reading above. Engagement with the self-designed portfolio helped instill a sense of purpose and meaning to the acts of reading and writing. The students did not see the work as mere assignments, but as purposeful, lifelong pursuits that continue long after graduation.

STANDARDIZED TESTING AND PORTFOLIOS

Teachers do not often find themselves in schools where the faculty works together to analyze the acts of teaching and learning and to design meaningful curriculum and assessment for their students. East Side is a place where teachers arrive early and stay late. We are well educated, experienced classroom teachers who understand the importance of constructing learning experiences with our students, and therefore do not accept prepackaged, "teacher-proof" curricula or standardized tests as fair and appropriate. With the recent push in New York State for mandated Regents Exams, our very existence as a school is in jeopardy.

The Comprehensive Regents Exams will be phased in until each student in New York City and State will have to pass a standardized test in math, global studies, science, English/language arts, and U.S. history and government. During the phasing-in period, students will be allowed to graduate if they pass the test with a 55 percent or higher. In the case of the new Math Regents Exams, the passing score has been lowered to 45 percent during the phase-in period. Students not passing even one test will not graduate from high school. Students who are designated English Language Learners (ELLs) or Special Education have very few safety nets built in to protect them. For example, ELLs can take all of the tests except the English/Language Arts Regents in their native language, *if* the tests are even available in their language, which is not a guarantee. Special Education students must take all Regents Exams. If they fail any of them, they are allowed to take a less rigorous version of the test, formerly know as the RCT, and they can graduate with a local diploma instead of a Regents Diploma. This local diploma is nothing more than an attendance certificate and is not recognized by colleges as a valid diploma for admission.

The reaction in schools like ours, where students must receive a 70 percent or higher to pass any test, paper, or course, is that the Regents are effectively lowering standards (45 percent to 55 percent is considered passing) to give the public the impression that they have raised them. When the New Standards and the New York State Standards were introduced by State Commissioner Thomas Sobol, they were designed to be open-ended guidelines that teachers and schools could use to design their own curriculum and assessments. Under the administration of Richard Mills, the businesslike quantitative measurement of student outcomes via standardized testing has debased the standards to nothing more than a list of content and skills to be covered. In New York City, Mayor Giuliani is even proposing that teachers be paid based on how well their students perform on these standardized assessments. The mood and tone set by these educational policies and policy makers is one of external pressure and intimidation. It is felt by students as well as teachers, and there have been some devastating affects at East Side Community High School.

As described earlier, the portfolios for my twelfth grade English class invited students to have some control over what they were reading and writing and how they would show this to others. The portfolios contained several genres of writing, and students made critical choices in their learning process about how to proceed in their reading and writing based on what they wanted to learn and based on what was required for graduation. In September of 1999, our school was told that the graduating class was required to take the English/Language Arts Regents Exam to graduate. Other students in the city and state had taken it as juniors, but we had not given the test as part of a petition we were filing to the state with the New York Performance Based Assessment Consortium. Our school and approximately forty others were requesting a variance from the exams until the state could gather data about our systems of portfolio assessment and decide, in fact, whether or not we were meeting the state standards. We argued that our assessments were more rigorous than the Regents Exams and that our students already had strict graduation requirements that reflected the standards assigned by the state. Richard Mill's office did not give an answer about the variance until three days before the test, so we had no choice but to prepare the students at East Side for the English/Language Arts Regents Exam.

The compromise made in preparing students for both the test and the portfolios created resentment on the part of teachers and students, and drastically altered the content, and therefore the student investment, in the portfolio process. The fatal flaw on my part, as a teacher, was in doubting that my own process was capable of preparing the students for the test. Instead of leaving the portfolios as they had been and simply occasionally drilling the students in the exam, I decided that the portfolio itself could prepare the kids, if I altered the contents. Since two out of four of the essays required for the Regents Exam involved writing comparative essays, this became the primary genre for the year. Students wrote comparative essays about their summer reading and their independent reading, and I selected books that could be read to facilitate the writing of this assigned genre. For example, instead of students choosing which form of writing they would like to use to express their understanding, they *all* had to write a comparative essay about *Like Water for Chocolate* and *The Glass Menagerie*. Instead of selecting to create a visual project for *The Bluest Eye*, students *all* wrote a "critical lens essay" (another form from the test) in which they interpreted the book through a quote from another writer.

As the year passed, students seemed apathetic, even angry, about the portfolios they were creating. Each student's portfolio was the same. They no longer took pride in the evolution of unique portfolios. When they wrote self-reflections of the pieces in their portfolio, they described trying to meet the requirements of the assignment, instead of recounting the process of discovering the criteria and drafting and redrafting until they were satisfied. The worst blow came in January, when we still had not heard from the state regarding the variance. The principal asked the eleventh and twelfth grade teachers to stop everything and drill the students in the test for the entire month. My classroom became a nightmare of photocopied forms and weekly drill. Attendance suffered. Tempers flared.

The students were disenchanted and disgusted. "Why are we doing portfolios if we just have to pass this test to graduate?" "When are we going to read a book again?" "My friends in other high schools only have to take the test, but I have to do a portfolio too?" "I liked Humanities better last year." Going to work day after day feeling as disempowered as they did was not easy. I came to realize that the students were not invested in the portfolio because I had changed the most basic element of student choice that had previously allowed them to individualize their learning experience. Without that, they saw the portfolio as exactly the same as the test: a hoop for them to jump through in order to graduate. In effect, I had orchestrated the same sort of top-down control over their work as the state had over mine. We were all miserable, and I feared the demise of the portfolios to the mandate of the test.

Just before the Regents Exams were given at the end of January 2000, Richard Mills granted a variance to several, but not all, of the schools belonging to the New York Performance Based Assessment Consortium. East Side was one of the lucky schools. The variance would last only one year and would include several visits from the state to "investigate" the "standard" use of portfolios at these schools. Because portfolios are not considered statistically reliable ways to measure the quality of student work, the state would be looking for evidence of interrater reliability across our portfolios. Would teachers in different consortium schools score the work in the portfolios in the same way? Would the portfolios used in all consortium schools contain a comparative essay, and would this essay be scored using the same rubric? Would teachers from different schools apply this rubric consistently to the work of students at different schools? These were some of the points the state wanted to look into.

Ironically, the Regents Exams are scored by board of education teachers. We grade the work of students in our own schools. When the majority of students in New York passed the New English/Language Arts Regents, the exact questions the state was asking the consortium were raised. Did the state really raise the standards, or was the scoring of the test subjective? Would teachers in one school give an essay a "3" and teachers in another school give a similar essay a "5"? The fact that the new testing has statistical validity is arguable, yet the lack of reliability of portfolios is the main argument the state is holding against us in our struggle.

The portfolios were again affected by the struggle against standardized testing. In an effort to speak to the state with a united voice, the schools of the consortium required a comparative essay in the senior English portfolio. This essay would be scored using a rubric designed by a representative body of consortium teachers. Now, the comparative essays my students had been writing all year to prepare for the exam had not been scored using this rubric. From January to June, I would have to assign more comparative essay writing and use the consortium rubric to score these papers. At this point the students and I were just going through the motions. One positive outcome was the discussion that I had with kids about political action and how groups organize to fight for what they believe is right. Several students attended rallies and made speeches about the negative effects of standardized testing, and many parents signed petitions and began to attend meetings on the topic. Teachers, including myself, spoke at state legislative hearings and documented how our curriculum is meeting the standards. In some ways the fight against the testing has mobilized the school around its mission, reminding us all why we are there.

Roundtable presentations would also come to be affected by the data gathering of the state. Previously, the roundtables were celebrations of a year's evidence of student creativity and learning. Students invited family, employers, and friends. I invited students and faculty from Teachers College, Columbia University, and other graduate schools of education in the city. It was usually a joyous occasion that students looked forward to. The students would give each member of the round-table a copy of their cover letter to read. After that, the questions, probing, and sharing of the individual pieces within the portfolio would occur, usually lasting for about an hour to an hour and thirty minutes. Each student left feeling proud of what they had accomplished, and guests wrote letters to the board and to us congratulating the students on their academic sophistication and poise.

This year, the kids seemed to dismiss roundtables. They had all passed the English Regents Exam already, only to discover that they didn't really need to take it because the variance had been granted in the eleventh hour. They just wanted to do what was required and stand on the stage at graduation the following Monday. Then, two days before the roundtables, I was informed that a statistician from the state would be attending. The consortium had been arguing that the students had to present and defend a comparative essay to a committee and that the committee would score the essay using the consortium rubric. This was a very different protocol than the roundtables our students were familiar with. We are indeed working towards this type of defense of the comparative essay, as this is already how students defend their research papers, but we were not there yet. The state was expecting to see this the day they came. The best we could do was to incorporate the use of the rubric in the roundtables. I decided that I had compro-mised the process so much already this year, that I could not change it anymore. So, the roundtables went on as planned, but at the end, I asked the students to take out the best comparative essay they had written that year. I then asked all participants to score this essay using the rubric provided. I collected these rubrics and we can use them to show consistency in scoring of our student work.

CONCLUSION

In altering my own teaching to prepare students for standardized testing, I led my students to produce weak, voiceless writing. This kind of writing actually enabled them to pass the Regents Exam, but it is not the kind of writing we have valued or taught in our school. As a faculty, we have worked to teach our students that hard work over time matters. Through creating portfolios, they have learned that process matters, choices occur over time, and that we should rely on dialogue and critical reading of our own work and the work of others to improve our writing. They have learned that writing is a socially constructed process, not a rote or solitary act. Using portfolios, students have developed critical self-reflection skills through looking back over their work and thinking and writing about what they have done. They have used evidence from individual pieces in their portfolios to prove to others, both orally and in writing, that their work demonstrates mastery of certain skills and ideas. Most importantly, the students at East Side have proven that when given the power to determine the path of their own learning, they will accept that challenge and meet higher expectations than any rigid curriculum or standardized assessment could ever hold for them.

We almost lost everything the year of the testing fiasco. Currently, we are still waiting to hear if the state will grant our school a "permanent" variance from all of the Regents Exams. At present, I have returned to the model of the successful portfolio used the first two years. My students passed the Regents Exam last year, as eleventh graders, so I am again free to design assessments that challenge and excite the students. In January and in June, each senior will complete and defend portfolios in history, English, science, math, art, and community-based organizing. They will also write and defend both a research paper and a comparative essay. To help them complete such rigorous exhibitions of their work, teachers, parents, and community members will again be asked to participate. Without the support of a critical mass of people involved in education and in the lives of these children, a portfolio system such as ours would dissolve. As well, if the testing is put in place, we will lose the time we use for presentations to the administration and scoring of the tests.

For schools planning on developing a portfolio culture, certain conditions must exist. First, faculty must share the philosophy that curriculum is more a means than an end. A content-based curriculum leads to memorization and shallow learning. A thematic-based, skills-based curriculum leads students to use their minds. This type of open-ended design will benefit the creation of a portfolio culture in that it is flexible enough to sustain student inquiry and concrete enough to allow teachers and others to see evidence of student learning. Because drafting writing takes time, students need to be asked to and allowed to revisit pieces throughout the year. The knowledge and skills students gain over the course of that year are then used to revise previous pieces, so that students are constructing part of the curriculum as they experience and understand new ideas and apply them to their own work.

Teachers in a school working to create a portfolio culture must be in agreement that the process is worthwhile. Partial commitment to using portfolios will create pockets of dissent. Without a unified vision and agreement that portfolios are the best way to provide students with personalized avenues for expressing their learning and teachers with a view of what their students are taking away from their classes, it will be difficult to convince parents and state organizations of their pedagogical validity. Admittedly, at East Side there has been somewhat of a rift between the math teachers and the humanities and sciences teachers. Math is a subject that is very content-based and sequential. Therefore, some of the math teachers have had trouble designing projects and portfolios that do not rely heavily on testing. Because of the commitment of the entire staff, the math teachers have begun to work together among themselves and with math teachers from other consortium schools to create more balanced and appropriate assessments and to design portfolios. This unified commitment to portfolios is invaluable to the students, as the process becomes more familiar to them and they become even more engaged in creating original work of the highest quality.

Support from the administration is also essential to developing a schoolwide portfolio culture. Scheduling during what other schools use as exam week needs to take place to enable all of the teachers to attend each other's roundtables. As well, senior defenses of research papers and comparative essays require teacher mentors. At East Side, the faculty has volunteered this, but in other schools, the administration might want to outline it as part of the basic expectations for all faculty members. However, administrative support involves much more than mere scheduling and writing up job descriptions and expectations. Support from the principal and assistant principal must also come in the way the school communicates to the public about what we are doing and why. Jill Herman, our principal, has publicly said that standardized testing will change the school she started so significantly that if the tests are mandated, she will leave. In addition, she has led the math and science teachers to analyze their practice and to develop portfolios in a similar manner to the humanities team. She and the assistant principal, Mark Federman, have done this by creating sacred meeting times, called vertical meetings, to be used for curriculum development and portfolio discussions. She has also urged the teachers to educate the parents, during our triannual parent teacher conferences, about the ramifications of standardized testing and to have parents sign petitions and letters to state representatives. She uses the existing structures of the school to advance her support of portfolios, and she invites important people to the roundtables to see what we are doing. Jill and Mark participate in the process with the teachers.

Another invaluable support system not to be overlooked when trying to create a portfolio culture is the work of other schools in the state or district. Becoming a member of the New York Performance Based Assessment Consortium has allowed teachers from the participating schools to join together for valuable professional development opportunities. Once a year, we use one of our professional development days for all of us to meet. Additionally, examining the student work from other schools during portfolio roundtables and defenses has provided insights about our own curriculum development, expectations, and portfolio content. I emphasize to my students that dialogue is crucial to the writing process, and the parallel is true for their teachers. The level of professionalism and collegiality among the teachers at these schools is like nothing I've experienced before. Our common goal is to gain acceptance for the processes we know to be pedagogically and socially beneficial and superior to standardization, not only for our children but for all children.

AN AFTERWORD

Since this chapter was written, the New York State commissioner of education, Richard Mills, has made a final decision regarding the Regents Exams. All New York State students are required to take and pass five Regents Exams to graduate from high school. The tests are in global history, American history, English, math, and science. Some schools belonging to the New York Performance Based Assessment Consortium were given a temporary waiver from the tests while a Blue Ribbon Panel, appointed by Commissioner Mills, researched the portfolio process and its validity as an alternative to standardized testing. It was the recommendation of the Blue Ribbon Panel (a body of policy makers, test makers, and educators) that East Side and the other schools petitioning for a variance from the Regents Exams be given more time to develop the processes of portfolio assessment currently used. Despite the recommendations from his own panel, Richard Mills has decided that portfolios lack interrater reliability; therefore, a model of educating that could be used to improve teaching, build community involvement in public schools, and provide students with the personalized learning opportunities so often missing in classrooms across the nation was deemed unacceptable.

As I sat grading essays for the English/Language Arts Regents Exam in January, I wondered how a test that grades writing on a six-point scale was raising standards when students could pass with a score of three or four on each essay. A score of three is equivalent to a 50 percent. If students answer a few multiple-choice questions correctly and write essays that all receive scores of three, they will pass. Is this really raising the bar? Is this really high stakes? Do the students learn anything about the power of the written word when forced to sit silently and write for six hours over two days? What does stopping the normal flow of school for a week and a half to administer tests accomplish for teaching and learning, when the results are not geared at improving instruction as much as at punishing students when they fail?

These questions frustrate my students. They have protested in Albany; they have spoken eloquently at legislative hearings about how portfolios have allowed them opportunities to learn; graduates have returned to take part in roundtables because they believe in the process; I have received e-mails from students asking if they can have their portfolios to show their college writing teachers. In short, we will continue the use of portfolios at East Side, despite the mandates of the tests. It will be difficult to do both. Some students will become confused by the mixed message sent by asking them daily to examine information in depth but then forcing them to write superficial formulaic essays on these tests. However, it is our hope that the truth about standardization will be recognized and that public pressure against the tests will continue to grow.

RESOURCES

Barton, David. (1994). *Literacy: An Introduction to the Ecology of Written Language*. Cambridge, MA: Blackwell.

Beauboeuf-Lafontant, Tamara, & Augustine, D. Smith. (1996). "Facing Racism in Education." *Harvard Educational Review 28.*

Boomer, Garth. (1992). "Negotiating the Curriculum." In Garth Boomer, Nancy Lester, Cynthia Onore, and Jon Cook (eds.), *Negotiating the Curriculum: Educating for the 21st Century*. Washington, DC: Falmer Press.

Bruner, Jerome. (1996). *The Culture of Education*. Cambridge, MA: Harvard University Press.

Carr, Wilfred, & Kemmiss, Stephen. (1986). *Becoming Critical: Education, Knowledge, and Action Research*. Philadelphia, PA: Falmer Press.

Cochran-Smith, Marilyn. (1991, August). "Learning to Teach against the Grain." *Harvard Educational Review 61,* 279–309.

Darling-Hammond, Linda. (1997). *The Right to Learn: A Blueprint for Creating Schools That Work*. San Francisco, CA: Jossey-Bass.

Darling-Hammond, Linda, Ancess, Jacquelyn, & Falk, Beverly. (1995). *Authentic Assessment in Action: Studies of Schools and Students at Work*. New York: Teachers College Press.

Delpit, Lisa. (1995). *Other People's Children: Cultural Conflict in the Classroom*. New York: The New Press.

Dewey, John. (1966). *Democracy and Education*. New York: Free Press (originally published in 1916).

Elbow, Peter. (1976). *Writing without Teachers*. New York: Oxford University Press.

Elbow, Peter. (1981). *Writing with Power: Techniques for Mastering the Writing Process*. New York: Oxford University Press.

Elbow, Peter. (2000). *Everyone Can Write: Essays toward a Hopeful Theory of Writing and Teaching Writing*. New York: Oxford University Press.

Freire, Paulo. (1970). *Pedagogy of the Oppressed*. New York: Teachers College Press.

Graves, Donald. (1992). *Portfolio Portraits*. Portsmouth, NH: Heinemann.

Gee, James. (1990). *Social Linguistics and Literacies: Ideologies and Discourses*. London: Falmer Press.

Hill, Clifford, & Parry, Kate (eds.). (1994). *From Testing to Assessment: English as an International Language*. London: Longman.

Hillocks, George, Jr. (1995). *Teaching Writing as Reflective Practice*. New York: Teachers College Press.

Hooks, Bell. (1994). *Teaching to Transgress: Education as the Practice of Freedom*. New York: Routledge.

Romano, Tom. (1995). *Writing with Passion*. Portsmouth, NH: Heinemann.

Schon, David. (1983). *The Reflective Practitioner: How Professionals Think in Action*. New York: Basic Books.

Sizer, Theodore. (1984). *Horace's Compromise: The Dilemmas of the American High School*. Boston: Houghton Mifflin.

Sunstein, Bonnie, & Lovell, Jonathon H. (eds.). (2000). *The Portfolio Standard: How Students Can Show Us What They Know and Are Able to Do*. Portsmouth, NH: Heinemann.

Stone, Deborah. (1997). *Policy Paradox: The Art of Political Decision Making*. New York: W.W. Norton and Co.

Wiggins, Grant, & McTighe, Jay. (1998). *Understanding by Design*. Alexandria, VA: ASCD.

CHAPTER 3

Personalization and Secondary School Renewal

ANNE FRIEDRICHS
Montpelier High School
DAVID GIBSON
Vermont Institute for Science, Mathematics, & Technology

A high school experience based on Personalized Learning Plans requires new knowledge and skills from both teachers and students, attributes that cannot be developed without changing the remaining structure of the high school experience.

Her legs dangling and swinging, Wendy Emerson slides happily onto the science lab table. As her mom and dad walk into the "beakers and tubes" room, her two advisors get up to shake hands and say hello. A rhythmic splash of water quietly bubbles in a nearby tank. All the adults find chairs around a glossy black table with gas valve cranes cocked at attention. Wendy rocks on her perch above the crowd, sitting on her hands. She brightly smiles at everyone, making eye contact. Her first Personalized Learning Plan (PLP) conference as a ninth grader is underway.

"Who are the most important people in Wendy's life?" her advisor Linda asks the gathering. Wendy's mom chimes, "Well, I'm the *most* important person." Everyone laughs. Wendy's father quickly adds, "Outside of your *parents*, that is," thinking of his in-laws, Wendy's grandparents. Everyone smiles. Ken, her other advisor, writes on a large pad of paper, "Mom," "Grandparents." Wendy adds "My friends . . . but also my Aunt Kathy. We did a job shadow in eighth grade and I went to O'Brien's Beauty School in South Burlington, where she works." Wendy slides off the table into a chair, where she is level with everyone else. Questions begin to draw out her history, strengths, fears, and bright ideas.

"Who is Wendy Emerson? What would others say when describing you?" Wendy looks to her mother and father for an answer and her father, sensing her reticence, encourages her to speak. "It feels like bragging." Mom moves in to help. "Wendy, you're fun! You have a great sense of humor. You're a dedicated friend, good listener, great athlete, top scorer on soccer team in 8th grade." Ken writes the words on the pad. Wendy doesn't protest. She smiles and looks around at everyone, engaged and pleased.

Her parents willingly share their understanding of Wendy and highlight her background and strengths. Her dad faces Wendy, offering, "I don't know if action describes you, but we're more wishy-washy." Then, addressing her advisors, "We are be-ers and she's a do-er. Uncle Ted sent her a phone. We didn't have the right hook-up. She wired the whole house, hooked it into an existing line. She is mechanical. Now she wants to know how to fix a car." Ken writes "Mechanical" on the big pad.

Wendy responds to most questions with short answers, and after most of her answers, her parents quickly expand on the idea while Wendy smiles and agrees. Occasionally, her parents start by giving an answer and then asking Wendy for her thoughts, which come readily. Together, the family forms a single voice about Wendy. Nothing seems impossible, and everything can be considered. "Is there anything you really want to do that you feel you can't do?" her mom asks, rephrasing a question from the advisors. "No, not really." Later on her dad mentions, "I remember you loved to draw and illustrate children's books." Wendy nods assent. "She's always liked drawing," her mom adds. Then Dad, "Doodling on everything." Ken writes "Artistic." Wendy agrees and adds, "I also like soccer and I might be in basketball this year."

Ken writes every important word and phrase onto the large paper, which later goes home with Wendy. Near the end of the meeting, Linda looks at Wendy and her parents; "Ken and I will be in partnership with Wendy and you for the next four years. Hopefully, we can be a link between you and the school and be a sounding board for Wendy as she makes her decisions. Four years from now, Wendy is going to be on her way someplace." Wendy purses her lips, nods her head and raises her brows. She mouths, but doesn't say aloud "College." "We're looking forward to this time in high school as a time for her to explore things," says her mom.

Everyone at the meeting has contributed to a chart that when completed, Wendy takes home to hang on her wall (figure 3.1). Her Personalized Learning Plan at Montpelier High School seems to be off to a good start. Or is it? Will the ninth grade program offer her a sufficient chance to be "mechanical," "hands-on," and "artistic"? Or will she have to go off campus for some of these experiences?

Supporting Wendy's personalized learning strengths, interests, and aspirations helped everyone become better acquainted. The atmosphere of acceptance and sharing of ideas allowed a new partnership to form

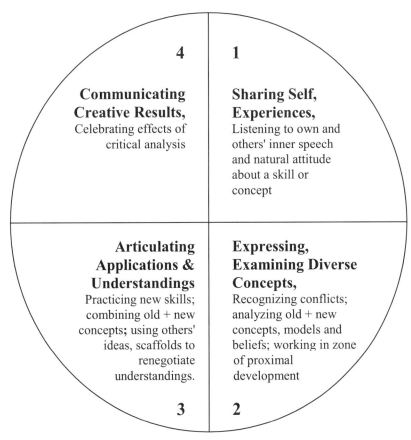

Figure 3.1.   Dialogue model.

Table 3.1.   Notes from Wendy's first PLP conference.

HISTORY	STRENGTHS	FEARS	BRIGHT IDEAS
• Apprentice in cosmetology, job shadow • Lived in River City all her life • Went to River City Middle School • 8th grade leader • Excelled at basketball and soccer • Recognized for writing • Illustrated over 30 children's books • Wired own phone through house	• Found her way by bus around Burlington in eighth grade • Mechanical • Friendly • Responsible • Learns through hands-on work • Artistic • Athlete: soccer, basketball, gymnastics, speedy runner	• Algebra • Word Processing	• Cosmetology • Photography • Dance • Sports: Basketball & Soccer • Art • Writing • Driving • Auto Maintenance • Job at Ben and Jerry's

along with an understanding of how they as partners could rely on each other during the coming year. However, a challenge also began to arise. Wendy's background and interests didn't connect closely with a typical ninth grade academic program at school. How could connections be made between her ninth grade year and these elements of personal interest and success? Could her advisors help make school a personal experience for Wendy? This is the enduring challenge of personalizing learning—finding ways for school and personal interests to coincide. The other two meetings of the year, one at the midway point and another near the end of the school year, provide a chance to check in on the school's effectiveness as well as Wendy's progress on personalizing education for her.

At times, personalization and secondary schooling seem like opposite approaches to learning. Personalization builds learning experiences on the foundation of the strengths, interests, and aspirations of the individual. Where would Wendy's interest in cosmetology intersect with algebra 1, or world history? In contrast, secondary schooling is focused on preparing groups, not individuals, as productive citizens bound for college and work. In traditional schooling, groups of similar-aged students move together each year from kindergarten through graduation, essentially independent of what they know and are able to do. Following the traditions of schooling, Wendy was already "placed" in a track of people headed for four years of mathematics and two years of foreign language. Her transcript was already planned to look like that of hundreds of thousands of other young people her age in U.S. public schools. Personalization, on the other hand, emphasizes that people are not easily grouped, even by age. Each individual learns in unique ways in their own place and time. Can these opposites attract, or do they repel one another?

While the goals of personalization and schooling don't have to be in conflict, in most high schools they don't happily coexist. In many schools, students are never asked to build their learning on their interests and aspirations for the future; it is simply assumed that their interests are inconsequential to the larger societal expectations for education. Schools so organized seem to question that a young person like Wendy would know what would be good for her; as if her current interest in cosmetology and art might be a waste of time. High school teachers have not been trained in or given the supports necessary to draw parallels between students' aspirations and the content standards students must reach. Instead, their training as experts in a content area builds a belief that their knowledge is at the center of instruction.

This philosophical position is not helped by the fact that some students, even highly successful students like Wendy, do not see themselves at the center of their school learning. During her first PLP conference, for example, Wendy focused her future school success on her ability to perceive her teachers' goals and grading system, not on her own ability to apply her strengths and interests to the subject being explored in class. Many students are indeed unable to enjoy the full fruits of a Personalized Learning Plan because they perceive learning as figuring out what a teacher wants them to do rather than how their ideas must be challenged, supported, applied to new ideas presented to them.

Interestingly, in schools where ongoing dialogues are allowing personal conversations to occur for all students, a healthy conflict inevitably arises between what students want to learn and what schools want to teach. In Wendy's case, cosmetology isn't on the menu. Maybe it would be available two years from now in the vocational center, but is that a "college track" option? What can the school do about it now?

How can Wendy's recognition of her own strengths as hands-on, mechanical, and artistic be applied to classroom learning, now? How can teachers and students see the individual student at the center of learning?

Can the opposites of personalization and schooling be reconciled? Can these streams merge in a secondary school?

Personalized Learning Plans put the student in charge of acquiring skills and knowledge that lead toward purposes they set for themselves.

Two issues help us see how personalization and schooling can work together. The first concerns the paths students take with advisors' help. The second concerns the links between extracurricular interests and the ongoing requirements of school. The next vignette illustrates both.

Wendy's friend Will came into his first Personalized Learning Plan conference feeling that he should be at the center of his education, but he was wary of his advisor's and his teachers' knowledge of and belief in this fact. Perhaps since schools up until now had not recognized this, Will was now suspect of any effort to build an advising relationship. Where Wendy made suggestions, Will primarily shrugged.

Ken began, "What are the things that have been really important in your life?"

"I had a good friend move away."

Ken, wanting to build the conversation, pursued this avenue: "So you miss him?"

"No, not really."

Ken tried another tack to engage Will in sharing experiences: "If I had remembered to ask you to bring a friend, would you have brought someone?"

"Not really."

Another dead end. Ken continued with similar stops. Finally, Ken stopped asking questions, and began to tell about his own interests, and that opened the door for the conversation. When Ken mentioned canoeing and camping, Will found a common interest, and that made a connection, a safe environment that began the dialogue. Will opened up to *share his experiences, his interests, and his aspirations*—that is the first step down the path of a continuous, open dialogue. They ended the first conference with one idea that seemed promising to Will, "camping for credit."

During the second conference, Will and his advisors laid out and *examined multiple options* to consider as he looked ahead to in-school and out-of-school learning: Community-Based Learning, a trip to Alaska, a vehicle built through an independent study or in a future physics class. Ken praised Will's interest in life and his self-direction. Will continued adding to his list of things he would like to continue working toward, "I like raising dogs. Boats are cool to work on. I like dirt bikes. I like target shooting from a distance." Building on the myriad choices laid out in front of Will, Ken thought about the conflicts that might arise when a choice seemed impossible, "The ultimate choice is how to respond to your fate, something that seems as though you have no choice in." Working one's way through the options and making preliminary decisions is the second step on the path of the continuous dialogue.

At his third conference at the end of the year, Will told Ken and Linda about his life during the second half of his freshman year. The relationships had grown since the beginning of the year. They communicated easily, sharing experiences, listening intently, building on each other's questions for higher-level thinking, and articulating new understanding. Will's voice was clear, animated, and expressed who he was as an individual and a learner.

Will initiated the conversations, "I went camping [last] winter with just a tarp. It was a zero degree wind chill. We had to keep everything on. I put my water bottle and other gear in my sleeping bag. The water heats up and stays warm. If you took a hot water bottle it would stay warm for a long time." Ken joined in by explaining calorie loss as water changes to ice or steam changes to water. He reminded Will of the burn that occurs when steam turns to water on your face.

Will continued on describing his own experiences then sharing his successes in school. "This year, I got mediocre grades, but I got an A in English. The only reason I got C's before is because I was bored. We did one thing that was somewhat interesting. We read *Into the Wild*. I like the book. What the main character did, I thought, was good because he wanted to do it and went out and did it. We did a project. We had to tell where we'd go, why we'd do it. Most of the kids went to Hawaii or the Bahamas. I went to Alaska. I said I'd go by canoe and I got a bunch of good grades on the project. It wasn't hard. I could do it any time. I could get an A in any class I'm in now." Will had found the third step in the path—a way to *directly apply his interests* to his in-school learning.

Will's path of development in PLP conferences shows a dramatic contrast from his reticent beginning to his glorious and open ending. He started his first PLP conference hesitantly, but during the last PLP conference he demonstrated how he used his personal strengths and interests to impact his academic success. Will had reached the fourth step on the path of a continuous learning dialogue—*communicating a new power*—by sharing his thinking and strategies for future action and study.

Over the course of a year, Will and his advisors built strong relationships through a learning dialogue that is facilitated by the PLP. Four distinct dialogue stages (refer to figure 3.1 earlier in the chapter) manifest themselves in the Personalized Learning Plan process:

1. Sharing Experience
2. Expressing and Examining Diverse Concepts
3. Articulating Applications and Understandings
4. Communicating New Powers and Creations

Classroom teachers can spiral through these same four stages to build students' relationships with content. Teachers who personalize learning allow student voices to stand out as strongly as theirs does. In addition, their classrooms assist students through all four steps along the path to an open dialogue about authentic, relevant learning. In short, personalized classrooms promote a continuous learning dialogue and bring students into a relationship with themselves as well as with the content under study. Will's English class and PLP illustrate this.

In his ninth grade Personalized Learning Plan, Will found the necessary ingredients for successful, personalized learning within his English class. His teacher designed a unit of study that allowed him to *share his strengths, interests, and aspirations* while reading *Into the Wild*. His teacher encouraged Will to *express himself as he worked through new ideas as they came into conflict with his previous knowledge*. Will *applied his new understanding* by writing adventure stories and by exploring ways of fulfilling his own aspirations. He *produced and shared a fictional canoe trip to Alaska* that not only inspired his interest in English class but also built upon his keen outside-of-school interests.

One year later, Will orchestrated his real-life Alaskan adventure by working in his uncle's Alaskan resort for the summer. His advisors and parents helped him think about the trip, connect it to classroom learning, and validate his personal aspiration. His Personalized Learning Plan had helped him take charge of his knowledge and skills toward a purpose he had set for himself.

STUDENT ATTRIBUTES: PERSONALIZED LEARNING PLANS PUT PRESSURE ON STUDENTS TO ASSUME CONTROL OVER THEIR EDUCATION

One of Wendy and Will's cohorts, Shannon, is a poster child for the arguments against personalizing learning. She is a student who does not see herself as the center of her own learning. It is instructive to compare the attributes of Wendy, Will, and Shannon to shed light on the skills students need to develop to take full advantage of the Personalized Learning Plan. It is also helpful to see how the PLP impacted her learning.

During the daily PLP advisory time where Shannon's, Will's, and Wendy's PLP team of fourteen students meets with Linda and Ken, Shannon sits so that she ever so slightly remains separate from everyone else. From the beginning of the year, advisors have a difficult time setting up her conferences. When each scheduled conference day comes, Linda and Ken routinely ask Shannon if she and her mom are going to be able to make it. Shannon says, "Can I call my mom?" to which Ken always replies, "Sure, Shannon." She picks up the phone, dials home, murmurs a question, and then usually says, loudly and melodramatically, "You were called in to WORK again? So, you're NOT coming?"

The first conference of the year has to be rescheduled three times because her mother can't miss work to attend. Finally, a meeting is held with Shannon and two friends, without a parent present. Chatter, laughter, and hopes are expressed among friends. Shannon admits, "The best thing I ever did was move to this school." Her friends agree, adding some information about Shannon's sisters. Attention turns to Shannon, but when her friends begin to stir and get ready to leave, she abruptly ends the conference asking, "Are we going to do this again with my mom?" The conference lasts about fifteen minutes, about a quarter of the time that other PLP conferences take. The strengths and interests chart is not complete; a parent has not been there. If we asked her or her friends what happened at the meeting, they'd probably say "Not much." Where Wendy had explored and thought about her strengths and found support from others she loved, Shannon barely touched the issues, but at least she was in the companionship of her peers and learned that another chance was coming.

Several weeks later, a second PLP conference is set up, this time with Mom. In a small counseling room where Shannon spends a great deal of time and feels at home, Mom and Shannon sit at a table near Ken and Linda. Friends are sprawled on a couch behind the table. Notes of the meeting are again being written on a big pad of paper on the wall. Shannon says, "I want to drop math. I already changed my science class, and I'm doing well in science now. I participate. It's a lot easier. Before, I didn't want to ask any questions; my boyfriend was in that class. Now, I don't care what people think. I just ASK." This sounds like a promising start for a dialogue.

However, when asked to say more or to help think of alternative solutions to her frustrations in math, she changes the subject, avoiding and dodging the complicated issues. After a while, one of her friends says that Shannon "definitely has mood swings." Ken asks, "What are they related to?" Shannon immediately replies, "Schoolwork." Ken tries to follow up. "If I'm not prying, let me ask you another question. Do you like going up and down?" Shannon doesn't answer. Her head droops. Her friends speak for her, "She doesn't know what you're talking about." Shannon shrugs and reiterates that all she wants to do is to drop math.

Has she considered what dropping math will do to her course selections for next year? Shannon sighs and in a resigned tone of voice says, "I've already talked to my counselor. She says I'll have 4.9 credits and I should have 5 by then. I'll be in every class but not be a sophomore." In spite of this problem, Shannon clearly does not want to examine alternative solutions. Instead, frustrated with her general placement in life, she says, "Mom, couldn't you have had me earlier so I could take driver's ed next year?" If she were older than she is, the credit problem would still be a problem, but she can't change her age. More blaming and defensiveness quietly creeps into the conversation, and there is little progress in examining strategies for success.

Given fours years of conferences, with two or three meetings each year, will Shannon eventually be able to sit and engage in a complex, continuous open dialogue with others? When will she be ready to take charge of her own learning? Will things improve or deteriorate and will it be because of, or in spite of PLP? Wendy, Will, and Shannon have remarkably different sets of attributes. What are those attributes, and what do their teacher advisors need to know and be able to do to work with these complex, diverse students? Will all students benefit from a more personalized education? Or will the school's PLP contribute to the gap between them?

STUDENT ATTRIBUTES

Like Shannon, students who have had little choice or success in conventional classrooms have not developed the skills or capabilities needed to undertake the personalization of their learning. Most students, rewarded over the years by school grades for their compliance rather than their individuality and creativity, choose to silently follow others' ideas (Sizer, 1985; Belenky, Clinchy, Goldenberg, & Tarule, 1986; Delpit, 1995). But silence is not on the skills list needed for a Personalized Learning Plan. Students who have not been able to speak about or receive help setting their goals may not know how or when a goal is reachable or unreachable. They may not be able to judge how long something will take to be accomplished. All students need their voices, their creativity, and their ideas to be heard and supported by others in order to gain these skills needed to personalize their learning.

Friedrichs (2000), in an in-depth study of the Montpelier High School Personalized Learning Plan (PLP) program, discovered five principal student attributes or capabilities that are needed for personalization:

- Having a belief in themselves as a center of their own learning
- Feeling physical, intellectual, and emotional safety
- Being able to explore and incorporate new words and the ideas behind the new words as they converse with others
- Holding one's own view while encouraging the views of others
- Dealing with change

The more that students have the above capabilities, the more successful they are in taking part in a dialogue about their learning, making and connecting goals to their lives, and taking actions to achieve their goals. Wendy and Will are good examples of students who entered their ninth grade PLP experience with the supports in place around them for success. Wendy's parents encourage Wendy to see *herself at the center of her learning*, helping her to identify her own learning styles and to apply them in school. Wendy's parents encourage her to talk with her advisors about *feelings of insecurities* that freshmen have in classrooms and in the cafeteria especially around upper classmen. They *ask her if their words and explanations are accurate* and listen to Wendy when she corrects their analysis of her. In those first three areas Wendy has support for the attributes that were most difficult for her. However, she easily takes action that helps her emphasize what is *best for her while accepting what others want or need as part of her schooling*. She also *adapts easily to change*. Her openness, her ability to apply her action-oriented strengths to learning, her ability to deal with change along with the supports her parents bring into her freshman year PLP conferences allow her to enter into PLP dialogues and apply all five attributes to her learning.

Will *accepts the PLP advisor and process as safe* thereby allowing him to demonstrate his strengths in the other attributes. He knows *he should be at the center of his learning*. Once the PLP dialogue focuses on his strengths and interests, he eagerly *seeks new possibilities and ways of expressing* his interests and aspirations. He strongly *stands up for what is true for him even though it may not be true for his friends, teachers, or his advisors*. This is perhaps why he receives C's in classes that do not ring "true" for him. However, when he directs his own path, he takes bold steps and *learns to deal with change*.

Shannon, on the other hand, is missing or lacking in most of the attributes. She does not believe in herself as connected to her classwork. She does not believe that if she works hard, she will be successful. She does not trust that what has been planned will occur or that she will be emotionally safe in school. She has far fewer feelings of safety and well-being than any young person should have to endure. Getting beyond these two attributes is difficult. Semantics are meaningless with regard to schoolwork, but she willingly discusses the nuances of social and family pressures with the student support counselor. She sees herself in a whole other world from others and seeks assurances from her school and her friends that she is not alone.

Students like Shannon have specific gaps that need to be addressed before she can concentrate on academics or her future. The gaps lead to an incomplete PLP experience, and therefore a need for skillful scaffolding by advisors and help from the student support systems in place elsewhere in the school. The Montpelier PLP experience shows that all students need encouragement in or support for developing the five attributes (Friedrichs, 2000). In spite of Shannon's gaps in the five attributes, her ninth grade PLP confirmed that the school and her friends could be counted on to care for her and help her think about alternatives. At Shannon's last conference of the year, her friends offered to provide safe havens for her when her housing and livelihood was falling apart. Evidence like this from schools with strong personalized learning programs shows promise for building the needed capacities in all students. Schools and communities that succeed in personalizing education turn students from passive to active participants in their learning both in and outside of school.

To bring the needed attributes into the toolkit of every learner takes good advising for every student and a structure that allows the time for dialogue and the freedom to invent learning experiences around the strengths and interests of the learner. Fortunately, teachers need the same set of attributes, so the whole school community can learn about them and support each other in developing the new skills and awareness (Gibson, 1999; Friedrichs, 2000). As demonstrated in figure 3.2, personalized learning occurs most easily when all participants have the five essential attributes and have the opportunity to engage in all four stages of a Continuous Open Dialogue.

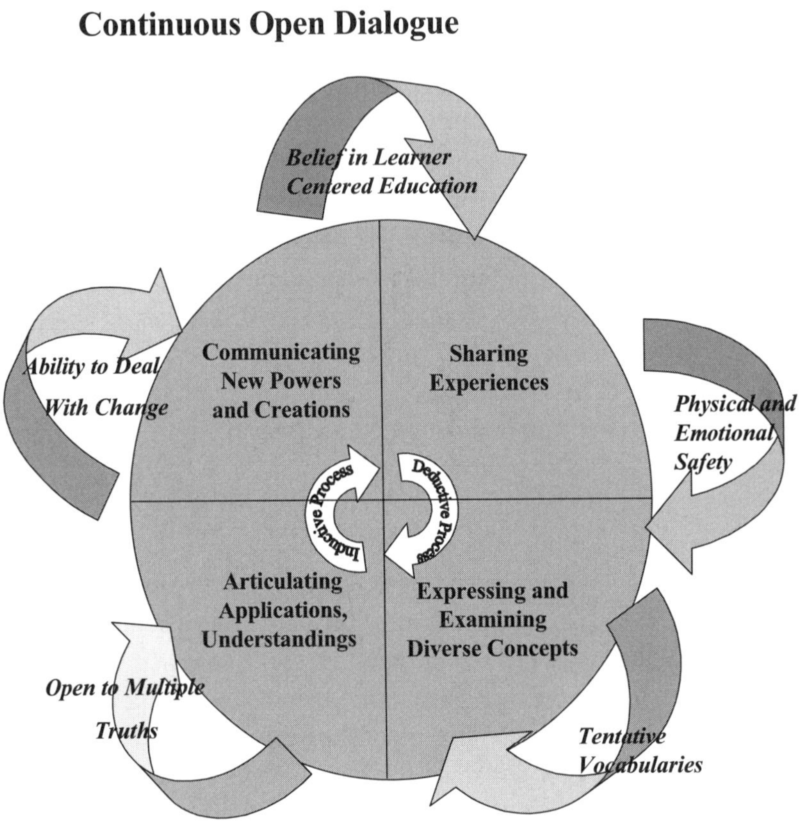

Continuous Open Dialogue

Belief in Learner Centered Education

Ability to Deal With Change

Communicating New Powers and Creations

Sharing Experiences

Physical and Emotional Safety

Inductive Process

Deductive Process

Articulating Applications, Understandings

Expressing and Examining Diverse Concepts

Open to Multiple Truths

Tentative Vocabularies

Figure 3.2.   Five essential attributes for a continuous open dialogue.

SKILLS REQUIRED OF TEACHERS AS ADVISORS

Ken and Linda worked with Wendy, Will, and Shannon. We learn from them that in the right atmosphere, adults can remain open to signs of self-direction in all students, no matter what attributes they bring to school. The atmosphere must allow the adults the time and support to focus on students as people who have promising hopes and aspirations, even if those are veiled or hard to draw out. The adults need to believe deeply that in those hopes lies all motivation for learning and that by attending to aspirations, teaching becomes ever more powerful. In addition, the adults need a personal toolkit of their own that helps them develop the sensitivities, responsiveness, and vocabulary of personalized learning.

TEACHER APTITUDES

The process of personalizing a student's education through an open dialogue involves letting go of the traditional means of control of the curriculum—that is, the textbook-based litany of the subject matter itself. Remembering that the intellectual discourse of the disciplines is an essential part of education, we must nevertheless face the fact that textual gatekeeping, which is appropriate for the professions, does not serve learning well.

Teachers need to first reenter their own professional disciplines as learners, recommit themselves to developing attributes of learner-centered education, building emotionally and physically safe environments, using tentative vocabularies, remaining open to multiple truths, and being willing to deal with change. Then teachers must extend personalized learning opportunities to others. They must be willing to enter into a learning dialogue that builds a relationship between the learner and the subject as well as between the learner and the teacher.

This is risky business, because as teachers, the "command and control" hierarchy has prevailed for so long. Taking and reporting class attendance, being responsible for parental notification, grading tests, proving fairness, and a host of other demands on a teacher have resulted in a highly defensive and isolating experience. Instead, teachers need a working environment that rewards inquiry and innovation, uniqueness, openness, and humility. Teachers need a personalized working environment as much as students need it for learning.

The four stages of PLP development—the path to a continuous open dialogue—mentioned previously (1. Sharing Experiences, 2. Expressing and Examining Diverse Concepts, 3. Articulating Applications and Understandings, and 4. Communicating New Powers and Creations) can serve as a starting point to talk about a model for building relationships between students and their own learning. The ideal is to have a teacher who can build a relational bridge between the student and learning. The entire school would support the teacher and the student in the building process so that if either the teacher or student needed support in the important attributes they bring to learning, the supports would be present in the school. The teacher would then be able to orchestrate the dialogue model successfully so that connections are made and personalized learning occurs for each student.

In what follows, we present what each PLP development stage is about and what a teacher can do to promote student growth within that arena. We will use the student-led Personalized Learning Plan (PLP) conference of Montpelier High School as the concrete structure to ground the concepts in a practical example. However, the conversational scripts and other ideas offered here can be adapted and applied in block scheduling, cooperative groupings, and other personalization strategies in secondary schools. Conversational scripts are merely starting points that should be surpassed as the teacher gains comfort with the new processes.

SHARING EXPERIENCES

Dialogue begins with a sharing of self and experiences. Throughout the PLP conferences, teachers can keep the conversation focused on the student's own view of his or her strengths, interests, aspirations, and concerns by asking open questions. The same is true for daily class-room dialogue. The teacher emphasizes her sincere interest in the students' thoughts, current focus, and future plans.

First meetings of the year:
"Tell me about yourself. Where were you born?"
"How did you come to attend this school?"
"What are you good at and what do you like to do?"
"What ideas do you have about the future?"
"Do you have any questions for me? Can I help you with anything?"
"What are you working on right now?"

Meetings later in the year:
"How's everything going?"
"What have you given your best energy to this year?" "Next year,

what do you see yourself getting involved in . . . ?" "Was there any excitement this year?"

"So what form has the anticipation of the end of the year taken?"

EXPRESSING AND EXAMINING NEW CONCEPTS

Teachers not only ask their advisees questions, they also express their own interests in relation to their students as a way to set the stage for students to examine new or different ideas. Talking with students at their levels of readiness to listen, skilled advisors empathize with a student's fears and offer suggestions that might not occur to the student. In addition, when differences are expressed, it brings out tensions. Teachers and students must then deal honestly with diverse points of view, be willing to examine the differences in meanings or words, and work to break down old conceptualizations so that new understandings can develop. Here are some "starter ideas and phrases" and some simple, basic advice. Listen to one another and check meaning by saying . . .

"I think I see what you mean. . . ."

"I too feel something like that when this happens to me. . . ."

"Have you thought about. . . ."

"I understood that to mean. . . ."

Help students look at the larger picture and then examine details that could assist them in getting what is needed. Help the student recognize conflicts and analyze old and new concepts, articulate and celebrate differences of opinion.

"I imagine you'd like doing this. . . ."

"Maybe you can do this. . . ."

"What would be interesting to see is the following. . . ."

"What are all the options?"

"What new information would help you figure that out?"

"Why doesn't that seem doable?"

Add personal stories that connect to common interests and provide models of new concepts and skills. Gather opinions in support of the student's learning.

"I like looking at things this way. . . ."

"If I were going to do what you are considering, here's what I'd consider. . . ."

"I think your parents agree with your thinking on this. . . ."

"The school will be proud of you for this. . . ."

"What I'd like to see happen. . . ."

ARTICULATING APPLICATIONS AND UNDERSTANDINGS

Teachers help advisees find the scaffolding support they need to work with their new academic challenges, their personal fears, and their new possibilities. What can teachers say to students who have the most difficult time working with new information, making choices, taking action on suggested directions?

"Will you come to me if you can't do this?"

"This is a suggestion; if you don't have something by next week, come in and we'll work it out with your friends."

Teachers assist students as they set academic goals. After sharing possibilities and encouraging a broad view of reaching personal and academic goals, teachers can encourage students to think and act in ways that support their strengths, interests, and aspirations. There is no need for teachers to force a new direction. Instead, teachers support the students' journeys through admiration of their progress even while guiding them more. Students gain confidence when teachers use open-ended questions to guide their reflections.

"How do you see your current plan fitting into your long-term goals?"

"How can we be providing you with some great service. . . ?"

"It seems that your ideas are integrated and have some direction. . . ."

"I'm impressed that you have as much interest in life as you do."

"Maybe for next year, we could build this approach into your schedule . . . if that will be in accord with your long-term goals."

"How has your wonderful performance affected your relationships with friends?"

A skilled teacher seeks a fuller understanding of her students by asking them about their train of thought and by explaining hers.

"Could you explain when you came to that . . . ?"

"I'd love to know what helped you figure that out."

"Would it be better if . . . ?

A teacher's questions can spark thinking and at the same time elicit an articulation of new understandings. The answers students develop empower them to continue their experimentation with new ideas. As students express themselves, they develop new understandings and take on new creative action.

COMMUNICATING STUDENTS' NEW POWER, CREATIVITY

When teachers openly admire the creative thought of their students, students explore and then take independent, empowered action. Some students need extra support. Their conferences and meetings can include supportive friends, who, when encouraged, can express how they can assist each other in multiple ways to solve real problems.

"Our paths diverge, but all of our paths are leading toward high school graduation. I want to encourage you to help each other."

"You don't have to be in class together, but you can still work together."

"Spend the time organizing your studying and working together on different work."

Teachers can encourage a continuation of creative, independent direction by expressing confidence in what students decide to undertake. Students look forward to further exploration of "What if?" questions with teachers who stay open and accepting in dialogue. Teachers show confidence, admiration, and belief in advisees' approach to learning with phrases such as:

"What if you presented this to others?"

"What if you published this work?"

"I admire you for your equanimity."

"Take pride in your own creativity."

When teachers and students learn together, they build common relationships—a relationship between the student and the teacher as well as a relationship between the people and the subject of study. This relationship develops through a learning dialogue that has distinct stages. When schools support students and teachers in the five essential attributes for successful learning dialogue, personalized learning occurs. Figure 3.3 presents PLP Dialogue stages and supporting attributes.

PRESSURE ON THE SYSTEM

Unlike individualized learning, which seeks to make external expectations palatable to learners, the Personalized Learning Plan begins with student interests, forcing the system to respond to diverse interests.

THE NEED FOR PERSONALIZATION

The argument in favor of personalization points out several essential facts. We now know that all learning is a personal construction that is

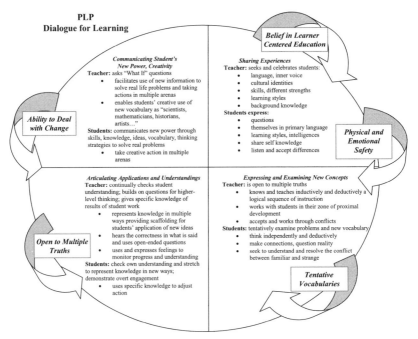

Figure 3.3.   PLP dialogue stages and supporting attributes.

facilitated within and by a diverse social setting (Irwin, 1991; Kohn, 1993; Dixon-Krauss & Friedrichs, 2000). I may arrive at school thinking that rain is caused by giants rolling bowling balls in the clouds, but as soon as I tell others about that theory, conflicting views are expressed. I then face a decision that will be faced many more times during learning and growth. Should I abandon my theory and take on the new one? If I am convinced to change my views, then I must reconstruct all the rest of what I know that depends on and relates to the new fact. Thus personal choice in a social setting is a crucial element of my learning. A school setting that recognizes and encourages me as an individual helps me make that choice to learn.

A learner's decision to reconstruct an understanding of the world is not only a complex intellectual problem, it is also vital to everything that already holds personal meaning and therefore is a highly emotional moment for the learner (Betts, 1906; Irwin, 1991; Sylwester, 1994, 1995; Goleman, 1995; Caine & Caine, 1997; Sprenger, 1999). For example, unless I feel mentally and emotionally safe, and possess the personal attributes to take advantage of those safe conditions, I may quietly decide to stay with my theory that giants with bowling balls produce rain. If I live in a social and personal setting in which I frequently step away from the decision to accept new ideas, I may develop permanent gaps in my understanding of the world. This might happen, for example, if my safety issues are constantly or effectively made uncertain. Unfortunately for many students, feelings of uncertainty, or worse than that, the experience of being isolated, labeled, mistrusted, and avoided, or even hated is not uncommon in school. This helps explain the well-documented relationship between these conditions that place students at risk, and the low level of their achievement (Kohn, 1993; Sowell, 1987). Thus schools need personalization so that all students feel that they belong within a social group that makes it safe to learn.

When schools believe that their central task is to aid people in the process of personalized learning within a socially diverse environment (Friedrichs, 2000), the benefits are numerous. All learners become supported in taking the risks of learning, which helps them develop a sense of being valued as well as fit for contributing to the group. As healthy, accepted members of groups, they then begin to make valued contributions to others and make the most of their individual learning opportunities. The school's resources are then utilized at their most effective level. Students who succeed in becoming productive members of small groups also transfer those capacities to society, which then fulfills the academic and social mission of schools. In the past, the personal assets of some learners allowed them to succeed in spite of the barriers present in traditional schooling. However, if schools could personalize learning for everyone it would lower barriers and raise possibilities for all students.

THE NEED FOR SCHOOL RENEWAL

Unfortunately, perhaps burdened by their public duty to educate the most people by the most efficient means possible, schools have usually sacrificed individuality, and nearly always systematically ignored personhood. This bureaucratic predilection has not helped many, least of all the most vulnerable students and families in society. It has instead led to traditional approaches to grouping students and even individualizing education that have solidified the unhelpful stance.

Many of the traditional approaches have forced the child to fit into the system. Tracking, for example, is an attempt to differentiate the school's program to meet various levels of students. However, it is well known that tracking also force-fits students into debilitating roles with limited learning opportunities (Oakes, 1992; Slavin, 1992). Renewal efforts combating these effects, such as heterogeneous groups and block scheduling, have attempted to address the bad side effects of tracking, but have sometimes ignored the main symptom that led to tracking in the first place. The main symptom is large numbers of individual students who are not being personally well served by the standard curriculum approaches, timing, sequencing, and support systems of schooling.

Another example of forcing the child into the system comes from "pullout" approaches intended for remediation. The child is labeled deficient and is removed from a regular setting in order to get "fixed." What do you suppose is going on in the regular classroom while the "pulled-out" student is away? If the classroom activity is either an enhancement or essential, then the pullout student is a loser. On the other hand, if the classroom activity is either nonessential or irrelevant, then the rest of the students lose out. If there is a win-win to be created here, it will take a renewal of our ideas about service delivery.

Or, consider a typical "independent studies" program. This seems like it would be one of the most advanced and flexible ways of meeting individual needs. However, when discipline area teachers grade the study and the content and the study design must meet academic requirements, the approach becomes limited to the conventional control of ideas, subjects, and assessments. As a result, many independent studies programs work with only a small segment of the already successful academically oriented students.

All of the above approaches create "haves" and "have-nots" within the system. For example, tracking creates a group of people that is expected to go to college and another group that is not. Pullouts create a group of people who are so "special" that a whole support system of separate teachers, counselors, specialists, materials, and rooms are needed. Independent studies, it is often claimed in the handbooks, are "not for everyone." It seems that the traditional ways of "individualizing the curriculum" have some serious drawbacks and side effects.

To address these ill effects, schools that seek to personalize education need ways to ensure that 1) activities are geared to the individuality of each student and 2) no individual or group will miss an important learning opportunity. To deliver on the first promise, teachers need new skills and abilities of assessing students and designing instructional experiences with the individual as the "unit of change." The new skills go beyond a teacher's typical training, experience, and support systems for professional growth that have been focused on group-based classroom management and curriculum presentation. To deliver on the second promise, the school needs a new way to open sustained dialogues with students and parents, and new ways to account for and monitor student progress. Key to the full acceptance of personalized goals within the school is an acknowledgment of the common core of skills and abilities that are addressed and assessed through a multitude of new learning avenues. Thus, there are both professional development as well as structural and organizational aspects to the problem of establishing personalized learning in a school setting.

RESTRUCTURING TO SUPPORT PERSONALIZED LEARNING: WHY THE WHOLE SYSTEM MUST CHANGE IF WE ARE GOING TO PERSONALLY ENGAGE ALL STUDENTS

Some might argue that schools do not need the additional burden. Schooling is well established in its role of transmitting basic information. Learning how to read, write, and do arithmetic still rings a valued note within the politics of education. Schools have their hands full, this argument goes, in carrying out this role. In addition, schools have taken on a bewildering array of other social missions, which up until now have not necessarily had much to do with personal fulfillment. For example, making healthy choices about sex and drugs and learning to get along with others are essential for a person's role in a democracy, but as personal goals, they don't capture the imagination and lead to creativity, a sense of calling, or happiness. Why do schools need to capture the heart of learners in these ways? Why do schools need "personalization"? Isn't it enough for schools to meet their traditional basic academic and social mission?

THE STRUCTURAL AND ORGANIZATIONAL CHALLENGE

"Personalization" and "individualization" are not the same, so the first challenge is to not create a structure that confuses the two. A school that solves the structural and organizational issues of individualization, for example, may still not make the connection to the level of personal meaning within the student. For example, a "pullout" program may effectively remediate below-grade-level readers without linking to their strengths, interests, and aspirations. Few schools rigorously ask their students and their parents about these sorts of things in order to make relevant, immediate adjustments in the school's offerings, approaches, and in the individual educational program of every child. Even in schools that "do" individualization well, the personal goals of families and students are often left unattended. A school might offer a wide array of enrichment and support services and still never ask its students who they are, what they are good at, and where they want to go in life.

Structurally, personalization can occur without individualization of the curriculum. In fact, if students feel a strong personal connection to the content and material under study, then the size of the group they are in doesn't matter as much. Witness the throngs at a music concert, theater performance, or a memorable school assembly and you'll see an example of personalization within a large group setting. To individualize the same settings, the music or theater group would have to produce hundreds or thousands of separate simultaneous performances. The fear of having to produce hundreds of separate classroomlike "performances" may be the prospect that frightens educators away from addressing personalization, but it obviously needn't be the case. Personalized learning experiences needn't be unique in order to be meaningful. This raises the possibility that a school can create structures for personalization of education for all students. But how?

To build meaning into learning experiences, the structure of the school needs to allow collaborative "customization" and "identification." Consider, as a metaphor, the custom-ordered consumer good. The choice of which item you want is made among several options. The very choice of buying today or not is yours. The items to consider are available in different "flavors," with special "editions," and can be "configured" to your liking. To allow these same kinds of choices to students, schools need to structure their time and organizational expectations to acknowledge students' vision, imagination, and ability to choose. To leave this arena to the individual classroom teacher is to invite unevenness in the school experience, create inequities within the learning opportunities, and consign other students to a "one-size-fits-all" mentality of schooling. The extent of choice and identity in a school setting and curriculum is a good measure of its meaning or relevance to students. Making and recognizing one's choices is essential to making meaning, which is essential to the personalization of learning.

Compare this to the average day in the life of a secondary school student. Studies that have shadowed students for a day or more discover that the day is pretty boring. Students pick up their books, supplies, hats, and coats—everything they have with them—and move from place to place six to eight times a day. They make sudden shifts in context and requirements, operating under pressure. On a moment's notice they are asked to perform at peak or recall numerous details from several days or weeks before, and if they can't perform or recall the details, they are punished (Sizer, 1985; DiMartino & Clarke, in press). To counter this, a school's structure of time and expectations can help "ensure that learning is a personal enterprise in a collaborative setting rather than a depersonalized, individual competition" (Friedrichs, 2000).

Of course, there is a place for learning to "do things that you have to, even when you don't want to." Life is not a custom-ordered good experience. It doesn't hand us everything we want. But neither is it a prisonlike experience where everything is ordered or demanded. Traditional secondary schooling, coming from its roots in the factory era, has a plentitude of structures devoted to an ordered and demanded curriculum. Personalization is an attempt to introduce a measure of humanity and individual democracy in the depersonalizing experience of secondary school.

Additionally, note the relationship between "choice" and "commitment." When the consumer—the learner—makes choices, a personal level of commitment is involved. At each step of the process of configuring the desired good, a stronger commitment is being built.

If the school can structure its time and expectations to allow for a personal experience—one with choice and identity for the student—then the attention can shift to the aptitudes of the students and teachers for interacting in a new way. For teachers, the new aptitudes are helpful to traditional teaching, thus supporting their current responsibilities while they retool themselves for the future. For students, it turns out that the aptitudes are also needed for success in academics and life. So, there is no sacrifice of the secondary school's cherished and important traditional mission of preparing students for further study and the social responsibilities of citizenship. The difference is that the aptitudes, instead of being assumed as an asset of every child and teacher, are systematically developed as part of the structure of schooling.

The Personalized Learning Plan is built on one promising structure borrowed from elementary education, the student-parent conference. At the secondary level, those conferences can eventually be student led, allowing a large measure of self-direction and responsibility to develop. In addition, because the conversation takes place outside of the regular classroom, teachers can fulfill their new roles without threatening their control of the curriculum and classroom. Teachers find it easier to experiment with new advising skills and can better help students toward new aptitudes in a low-risk conference structure. In Personalized Learning Plan conferences, the idea is to treat the meetings as a sorting table of ideas for the student to make sense out of in-school as well as out-of-school learning in conjunction with their aspirations and immediate life goals.

Educators and parents, as long-term partners of the learner, need to build relationships to become better listeners and facilitators of learning grounded in and motivated by learners themselves. The central component of those new relationships is a continuous open dialogue about learning and growth. The structure of schools must change in order to allow the time and support for such dialogues to evolve in order for all students to become more engaged and successful in learning.

RESOURCES

Belenky, M.F., Clinchy, B.M., Goldenberg, N.R., & Tarule, J.M. (1986). *Women's Ways of Knowing: The Development of Self, Voice, and Mind.* New York, NY: Ballantine Books.

Betts, G.H. (1906). *The Mind and Its Education.* New York, NY: D. Appleton and Company.

Caine, R. N. & Caine, G. (1997). *Education on the Edge of Possibility.* Alexandria, VA: Association for Supervision and Curriculum Development

Delpit, L. (1995). The silenced dialogue. In *Other People's Children.* New York: The New Press.

Dimartino, J., Clarke, J., & Wolk, D. (at press). *Personalized Learning: Preparing High School Students to Create Their Futures.* Lanham, MD: ScarecrowEducation.

Dixon-Krauss, L. (Ed.). (1996). *Vygotsky in the Classroom: Mediated Literacy Instruction and Assessment* (paperback ed.). White Plains, NY: Longman.

Friedrichs, A. (2000). Continuous Learning Dialogues: An Ethnography of Personal Learning Plans' Impact on Four River High School Learners. Unpublished dissertation, University of Vermont.

Gibson, D. (2000). Growing Towards Systemic Change: Developing Personal Learning Plans at Montpelier High School. In *Dynamics of Change in High*

School Teaching: A Study of Innovation in Five Vermont Professional Development Schools. Providence, RI: The Regional Laboratory.

Goleman, D. (1995). *Emotional Intelligence: Why It Can Matter More Than IQ for Character, Health and Lifelong Achievement.* New York, NY: Bantam Books.

Irwin, J. (1991). *Teaching Reading Comprehension Processes.* Boston, MA: Allyn and Bacon.

Kohn, A. (1993). *Punished by Rewards.* New York, NY: Houghton Mifflin Company.

Oakes, J. (1992). Multiplying Inequalities. In *Relevant Research, 2.* Washington, DC: National Science Teachers Association.

Sizer, T. (1985). *Horace's Compromise: The Dilemma of the American High School.* Boston: Houghton Mifflin Company.

Slavin, R. (1992). Achievement Effects of Ability Grouping in Secondary Schools. In *Relevant Research, 2.* Washington, DC: National Science Teachers Association.

Sowell, T. (1987). *Conflict of Visions.* New York, NY: W. Morrow.

Sprenger, M. (1999). *Learning & Memory: The Brain in Action.* Alexandria, VA: Association for Supervision and Curriculum Development.

Sylwester, R. (1994, October). How Emotions Affect Learning. In *Educational Leadership.* Alexandria, Virginia: Association for Supervision and Curriculum Development.

CHAPTER 4

Personalized Learning and Personalized Teaching

JOHN CLARKE
Professor emeritus, University of Vermont

"How do you want to die?" I hadn't thought about that question at all until I started teaching high school English nearly 35 years ago.

Equipped with a lesson plan on Frost's use of symbolism in "An Old Man's Winter Night," I thought I could disrupt the afternoon apathy of our classroom by asking my students to help me draw pictures of all the things Frost described in the old man's house—barrels, a fading lamp, a damp cellar—then help them guess what these things might represent from his earlier life. Most kids like to draw more than they like to read poetry. I would draw the poem. They would interpret my drawing.

I had drawn a rough shack on the board to represent the old man's house. "What do the barrels mean?" I asked, pointing to a barrel I had drawn in a lower room, where the old man sat. I waited. Eyes were dropping away from my sketch, or shifting toward the bright sunlight slanting in through a crack between shade and sill in our darkened classroom. Noise of chairs moving. Apparently, this afternoon crowd had not come to believe that barrels "mean" anything. I waited, letting the pain sink in. A hand shot up from the front of the room, at last.

"How do you wanna die?"

Silence still shrouded the room, but eyes had returned to me. How could I divert this irrelevant question back to Frost's poem?

"How does Frost show the old man's attitude toward death?" I queried, searching the center of the room for some bright face. Faces faded again into sullen withdrawal. Heads dropped. But Bruce's hand was back in the air, for all to see.

"How do you wanna die?"

Bruce was something of a pariah in our class, often homeless and sometimes dirty. He slept in parked cars, they say, and came to class smelling of gin. He also experienced episodes of hallucination that could be frightening if you didn't expect them, particularly if he was frustrated. Students have a defense compact with each other, but I do not believe I was alone in that room, worrying how close Bruce might come to frustration. We were all a bit scared of Bruce.

"How you want to die?"

I may have been the only one of us thinking that Bruce might have some particular answer in mind—for me. My mouth began to dry up. Still, Bruce had broken the pall of silence. A question had been asked, so I had to persist.

"How do you think the old man would answer Bruce's question?" I asked, trying once more to turn our exploration toward the poem. Some eyes had turned back to the blackboard. Others were scanning the room to see what might happen next. I saw a wave of smirks and whispers pass across male faces in the back row.

Bruce's hand was back in the air. "I mean, how do you wanna die?

A teacher's nightmare. I was frozen. I had no answer. I had no questions. I had no clever ideas. No jokes came to mind. I felt only fear. Images flashed through my mind suggesting the hundred ways in which I did not want to die. I suddenly felt cold beads of sweat running from armpit to belt line. Bruce looked cool and composed. No hallucinations, yet, but his hand remained upright and all eyes were on me. After several seconds of helpless silence, I turned back to the board.

"How do you want to die?" I wrote in broad, unsteady letters across the top.

We took two minutes to write out our thoughts, and the work began. Some thought dying would be OK if they had lived a good life. Others thought a bunch of possessions might help. Several cited religious reasons for not being afraid. Some imagined a heroic end with public applause. Everybody had something to say. Then, we began to read Frost. If the barrels represent memories, how much comfort do they offer the old man? Us? Is death cold, like the surrounding night, or is it warm like the lamp flame? We read other Frost poems for clues: "Fire and Ice," "Death of the Hired Man," "After Apple Picking."

How do you want to die? By looking at Frost's efforts to answer that question, in comparison to our own beliefs, we all began to assemble some vision of life that would make death acceptable, using Frost's lines to anchor our thoughts. We began to write. We began to think. We were thinking about ourselves, through Robert Frost. And I had begun a lifelong quest to discover how to engage young adults in discovering how to use their minds to control the direction of their own lives.

All learning is personal. High school learning could not produce such a broad range of unique results, whether measured on standardized tests or creative projects, if it were not unique to each of us. Learning begins with personal questions. All learning engages what we already know in pursuit of what we don't know yet. Learning forces us to look closely at information that may not support our initial beliefs. Learning forces us to entertain several choices and make a stand. Reconciling divergent views into a personal perspective, or selecting one choice from many options, produces the stress of disequilibrium. Learning makes us reorganize information into patterns that yield personal meaning. Learning forces us to present what we know in a manner that brings us clarifying feedback. Learning asks us to produce something new that represents new understanding. Learning is active. Learning is effortful. Learning is idiosyncratic to the individual learner. Learning follows personal engagement.

Learning, in brief, is always personal. Yet we have established a nationwide system of high schools that channels all learning and assessment toward one mode: abstract, text-based, inert, uniform across schools and individuals, bolstered by standardized tests measuring the acquisition of uniform content. As long as we insist on uniformity among young adult students who are growing toward their distinctive purposes, our results will adhere to the normal curve: a few succeed nicely; many fill the ambiguous central quartiles; and an alarming number will fail or drop out to pursue their aims without adult guidance, or to drift aimlessly into another decade of dependence. To the extent that high school teaching insists on uniform answers across a population that grows increasingly unique as students move toward adult roles, it will fail a large proportion of the students that public education is mandated to serve. To reform the high school experience, we need to base high school reform on increasingly complex ideas about how young adults learn, and how individuals learn differently.

Several decades of research and theory on learning have produced a framework called constructivism that connects teaching to what we know about how students learn. From a constructivist perspective, the bits of knowledge that make up high school courses can be learned only to the extent that they extend what the learner already knows and provide a platform for further elaboration. Fosnot (1989) offers this explanation:

> A constructivist takes the position that the learner must have experiences with hypothesizing and predicting, manipulating objects, posing questions, researching answers, imagining, investigating, and invention, in order for new constructions to be developed. From this perspective, the teacher cannot insure that learners acquire knowledge just by having the teacher dispense it; a learner-centered, active instructional model is mandated. The learner must construct the knowledge; the teacher serves as a creative mediator in the process.

In a constructivist classroom, students spend the greatest amount of time making explicit what they already know, working with others to make new knowledge fit an expanding sense of how things work, and projecting their new conceptions into the world around them where those conceptions are tested against new experience. Personalized learning allows individuals to understand the world they are preparing to enter and develop the skills and knowledge they will need to succeed.

PERSONALIZED LEARNING IN FIVE VERMONT HIGH SCHOOLS

From 1997 to 1999, a group of high school educators in Vermont began a research project on high school teaching that engages students in learning (Clarke, Bossange, Erb, Gibson, Nelligan, Spencer, & Sullivan, 2000). We selected specific teaching projects in five Vermont Professional Development High Schools that were recognized in those schools as highly engaging. By observing students in those classes, and interviewing teachers and administrators who had supported their development over six years, we aimed to describe the processes that produce standards-based reform at the high school level. Although our study focused primarily on the processes of change that allow a high school to move toward standards-based learning, the projects themselves represent the wide diversity of teaching techniques that engage students actively and support personalized learning. A quick review of those projects may represent the diversity of approaches to teaching and curriculum that may be required to engage a diverse student population.

Otter Valley High School: The Land Use Project "One Hundred Acres"

Until Ellie Davine and her university intern began to redesign Otter Valley's course "Vermont Geography" to fit Vermont's "Framework of Standards and Learning Opportunities" (Vermont Department of Education, 1996), the course was an overview of the geographic areas that make up the state's landscape. Students read books and maps, and then took quizzes and tests on the differences among sections of the state. Because "Vermont Geography" was not part of the college preparation track, the students who filled the desks tended to come from families in which college was not a real choice. Most of these students in the course had difficulty attending school regularly; many had long records of infraction in the vice principal's office; many lived in trailers and small houses scattered among the rugged valleys of this fading agricultural region or in villages that once relied on small industries or marble and limestone quarries. Most hoped to remain in the area served by the high school, developing roles in the local economy.

Bill and Ellie began redesigning the course by selecting standards related to geography and decision-making. For a culminating task in the course, they "gave" each student a plot of land described in a topographical map, perhaps 100 acres. The student's task was to assess the condition of the land and propose a land use plan for its development or preservation. Some lucky students received a crossroads in one of Vermont's five geographic regions. Others received a ledge hillside surrounded by impenetrable swamp. All students conducted the assessment steps required by Vermont's Act 250, an environmental law that defines the process for any land development scheme in the state. Each was responsible for making a presentation to a simulated Act 250 review board late in the semester. Getting ready to pitch their idea for development made up the body of the new course.

Vermont Geography students develop a portfolio on their land over two months or more. The portfolios had to include a table of contents and 25 artifacts, including:

- an analysis of topographical variation in the site
- watershed maps
- analysis of glaciations on topography
- wildlife and vegetation inventories
- existing environmental restrictions and laws
- an analysis of transpiration systems
- existing infrastructure
- energy availability
- ethnic, religious, and racial characteristics of the population
- economic characteristics of the population
- agricultural characteristics of the region
- commercial and industrial developments in the area

The land use project allowed students to demonstrate how their final proposal met six of Vermont's standards, assessed by a rubric distributed as the course began. Students also practiced computer analysis of census data and the development of graphs, charts, and maps for their Act 250 hearing. In the year of our research, all students completed the culminating task and passed the course: ESL students, special education students, habitual truants, and quiet students who seldom spoke in any class (Spencer, 2000).

Global Perspectives at Essex High School

More than forty-five students fill seats in a doublewide classroom in a daily eighty-four-minute English and social studies class, managed by Kevin Martell and Sue Pasco at Essex High School. Many students who excel in Global Perspectives have not experienced success in more conventional courses. Kevin and Sue decided years ago to teach the students to teach themselves, and to organize their expanded time together around projects and presentations presented by students to each other. They integrated English and history to gain a broad perspective, open to students who think and learn differently. Student maps, graphic organizers, collages, models, papers, posters, and homemade artifacts cover the walls and hang from the ceiling. Television monitors, CD players, overheads, computers, and tape recorders fill the corners of the room, ready for students and small groups to use in teaching the class. Over the year, materials developed by students to explain themes from history and literature begin to cover each other on the walls, forming unwieldy stacks on filing cabinets, like archaeological artifacts from the strata of accumulated human experience.

The course focuses on ideas that have arisen over thousands of years to change the human condition. Most of the course assignments ask students to assume the perspective of literary or historical figures along the trail of human events. Students replicate cave paintings, dance the rituals of their tribe, compose and sing the songs that praise or lament their people's fate, design graphics that explain the transitions that open new eras, new ways of thinking. Students work in small groups to develop their presentations. They finally work alone to express the personal perspective they have developed from their studies. Sue and Kevin continue to redevelop their course each year, using learning theory to create projects that engage all students and also represent the achievement of Vermont's standards. Most students see Global Perspectives as their favorite class, the one in which they can become successful.

Because Kevin and Sue use their Global Perspectives experience to guide their own professional development, their approach to teaching incorporates constructivist techniques developed over 15 years or more, from Writing to Learn (Fulwiler) to Multiple Intelligence theory (Gardner). They design their units to match the learning styles of different students, derived from Bernice McCarthy's 4MAT learning cycle. They employ Cooperative Learning extensively, so students support each other in developing a perspective on the human condition. They integrate thinking strategies instruction (Clarke, 1990). They practice interdisciplinary, cross-disciplinary teaching, so each student can find a point of access to the content, supported by a teacher who understands and respects their personal perspective. Finally, as the standards movement gained momentum across the country, they connected their projects to standards and designed rubrics for assessing student presentations and papers.

Global Perspectives continues to grow because an English and a history teacher have developed a reliable course structure that also allows wild proliferation in the ways students learn and present information. As students practice different learning techniques, they also discover new ways to convey their ideas, creating new opportunities for their classmates and for their teachers. As Kevin and Sue see what students can do with information, they change their assignments to allow greater flexibility. This year, for example, they adapted their "Medieval Journey" assignment to accommodate the social class perspectives of Europe and Asia after the last millennium. Students adopted a clear perspective that matched their own interests: pope, knights, kings, merchants, serfs, or priests, then set off on a pilgrimage to any "Canterbury" in the medieval world. Their task was to describe their pilgrimage in detail from a chosen "persona"—and bring home relics they could use to educate other members of the class system. The festival that ensued after their return was worthy of any medieval town, allowing each student to develop a perspective on a neatly regulated social system that contrasts markedly with our own.

The Imaging Lab at South Burlington High School

Tim Comoli, the English teacher who conducts electronic arts, advertising, and video production classes in South Burlington High School's Imaging Lab, likes to deny that he knows anything about computers or the software his students use to create graphics and video for local businesses and service organizations. Tim began his media career in radio and wrote with a pen more than thirty years ago. Nevertheless, his students learn to use state-of-the-art technology to prepare films and other media for presentation to the larger Burlington community. The Imaging Lab, a converted classroom, glows with the strange light of many state-of-the art computer screens. A projector allows individuals to project their work to a ceiling monitor, receiving criticism and suggestions. His students borrow knowledge and technique from each other, testing new software programs and growing their way into the world of technology that is expanding around them.

Tim can be found in the back room, consulting with students on how to get messages to carry and stick. He has assembled a vast library of current computer magazines, from which students glean examples of interesting effects to fit their own ideas. As they develop expertise with different programs—Power Animator, Softimage or D-Paint, for example—they can show others the advantages and limitations of the newest options in software. Tim's students teach themselves, then teach each other. Tim wanders from student to student in the darkened lab, encouraging and asking questions that help his students understand their own work. "Unlike other teachers," a young woman explained, "Mr. Comoli understands the way we think and understands the gaps between high school students and the adult world." Tim's courses bridge that gap, bringing students into contact with the world they will soon lead (Bossange, 2000).

Tim's students have already assumed leadership roles in the school and community. Even in the early years, they were recruited to help the high school faculty understand how to use word processors and the precursors to the World Wide Web. They have helped teach university students to understand communications software and solve network problems. They join graduate courses in the summer as consultants and guides. As one student commented, after confessing he had been a marginal student with some personal problems, "Before I got in here, I didn't have any direction. I thought school was a big joke. Now I realize what I want to do with my life" (Bossange, 2000). Tim Comoli's students learn to assume adult responsibilities by experimenting with adult roles.

Community-Based Learning and Personalized Learning Plans at Montpelier High School

Montpelier High School's Personalized Learning Plans (PLPs) are designed to allow each student to set a direction toward engagement in the community that will lend coherence and purpose to their coursework in school. The idea of helping each student assess her own strengths, review her own history, and establish hopes for adult roles emerged from the discovery that a vast number of students were already engaged in community service, business, government, or education projects in their own city. As students converted voluntary projects into academic credit, the school's faculty began to collide with each other in the doorways of local institutions. Driven by student need for engagement, Montpelier's campus expanded gradually to encompass the entire community. Rather than spending their days in a series of high school classrooms, students run back and forth from school to local businesses or community organizations, weaving the two into one system. Experience in the community began to influence the way teachers designed their courses. Personalized Learning Plans are emerging now to provide systematic support connecting high school learning to adult engagement—for all Montpelier students.

Do Montpelier students like Community-Based Learning (CBL) because it gives them a way to escape school? "Well, yeah, that's part of it," one student explained, who had been drifting aimlessly through high school classes for three years. "But I go to my site even on weekends." This student was working with his adopted grandparent, who can no longer leave his home without major assistance. "Some of my friends don't get it. They think I'm just wasting my time sitting there quietly watching the clock. But Charlie needs me, you know—for food and medicine and stuff like that. Little things, but they matter" (Gibson, 2000). The Montpelier Community-Based Learning and independent studies students range widely across their city. This year, four women are setting up a community awareness program about date rape and violence. Another is assisting in a scientific study of ravens and crows. Directing one's own learning is difficult to achieve in a setting where someone else makes all the assignments and grades all the work.

In Community-Based Learning, Montpelier students are learning to gather information that fits a purpose they have set for themselves. Using a design for Personalized Learning Plans that begins with their own talents and interests, they are using experience to test their hopes, and reflection to adapt their personal goals. "When students without CBLs walk downtown," one teacher commented, "they look at buildings and do not know what goes on inside. With CBL, students are put into the buildings. They learn what makes a community and they gain an increased sense of belonging. They learn about who they are. They learn responsibility" (Gibson, 2000). Montpelier classes remain patterned to the established academic subject areas, but students can use both classes and experience to search for their own futures, and also understand what it will take to get there.

The Physics War at Mt. Abraham Union High School

Each year, Tom Tailer's physics war rages on the playing fields of Mt. Abraham High School in Bristol, Vermont, usually on a Friday just before Halloween. To prepare his 100 students for "War," Tom uses the laws of physics to teach them how to design, field test, and calibrate a weapon that fires tennis balls—some laden with grease or paint—to distances that may exceed 100 yards. PCV pipe, two-by-four lumber, yards of surgical tubing, and items rescued from dumps and attics make each weapon unique. If a student's weapon proves accurate and reliable during calibration, the student is assigned to a rich country, the U.S. or China, for example. If a weapon fires short or wild during calibration, the student is assigned to a third world nation. First world armies feast on pizza. Third world armies get a handful of rice. An army that destroys an enemy ammo dump or food supply receives that country's store of goods. The chance to share pizza or recruit weapons from neighboring countries leads to alliance-building that is as lively as hostile aggression—or nearly so" (Clarke, Aiken, & Sullivan, 1999).

The "Armed Aggression" Unit focuses first on physics, but quickly expands to include history, geography, English, philosophy, economics, political science, and anthropology. Each year, Mount Abraham students use an integrated approach to mathematics and science to develop an arsenal of nonlethal weapons; they then use information from history, political science, economics, and geography to enact global conflict and divide wealth among the world's nations. After the war has ended, they meet as a physics class again to assess the meaning of what they did on the battlefield in light of their understanding of real global conflict (Sullivan, 2000). Many students in the physics war choose to put down their weapons and work for peace. Some form a small version of the Red Cross. Some become UN negotiators. Some spend the day as anarchists, refusing to join the conflict under any flag.

After some alliance has managed to conquer the world, Tom's 100 students gather in the auditorium to assess the battle. They are joined by a sample of adults from the community who either work in the military or in organizations that repair the destruction war brings. Adults and students face the same questions: How does technological acumen affect conflict? Morality? Can peace activism affect human conflict? Do we fight for values, or for the thrill of the battle? Is war a male event? Should women be required to serve? The questions range wildly, as students struggle to adopt a personal perspective on what has happened to them and through them. To understand the place of "force" in Newtonian physics, Tom creates a personal context in which "force" may appear in all its forms. How can we use "force" to improve the human condition?

IMPERSONAL HIGH SCHOOL SYSTEMS

Decades of research on learning—from Freud to Ericson and from Dewey to Howard Gardner—show that each human mind develops its own structure and content from birth to adulthood, but schools hold fast to a uniform structure that treats all learners as if they were the same. Learning depends on processes of skill development that become increasingly unique as individuals pursue their own interests and solve their own problems. Yet high schools teach and test a discrete body of information, obtained through a very narrow range of learning opportunities. Learning requires the active engagement of the individual mind, but high schools are designed to ensure general passivity from early morning until mid-afternoon. Learning is social, but high schools teach and test as if each mind grows in isolation from others. Learning brings the joy of discovery, but high schools still emphasize rote learning and recitation. For high schools to become effective for all students, they must develop an approach to teaching and learning that lets each mind make sense of the world in which it grows—and test new ideas in the real world in which young adults will experience both freedom and responsibility.

The net effect of uniform expectations for all students is that many high school students refuse to respect or accept our prescriptions for their learning. Many students see high school as an impersonal experience, forced upon them by an uncaring world at the very moment in their lives when they begin to imagine their independence and yearn for opportunities to expand and express their own talents. Schools emphasize uniformity; the students want to develop a unique identity. Strife is inevitable, except perhaps for the minority of students whose families can assure them that conformity will bring future rewards.

Facing an endless flow of adolescents who are learning to become adults, schools have erected an impressive system of control and monitoring to maintain order in the halls and classrooms. Unfortunately, many of the structures high schools use to sustain order also contribute to inequities that characterize both school and adult life. We use grades and test scores to rank students according to ability, though we only measure the ability to use the symbol systems of mathematics, science, and English. We "track" students into levels that tend to keep the disciplines intact, but reduce the level of challenge to fit the apparent disinterest of students who may have distinctive interests beyond the conventional subject areas. We prepare students who work well with abstractions for college study, but pass the rest into the realities of adult life without preparation. We insist that all students meet graduation requirements measured largely by seat-time and Carnegie units, but many do not learn effectively while sitting at a desk, or understand how four years of English, three of math, two of social studies, and two of science will lead them toward adult autonomy. Students who cannot imagine how the abstractions taught in school relate to their own experience may become unruly.

Unruly students show up as discipline referrals in the vice principal's office. Figure 4.1 is a list of all the disciplinary referrals made to the central office at a small rural high school of about 800 students during one academic year. I have arranged those referrals into coherent categories and rank ordered the categories by frequency. Of 2,096 disciplinary referrals, nearly half of the infractions (982) resulted from the students' attempt to avoid the imposition of adult authority at the school: truancy, cuts, skipping, and tardiness. Another large number (460) represents attempts to resist authority: insubordination, disrup-

Categories of Disciplinary Infraction			
Why do they get sent to the principal's office?			
Avoiding authority		**Disrupting order**	
Tardy	358	Bus problems	44
Truant (from class)	290	Excessive talking	33
Cut detention	136	Vandalism	22
Left class	43	Theft	10
Left School	42	Horseplay	10
Truant: school	23	Public display of affection	6
		Driving violation	4
Resisting authority			
Insubordinate	230	**Violence & Threat**	
Disruptive	171	Fighting	61
Area without permission	125	Danger to others	20
Uncooperative	30	Threatening	14
Inappropriate behavior	4	Harassment	5
Injured staff member	1	Weapon violation	4
		Safety violation	3
Offending authority		Assault	7
Rude	100	Sexual harassment	7
Foul language	76	Extortion	2
Discourteous	9	Injured staff member	1
Annoying	9		
Spitting	4	**Academic Infractions**	
		Unprepared	18
Substance Abuse		Plagiarism	8
Tobacco use/possession	69	Academic dishonesty	4
Marijuana use/possession	4		

Figure 4.1.   Discipline referrals.

tion, disobedience, lack of cooperation, and inappropriate behavior. A lesser number (198) reflect the students' desire to offend adult authorities: being rude, using foul language, being discourteous, and being annoying or spitting. A smaller number (129) are for disruption: bus problems, excessive talking, vandalism, theft, horseplay, and incidents with driving or with public affection (PDA). A similar number involve student violence and threat, usually among peers: fighting, threatening, and creating danger for others, for example. Only a few infractions were for drug use (4), with tobacco being a greater problem (69). Only a very small number of infractions result from the learning enterprise itself (30): plagiarism, being unprepared, or being dishonest. Rather than responding to the unique interests and talents individuals bring to school, we force compliance and suppress their anger. We have assembled structures and processes that make high schools "impersonal" to control their potential for anger and hostility, but the result may be rebellion and resistance, or passivity and avoidance.

By paradox or intention, the large impersonal systems developed to control young adult anger fuel that anger and produce a mass of effects that run counter to our purposes—and theirs. Dropout rates are highest among those students who cannot relate school processes to their own experiences: poor students with little hope for college, minority students whose culture does not appear in the high school curriculum, and male students whose pride prevents them from complying with requirements leading to no predictable end. The more disengaged students appear to be, the more we impose controls on their behavior: metal detectors, body searches, and locker checks. In some Vermont schools, the arrival of drug sniffing dogs early in September signals the tone for the year. Bomb scares, truancy, and a wide spectrum of ritualized rebellions then ensue. Compelled by the drive toward adult autonomy, our students find ways of expressing their restricted freedom in small, symbolic acts that defy the elaborate systems developed to suppress their anger.

To be effective for all students, we must begin to apply what we know about how individual students construct their learning to the design of educational processes. Rather than suppressing individuality, we should create opportunities for students to express their knowledge. Rather than confining "choice" to a narrow range of courses in the subject areas, we should design experiences that help students assess their situations, understand their choices, explore options, test their skills, and express their growing confidence in particular directions they have set for their own lives. Rather than confining high school students to only one kind of learning, we should connect them to activities in their communities where learning does make a difference. We should develop programs that let students personalize their learning. Learning is always personal. Denying that maxim condemns us and our students to a frustrating cycle of oppression and rebellion.

PERSONALIZED TEACHING FOR PERSONALIZED LEARNING

After searching out a national sample of exemplary high school practices with my friend, Russ Agne, I compiled a rubric to describe the criteria we might use to assess how well teaching engages high school students (Clarke & Agne, 1998). Good teaching starts with a problem and raises a question. Questions should be personal, inviting each student to explore a wide range of information from a variety of sources. Answers should keep the flavor of the individual perspective, inviting students to express what they have learned in a variety of media. Student expressions of understanding should be assessed against clear standards, with criteria that students can use to evaluate their own work. Focusing on problems, questions, information, expression, and standards, learning can become personal for each high school student—and each teacher.

As the years went by, I began to lose my fear of personal questions in the classroom and began to use them to guide students through language and ideas. To understand *Walden*, we camped in the winter woods, living off dried peas and rice. Then we wrote transcendental poetry in the snow. When we read *The Scarlet Letter*, each of us designed and wore for a full school day a letter from the alphabet that represented our most protected sin. A big black K for "kleptomania." Blue L's for "Lonely." A garish red A for "angry." I designed for myself a yellow A, and called it "anxiety." At the end of our day, we all had experienced some level of cure. Like Hester Prynne, we had used our worst fear to elevate ourselves, with the help of all those others who challenged us in the halls and cafeteria of the high school. Then we began to read with intense interest the almost impossibly dense prose of Nathaniel Hawthorne. Learning begins with a personal question.

Start with what you already know. Then, create an experience that challenges that knowledge and evokes a main question. When the question was, "Should I live within society or outside its bounds?" we ate a handful of dried peas and corn, laden with sugar, in snowy woods far from the city. Then we read *Walden*. "Are you a Realist or are you a Romantic?" First we took our own temperatures on scales representing realistic and romantic orientations to experience; then we read Kubla Khan and Ernest Hemingway. How does propaganda work? We created a multimedia extravaganza aiming to inspire generalized hate and tried it out on a study hall full of seniors. Then we read *1984* and began to think about the malleability of the human mind, its susceptibility to influence by government or media. School learning must be tested in the surrounding world, where knowledge may, indeed, make a difference in how we direct our energy.

How do you want to die? How do you want to live?

REFERENCES

Bossange, J. (2000). Pioneers and Partners in South Burlington High School's Imaging Lab: Adapting Systems to Standards. In Clarke et al., *Dynamics of Change in High School Teaching: A Study of Change in Five Vermont Professional Development Schools.* Providence, RI: LAB at Brown University.

Clarke, J. (1990). *Patterns of Thinking: Integrating Learning Skills with Content Teaching.* Boston: Allyn and Bacon.

Clarke, J. (1999). Growing High School Reform: Planting the Seeds of Systemic Change. *NAASP Bulletin, 83*(606), 1–9.

Clarke, A., & Clarke, S. (1999). Interactive Leadership in High School Reform. *NASSP Bulletin, 83*(607).

Clarke, J., Bossange, J., Erb, C., Gibson, D., Nelligan, B., Spencer, C., & Sullivan, M. (2000). *Dynamics of Change in High School Teaching: A Study of Innovation in Five Vermont Professional Development Schools.* Providence, RI: LAB at Brown University.

Clarke, J., & Agne, R. (1997). *Interdisciplinary High School Teaching: Strategies for Integrated Learning.* Boston: Allyn and Bacon.

Clarke, J., Sanborn, S., Aiken, J., Cornell, N., Goodman, J., & Hess, K. (1998). *Real Questions/Real Answers: Focusing Teacher Leadership on School Improvement.* Alexandria, VA: ASCD Publications.

Fosnot, C.T. (1989). *Enquiring Teachers, Enquiring Learners: A Constructivist Approach for Teaching.* New York: Teachers College, Columbia University.

Fulwiler, T. (1987). *Teaching with Writing.* Upper Montclair, New Jersey: Boynton/Cook.

Gardner, H. (1983). *Frames of Mind: The Theory of Multiple Intelligences.* New York: Basic Books.

Gardner, H. (1993). *Multiple Intelligences: The Theory in Practice.* New York: Basic Books.

Gibson, D. (2000). Developing Personal Learning Plans at Montpelier High

School: Linking Change from Bottom and Top. In Clarke et al., *Dynamics of Change in High School Teaching: A Study of Change in Five Vermont Professional Development Schools*. Providence, RI: LAB at Brown University.

Lee, V., Smith. J., & Croninger, R. (1995). *Another Look at High School Restructuring: Issues in Restructuring Schools* (Report #9). Center on Organization and Restructuring of Schools.

McCarthy, B. (1990). Using the 4MAT System to Bring Learning Styles to Schools. *Educational Leadership, 48*(2), 31–37.

Nelligan, B., & Erb, C. (2000). Adapting to Learning Styles at Essex High School. In Clarke et al., *Dynamics of Change in High School Teaching: A Study of Change in Five Vermont Professional Development Schools*. Providence, RI: LAB at Brown University.

Newmann, F., Wehlage, G., & Lamborn, S. (1992). The Significance and Sources of Student Engagement. In Newmann (Ed.), *Student Engagement and Achievement in American Secondary Schools*. New York: Teachers College Press.

Perkins, D. (1992). *Smart Schools: From Training Memories to Educating Minds*. New York: The Free Press.

Spencer, C. (2000). Developing a Standards-Based Geography Unit: Working Change from the Top. In Clarke et al., *Dynamics of Change in High School Teaching: A Study of Change in Five Vermont Professional Development Schools*. Providence, RI: LAB at Brown University.

Sullivan, M.J. (2000). Developing the Capacity for Systemic Change at Mount Abraham Union High School. In Clarke et al., *Dynamics of Change in High School Teaching: A Study of Change in Five Vermont Professional Development Schools*. Providence, RI: LAB at Brown University.

Vermont Department of Education (1996). *Framework of Standards and Learning Opportunities*. Montpelier, VT: State Department of Education.

CHAPTER 5

The Path to Personalized Learning

A Teacher's Perspective

EDORAH FRAZER

Teacher Quality Network of Vermont

Personalized learning is rare in all but the most successful schools and classrooms. To introduce practices that will engage the unique talents, interests, and aspirations of all students, schools need to examine their practices on many levels. As we change schools to facilitate personalized learning, we must also prepare our students for the transition. Innovations in education are all ostensibly for the sake of students, but students are often shielded from the planning process, only to feel confused or disenfranchised by the result. Students will benefit most from reforms aimed at personalizing learning if we consult with them and involve them in change incrementally, just as we prepare school personnel.

I have been working with members of an urban high school faculty to help them deepen their professional collaboration. Their school has undertaken sweeping changes over the past year with the arrival of a new principal. Extensive resources have been committed to professional development to support the faculty in the restructuring effort. The professional collaboration group, however, recently expressed resentment about the manner in which change had occurred. When we took the time to chart all of the issues and prioritize them as a group, it turned out that the most compelling concerns of teachers were the behavioral issues that had broken out among the older students. The conclusion of the group was that these students had undergone too much change with too little support along the way. Though the reforms were ostensibly for the good of the students, the students were suffering. While the educators were struggling with their own feelings of confusion, fatigue, uncertainty, and lack of control, they forgot to prepare for the same responses, and the adolescent behaviors that would accompany them, from the kids.

This chapter focuses on how schools can personalize learning, first by creating environments that help educators know their students well, then by crafting learning experiences that allow students to drive their own educations. I narrow the focus to a tale of my own classroom, linking the school structures that support personalized learning to the responses of students as they encounter a new environment of voice, choice, and responsibility.

THE HIGHWAY OF ANONYMITY

I attended a suburban, regional high school of nearly 4,000 students. My memories of the school include the crushing flow of adolescents that filled the halls during the four minutes between classes, the neglected walls of classrooms that belonged to no one teacher, and the intensity of competition required to receive recognition in such a vast population of students. Against all odds, several talented and committed educators picked me out of the crowd and came to know me well, and I learned a great deal from them about life as well as the academic subjects they taught. On an institutional level, however, I was aware of my anonymity. In a culminating event during my senior year, a guidance counselor accused both my mother and me of lying about a parking infraction. I railed at the injustice to my two trusted teachers, but they were powerless in the bureaucracy of parking officials and disciplinarians. Years later, the memory of that event taught me to look deeply into the eyes of my students and to strive to know them as individuals.

THE PATH TO PERSONALIZATION

My experiences as a high school student stand in sharp contrast to my professional experiences in personalized schools. I have had the privilege of working in three schools that focus their efforts on personalizing students' educations. At Thayer Jr./Sr. High School in Winchester, New Hampshire, the principal stood at the front door upon the students' arrival to school and called out their names, asking questions. "Is your mom feeling better?" "Did you study for your big test today?" "Unbelievable three-pointer yesterday! That could get us to the championship!" Inside classrooms, the teachers worked to know their students well. Each teacher had no more than eighty students, fewer than twenty per class. Many students arranged for apprenticeships outside the school, keeping reflective journals and earning high school credit as they learned job skills. All seniors wrote their autobiographies in order to reflect on their lives' lessons.

At Souhegan High School in Amherst, New Hampshire, there are too many students for anyone to know all their names, but grade-level, interdisciplinary teams are formed so that a group of teachers will have all of their students in common. Common planning periods among the teachers allow for conversations about individual students and team conferences with parents. All adults in the school are addressed by their first names, and each member of the school community is understood to be an active learner. In this way, students and faculty members become colleagues in the education of all. The mission of Souhegan High School, engraved in the front hallway and known well by every student and adult in the school, reads in part, "We consciously commit ourselves to support and engage an individual's unique gifts, passions and intentions." The student handbook is entitled "Souhegan High School Owner's Manual," emphasizing the students' roles in the co-creation of the school. Extensive senior projects are designed by students, allowing them to pursue a subject in depth and present their developed expertise to an audience of faculty, family members, and peers.

At the Gailer School in Shelburne, Vermont, all eighty students are known by every teacher. Students are greeted cheerfully at the front door each morning by two teachers who call them by name and shake their hands. Like Souhegan, Gailer is built on a model of a schoolwide learning community. Here, too, first names are used for all adults, and faculty members actively model their own learning process. At the core of Gailer's academic life is the seminar, a forum that engages all students in daily dialogue in order to help them develop their voices and perspectives, incorporating the wisdom of their classmates and texts into their understanding. Each Wednesday, the Gailer faculty gather for "Student Concerns," a time to discuss the needs of individual students. This allows fifteen teachers and two administrators to bring their professional expertise and personal care to bear on the needs of individual students. Each student attends a community service placement and engages in an independent inquiry of his or her own design one day per week. A faculty member coordinates these programs, developing ways for students to develop their interests and self-knowledge. A student serves on the Board of Directors of Gailer, and the School Forum, comprised of the entire faculty and some student representatives from each grade level, makes substantial policy decisions for the school.

In all three of these schools, teachers write curriculum appropriate for the students before them, engaging students in the curriculum development process. Textbooks are rarely used as the basis for a course, and bells do not ring to delineate periods of time, since time is crafted to the needs of individual classes and/or teams. In each school, students can be found actively negotiating their assignments if they are asked to do something that doesn't seem relevant, challenging, or interesting to them. While many members of a class are writing essays to express their understanding of a text, for example, another student might be creating a work of art, a model, or an oral presentation. Students in all three schools engage in advisory groups designed to link each student closely and personally to an adult and a small group of peers for support. These advisory groups frequently enjoy social outings beyond the school day.

These schools provide vibrant alternatives to the alienation and anonymity frequently found in high schools. While they employ a variety of approaches to personalizing the students' experiences (figure 5.1), they share an educational belief that in an environment of trust and mutual respect, in which students are encouraged to develop their own paths of inquiry, profound learning takes place.

Each of these schools provides a small community in which students are well known and considered by thoughtful and caring adults. Gailer and Thayer are small schools, and Souhegan has created small learning communities via interdisciplinary grade-level teams in the ninth and tenth grades; junior American Studies teams; and small senior semi-

Souhegan High School

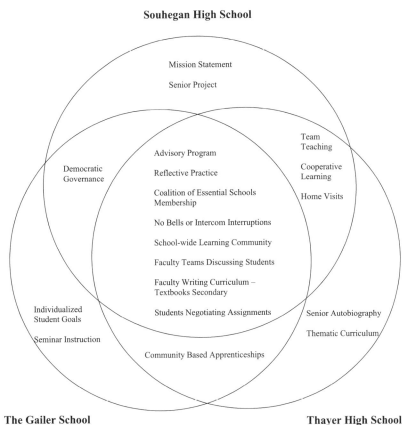

Figure 5.1.   Structures and practices supporting personalized learning.

nars. In each school, adults gather regularly to discuss the needs of individual students and how they can best be served.

The personal attention afforded students in these three schools sets the stage for academic engagement, but close relationships between educators and students do not necessarily yield powerful learning in themselves. Working in these environments has secured my conviction that high school students become most engaged in their learning when they are given responsibility, respect, and the elements of choice and flexibility in their education. Thus, once we have established an atmosphere of caring, we need to begin to encourage kids to steer their own education. High school teachers frequently observe otherwise apathetic students spending hours poring over driver's manuals when they are learning to drive. Why? Because driving represents freedom, power, and self-determination, and it is inherently engaging. Similarly, teachers can fully engage students by developing incremental means by which students can gain control over, and take responsibility for, their own intellectual pursuits. Driving instructors employ patience, guidance, and vigilance as they prepare students to become independent drivers. Complicated intersections and high-speed highways don't come in the first lesson, but they are guaranteed before the course is over. The promise and the responsibilities of independence motivate both teacher and learner to do their best work.

A CLASSROOM EXPLORATION OF PERSONALIZED LEARNING

Several years ago at Souhegan High School, a colleague and I committed ourselves to sharing control over the learning environment and the curriculum with our students. My teaching partner Barry Ehrlich and I began our integrated senior seminar in Human Nature & Human Behavior with forty-seven high school seniors, two adjoining rooms, and the last 110 minutes of the day between us. We spent the final week before school opened planning our course. We had never taught together before, but we had requested to do so, and we had the flexibility of developing the curriculum for the course as we saw fit.

After developing the essential questions (Sizer, 1992) and skills that we would address in the course, we chose a study of free will and obedience as our first topic (Appendix 5.1). In the first week of school, we assigned Thoreau's "Civil Disobedience" essay, and through cooperative learning activities and student-led discussions began to develop a dialogue around the questions, "What is the individual's responsibility to society?" and "What is society's responsibility to the individual?" Most of the students initially developed a fierce antigovernment stance as they wrestled with the Thoreau reading. They brought into our discussion examples from their own lives of ways in which they felt the laws that governed them were unjust and limiting.

When we had completed the essay, Barry and I posed to the class the task of developing behavioral guidelines for our class (Appendix 5.1). We taught them skills for consensus decision-making and showed them a simple tool for assessing the group's response to a proposal. We told them that we would participate in the work as equal members of the learning community, but not as leaders. Then we sat down. After a few minutes of uncertainty, the class set to work. They were to present their results to a panel of school administrators and students from the school council two weeks from the starting day.

Initially the class chose to work together as a large group of forty-seven. They nominated and elected two facilitators, a boy and a girl, to manage their discussion. Quickly the conversation became cumbersome, a majority of the students began to lose their focus on the task, and people started to complain about the facilitators. Finally someone suggested that the class split into working groups. After a brief discussion, three groups were formed to develop proposals: a mission statement, behavioral guidelines, and an approach to developing curriculum.

I sat with the curriculum group. Their discussion was deep, wise, and moving. I listened and observed as my students developed a format for developing curriculum with the class that was inclusive and creative. The level of discussion regarding what curriculum is and should be would have been impressive among teachers or graduate researchers; in this student context, it was striking. The group prepared to present their proposal to the rest of the class.

Barry sat with the behavioral guidelines group. After the first day of group work, he commented that the most dogmatic and traditional of our students seemed to have collected there. He expressed frustration that the students couldn't seem to think beyond the rules they had experienced previously in their education, so they had come up with a basic collection of penalties for tardiness and late papers.

After three days of group work, the class reunited to present their reports. The mission committee led us line by line through the mission statement they had written. We approved it with revisions, using the consensus process. The result was an inspiring document that was laminated and put up in both classrooms (Appendix 5.2).

Next, the behavioral guidelines group presented their work in a somewhat militaristic manner. The class erupted in fierce debate.

Through an exhausting process of consensus blocks, counterproposals, and eventually many expressions of fatigue and apathy, a list of behavioral guidelines was passed.

The next day the curriculum group presented their work. It was a complicated proposal, and the group's presentation wasn't very clear. A challenge arose that became the crux of our learning experiment: the students did not want responsibility for developing curriculum. They said boldly and clearly that developing the curriculum was the teachers' job and that they trusted us to do it well. They wanted to be told what to do and exactly what would earn them good grades. Our curriculum committee eventually managed to bring the class to an agreement. Any student or group of students would be welcome to propose alternative approaches to any unit, once the teachers had presented a written overview of the next unit to the class. The teachers would work with any student(s) to ensure the academic viability of their proposal. The class also agreed that they would choose as a group the themes they would like to study from a list of options we had placed on the syllabus.

The final presentation to the panel was impressive, and the principal declared that the class's mission statement was among the best he'd seen in any organization. If we conducted ourselves by it, he said, we were bound to have a powerful learning experience. The dean of students was impressed by the students' willingness to assign themselves stringent behavioral guidelines. The students on the panel asked probing questions to uncover the group's decision-making process and subsequent investment in the outcome. All four panelists congratulated the class for their careful and original work.

We finished our unit by reading Ayn Rand's novel *Anthem*, which depicts a totalitarian society. While I worked with the novel, Barry showed videos of *The Milgram Experiment* and *The Wave*, both films dealing with obedience taken to an extreme, and led discussions supplemented by *Facing History and Ourselves* materials on free will and obedience.

In the final reflection paper of the unit, we asked our students to synthesize what they had learned from our study of free will and obedience. They expressed a range of responses, but most of them demonstrated deeper thoughtfulness about the responsibilities that society and the individual had toward each other than they had expressed in our initial class discussions. Some came to the conclusion that Thoreau was essentially a complainer and that people need rules in order to work effectively together. Others concluded that while tedious, group consensus ultimately results in a stronger commitment to uphold the values of the community. Still others felt that they preferred to live in a society in which their behavior was prescribed and their choices limited in exchange for less responsibility for making difficult decisions.

Barry and I reflected on the unit also. We were pleased with the learning that had taken place, although we had weathered many complaints along the way. We recognized the skills of negotiation, consensus, and organization and recognized the content knowledge of political science and literature that our students had acquired and exhibited. We were dismayed, however, by the class's disinterest in becoming involved in the creation of its own curriculum. We had thrown them the keys, and they had thrown them back.

In assessing our situation, Barry and I began to realize that the students hadn't been prepared for the opportunity we had presented them. They were attending an unusual public school, one in which they were frequently asked for feedback, input, critique of the curriculum, and their own choices regarding the format of their work. We had asked them to participate more extensively in the creation of this course. Our challenge was to scale back their responsibility to a more manageable level, incrementally increasing their independence as the course went on.

According to plan, the class chose the theme for the next unit. The students picked "sanity and insanity" for their next topic of study, and Barry and I set to work preparing curriculum. We wrote essential questions, determined the skills we would target, brainstormed activities, chose readings and films, and determined the format for the students' final exhibition of their knowledge. We decided that we wanted to use this unit to develop strong research skills so that our students would be capable researchers when it came time to work on their senior projects.

The students did extensive research on mental health and illness and ultimately shared their findings via oral presentations. Barry and I acted as coaches in the classroom and media center, assisting small groups and individuals as their personalized inquiries took shape. It wasn't until school had disbanded for winter vacation that I looked around the room and realized that the personalization we had hoped to achieve in allowing students to develop their own curriculum had finally occurred. Our mission statement was on the wall, covered by brainstormed lists of essential questions, flow charts of research strategies, and schedules for group work. The final presentations displayed a wide diversity of student interests within the theme of mental health and illness, and demonstrated the research and presentation skills that we had targeted with the unit.

The planning sequence that we followed in creating these units can be gleaned from Appendix 5.3. Working from essential questions and a list of skills that are authentically employed in the adult world, we created a curriculum structure within which our students could personalize their learning. Drawing ideas from the Foxfire training that we had attended together, we listed the "givens" for the course—the information and skills that we felt our students needed to gain by the end of our course. Then we looked for ways to give our students choices regarding the way they learned the material and any additional inquiries they would like to make into the subject of human nature and human behavior. What our students taught us along the way was that they needed to be given more carefully circumscribed choices at the beginning of the course and a broader range toward the end.

The lessons in democracy that Barry and I explored with our students derived from our commitment to personalized learning for our students. The school in which we worked provided the context for innovation in our classroom. Souhegan High School was founded on principles of high school reform that provided multilevel support for our work. John H. Clarke describes the structural and attitudinal changes required to create a personalized environment in schools:

Mission: From academics to a community of learners
Systems: From efficiency to responsiveness
Organization: From hierarchy to collaboration
Curriculum: From covering content to pursuing lines of inquiry
Instruction: From subjects to students
Student Learning: From seat time to self-direction (personal communication, November, 2000)

Each of these principles was reflected in the course work and class-room culture Barry and I cocreated with our students. In handing our students the keys to our course, we learned that students can learn to drive their learning, take responsibility for their lives, and support the growth of their peers if we help them learn to do so incrementally, and adapt the school's systems to that purpose.

RESOURCES

Sizer, T. (1992). *Horace's Compromise.* Boston: Houghton Mifflin.

For additional information on educational practices that support personalized learning:

Coalition of Essential Schools
1814 Franklin Street, Suite 700
Oakland, CA 94612
(510) 433-1451
www.essentialschools.org

Foxfire Network
P.O. Box 541
Mountain City, GA 30562
(706) 746-5828
www.foxfire.org

National School Reform Faculty
Harmony School Education Center
P.O. Box 1787
Bloomington, IN 47402
(812) 330-2702
www.nsrfharmony.org

Thayer High School
85 Parker Street
Winchester, NH 03470
(603) 239-4381

Souhegan High School
P.O. Box 1152
412 Boston Post Road
Amherst, NH 03031
(603) 673-9940
www.sprise.com

The Gailer School
4066 Shelburne Road
Shelburne, VT 05482
(802) 985-1276
www.eddos.com/gailer

APPENDIX 5.1: CLASS BEHAVIORAL GUIDELINES: A CLASS EXHIBITION

Essential Question: What guidelines will we use in our course in order to create and maintain a powerful and productive learning environment?

Now that we're three weeks into school and we've all gotten acquainted with each other, it's time to take a more careful look at our working environment. This week we are turning over the leadership of this seminar to the group as a whole to develop guidelines for our working relationships for the rest of the year. These guidelines will be presented to a panel in an exhibition next week.

We are hoping that you will draw on a number of experiences you have already had in this course: our discussion of peak learning experiences, your group work on creating a government, your readings of Thoreau, and your own experience of the group dynamic to help you come up with clear, realistic, appropriate, and helpful guidelines for our time together in this course. How do you want this class to be? What behavior can and should we expect from each other in order to get the most out of it?

Your answers to these questions should be determined as a class, resulting in a document that we can all agree to live by for the rest of the year. The document will describe behavioral and procedural guidelines for this class to be a powerful and productive learning environment.

When: This exhibition is to be completed throughout the course of this week and into next week. We have tentatively scheduled a presentation to a panel of evaluators on Tuesday, October 4, at 12:45. We anticipate that your presentation, followed by questions from the panel, will take 30–40 minutes. The time until then is yours to schedule as efficiently as possible. If we need more time to work on this, we can move the panel date, but we will need to know that by this Friday in order to give the panelists reasonable notice.

Who: All members of the class will be involved in and accountable for the product of this exhibition. Barry and Edorah will participate as members of the course, not as leaders unless they are requested to present specific information to the group. The evaluation panel will consist of the Principal, Dean of Students, and two students from other seminars.

How: That's up to the group to decide. This is an opportunity for you to make this class the way you want it to be. All we ask is that you approach this task thoughtfully and honestly. The process of your work on this is up to you to create. Remember that whatever process you choose should prepare you to present a finished document to the panel.

The guidelines you create for this class must address the following general areas:

- What learning environment will be optimal for the most powerful education possible?
- What expectations do we have for student behavior, attitudes, and leadership?
- What expectations do we have for teacher behavior, attitudes, and leadership?
- What are reasonable and effective consequences and methods of enforcement for violations of guidelines?
- What support services will be available for those in need?

- How will work in this class be assessed, including this work?
- How will these and future decisions be made by the group?

APPENDIX 5.2: MISSION STATEMENT

Our goal is to create a learning experience which will incorporate these common principles, and to enable each individual to maximize their learning experience.

Both teachers and students will:

- Strive to challenge themselves and to encourage others
- Be flexible and supportive of each other's individual needs
- Make a conscious effort to participate in all activities
- Ensure that the community and curriculum encourages individuals to use their unique gifts and talents
- Behave in a manner that exemplifies respect, trust, and thoughtfulness
- Be willing to assume the responsibility of leader and/or role model when necessary

APPENDIX 5.3: SENIOR SEMINAR

Senior Seminar: Human Nature & Human Behavior
Instructors: Edorah Frazer
              Barry Ehrlich

Essential Questions:
    What does it mean to be a human being?
    In what ways can we as human beings respond to the challenges of
       the modern world?

Skills:
    Taking multiple perspectives—suspending judgment, listening for
       understanding, building agreement, taking on and developing
       unfamiliar positions

Self-directed learning—identifying areas of interest, outlining tasks, planning and implementing timelines, self-assessment and reflection

Research—posing questions, gathering resources, consulting primary and secondary resources

Critical thinking—understanding and critiquing sophisticated, challenging materials and making meaningful connections, developing positions based on logic and evidence

Leadership—planning for group success, planning and leading discussions, contributing to course development, building community, resolving conflicts

Communication—speaking before a group; respectful dialogue; practical, analytical, and reflective writing

Creativity—combining ideas in new ways, seeing new ways to look at old problems, expressing an idea or point of view through more than one medium (visual art, music, dance, and/or drama)

I. Self-Discovery

    Who am I?

    What are the processes of self-discovery?

    How can I most effectively filter and incorporate new information?

II. Societal Forces

    What is the nature of the interactions between individuals, events, and ideas?

    How are individuals empowered or limited by societal forces?

    Where do new ideas come from?

III. Action/Responsibility

    What is my place in society?

    How can I influence it in a positive way?

    Themes: Free Will & Obedience

              Tolerance & Intolerance

              Community & Solitude

              Peace & Violence

              Sanity & Insanity

              Despair & Empowerment

Resources (assigned and recommended readings):
  Books: selected autobiographies
      Selections from Thoreau and Emerson
      Declarations of Independence, Howard Zinn
      American Dreams, Studs Terkel
      Their Eyes Were Watching God, Zora Neale Hurston
      Hamlet, William Shakespeare
      Black Like Me, John Howard Griffin
      Anthem, Ayn Rand
      Dinner at the Homesick Restaurant, Anne Tyler
      The Dogs of March, Ernest Hebert
      The Milagro Beanfield War, John Nichols
      Sula, Toni Morrison
      Wildlife, Richard Ford
      Housekeeping, Marilynne Robinson
      Native Son, Richard Wright
      One Flew over the Cuckoo's Nest, Ken Kesey
      A Yellow Raft in Blue Water, Michael Dorris
      The Little Prince, Antoine De Saint-Exupery
      Siddhartha, Herman Hesse

  Essays and short stories:
      "The Lottery," Shirley Jackson
      "The Last Night of the World," Ray Bradbury
      "Why War?" Sigmund Freud
      "The Melian Dialogue," Thucydides
      "Everything That Rises Must Converge," Flannery O'Conner
      "On Happiness," Aristotle
      "On Liberty," John Stuart Mill
      "Conscience," Immanuel Kant
      "Habits and Will," John Dewey
      "A Hunger Artist," Franz Kafka

  Films: *The Milgram Experiment*
      The Power of One
      Amadeus
      The Wave

CHAPTER 6

Democracy and Equity in the Classroom

A Team Design

PAMELA FISHER
Superintendent, Acton, Maine

Democratic classrooms exist and thrive in democratic schools. They emerge in high schools where a school community gracefully weaves teaching and learning into mutual inquiry, supported by a school organization and leadership structures that engage the entire community in self-development. In a democratic school, the world of teachers and students is very different from teaching and learning in a traditionally managed comprehensive high school. Those differences may be visible in the snapshots of teachers and a thousand students who work and learn at Noble High School, a rural, regional Maine high school, guided by the Ten Common Principles of the Coalition of Essential Schools. The snapshots that follow are drawn from my years of supporting the school through its transformation to a democratic model of schooling, organized in teams of students and teachers.

SNAPSHOT OF MARY'S TEAM

In this early morning, with coffee and bagels in hand, teachers are putting the finishing touches on their "Neaotaquit Nature Center Unit." Jenny is presenting her latest draft of the lab packet for a "tuning" with her colleagues, including the team's special education teacher and guidance counselor. Teachers use a tuning protocol as a way to gain feedback on work in progress—particularly on units in the early stages of design. Mary's team meets for a ninety-minute planning block every other day. Her teaching team, including English (Jim), geometry

(Kevin), biology (Jenny), and history (Mary herself) teachers, creates a learning hub for about eighty-five sophomores, making up one of three sophomore teams in the 9–12 school. Mary's team, as well as all other learning groups at Noble High School, thrives in a learning community guided by shared vision and a well-maintained democratic governance process.

As the team works through the new lab, the tuning protocol focuses collective energy on the work at hand. "Are the criteria for honors options clear?" "Will all students understand the directions?" "How can we improve the final project rubric?" Later, at the conclusion of the project, teachers will look at student projects together, gaining insight into student understanding—and into the effectiveness of their own teaching strategies. At Noble High School, teachers clearly see themselves as leading a small learning community within a larger one. The structures and governance of the school support their role as designers and inventors of rich, engaging curricula, and as self-managed leaders of learners.

A democratic school's learning environment consists of three nested structures that support student learning: 1) curriculum, instruction, and assessment (the classroom); 2) structural and organizational features (schedule, teams, grades, length of day); and 3) leadership and decision-making practices (faculty leadership groups, planning teams, vision-keepers). In a democratic school, synergy among these nested structures ensures that all learners have equitable access to an elite education. Interaction among nested structures builds the capacity of teachers to become leaders, to work collaboratively in critical friendship, and to continuously renew their personal vision of a good high school. Democratic schools provide all teachers and learners with an opportunity to lead and to refine through action the common purpose of their school.

As we look closely at Mary's team and other features of Noble High School, withhold assumptions regarding similarities to other well-known team teaching models. Teaming, especially in this setting, does not equate with "middle level" team teaching. Recall that middle schools seek to provide young teens with a richly diverse learning experience in a teamed setting, attending carefully to the students' level of development. Teaching teams may or may not exist in a democratic school or be democratically organized themselves. In Mary's school, teaming is one structure used to personalize learning in a large high school and to provide teachers with the means of leading their own organization. The stories in this chapter begin with the classroom, with what happens between students and teachers, followed by illustrations of the structures and programs that support democratic teaching and learning.

MARY'S CLASSROOM

Mary is the history teacher on her team. The history curriculum for sophomores is the second year of world and American history. Developed in collaboration with the other two sophomore history teachers, the essential understandings to be gained from the curriculum have been aligned with the state's learning standards. Within these general guidelines, different teams construct their own themes and learning experiences for their students. On this particular day, Mary's students have prepared to present their political party conversations before a panel of teachers. Using a collaboratively designed rubric to evaluate the performance, panelists assess the conversation's historical accuracy and look for indications of students' understanding of key concepts.

In this culminating assessment for the unit "Understanding Political Parties" (Johnson, 2001), students assume the persona of a political figure from early 19th-century America. (These history performances follow completion of individual persuasive essays, guided by essential questions on state versus federal control.) Mary's teaching partners help recruit panelists to score and respond to student work. Using a similar rubric for peer editing, the students have worked in teams to practice their political presentations. All students in these heterogeneously grouped classrooms participate in reading, note taking, and lecture/discussion groups to understand what is required to achieve the expectations described on common assessment rubrics. As each student presents, the rest of the students on the team also participate, by scoring each performance and engaging in discussions of their scoring over several days. Since a final assessment in any unit requires several hours to complete, Mary's teammates give up their classes for the morning to focus on history. The team has grown comfortable sharing time and taking turns launching major assessments, recognizing the crosscutting competencies being taught and assessed with authentic, performance-based rubrics.

In a democratic classroom, rubrics reflect the purpose shared by the school community, reducing the tendency of other student-oriented techniques to stall and diverge from a goal. In such classrooms, freedom is modified by collective purpose and individual accomplishment is recognized by shared standards:

- Democratic classrooms are places where students have choice not necessarily in what they learn, but in how they learn it and how they demonstrate understanding of what they have been asked to learn.
- Democratic classrooms provide learning experiences that celebrate the diverse talents of all learners and provide multiple opportunities to stretch thinking without penalty when students initially fall short of their goal.
- Democratic classrooms are collaborative—as opposed to competitive—workplaces, where students demonstrate respect for diverse views, styles, and abilities.
- Avoiding chaotic individualism, democratic classrooms celebrate high performance by each student using rubrics that apply to all.

MARY'S TEAM EXPLORES BIOETHICS

"Just because we can, should we?" Such is the essential question for the team's unit on bioethics. Jenny, the team's biology teacher, has been the point person for this work, helping her colleagues figure out appropriate entry places for the other classes as this unit begins. The bioethics unit allows students to work on real-world problems our society is struggling with, connecting the content required by biology standards to major decisions faced by the larger society. Genetic engineering, cloning, organ banks, population control, and living wills—each provides a backdrop for individual and team research, debate, interviews, and persuasive essays. Because academic skills vary widely within the team, Jenny has grouped students to ensure their success with highly complex problems.

The special education and enrichment teachers support work groups in the lab and the library. Students prep each other for quizzes along the way. During the team's "interact period," an extra block of time used for academic support, advisory, and portfolio development, the team's geometry teacher helps students analyze statistical data while the team's English teacher organizes peer editing and practice sessions for final presentations. When students begin struggling with reading assignments or lab work, additional support is provided from the school's Learning Center. Culminating assessment for the bioethics unit will include participation in a world council on bioethics where students present their research findings to a collection of world leaders, represented by teachers, local business leaders, and religious leaders. Later, students will publish "World Council" results in the school newspaper as a culminating writing assignment for the English teacher.

While the bioethics unit gives focus to study across the curriculum, it seeks diversity rather than uniformity in student expressions of understanding. Culminating assessment tasks require quality results, but they allow for rich personal interpretation.

- Democratic classrooms support students exploring and developing personal responses to real problems in the world where they live.
- Democratic classrooms provide all students with the supports required to ensure that they meet common, rigorous academic standards.
- Democratic classrooms are fearless. They respect and celebrate different views, occasionally passionately debated.
- Democratic classrooms may promote individual expression, but they also consistently require a high standard of knowledge.

MARY'S STUDENTS IN SOCRATIC DIALOGUE

"How can we learn to live together?" The overarching theme for all sophomore teams, this question engages sixteen-year-olds in dialogue connecting their experience on many levels. How do we work together as a team of students and teachers? As a community of diverse talents and interests? How does our school community cooperate; how does it tolerate and celebrate each of its members? How may our world become safe and peaceful for all humankind? Should wealth among Americans be more evenly distributed? For these and other questions, Jim, the English teacher on the team, uses Socratic Seminars to organize his English units as well as a central strategy for engaging students in understanding challenging texts. Having read *To Kill a Mockingbird* with essays from De Toqueville and Malcolm X, students begin their inquiry with the question, "What is justice?"

In a Socratic Dialogue, the students direct the discussion to answer a focusing question using several sources of information. Since student groups in the class have all read different texts, the Socratic Seminar allows everyone in the groups to bring a special perspective to common questions and themes. The goal is to increase everyone's understanding of the readings, not to come to a particular understanding of the questions. Jim acts as the observer and recorder of the conversation, making mental notes on the degree of their preparedness and on the participation of each student in the dialogue circle. As the Socratic dialogue ensues, students respond to each other's comments, guided by a student facilitator within the circle. From many similar experiences with leadership at school, student facilitators require little coaching at including most everyone in the circle, and they often probe those who are reluctant to speak. From outside the circle, Jim may record comments, clarify statements, and refocus the group if necessary. Students are encouraged to use citations from the texts to strengthen their personal assertions. Guided by the Socratic process, students inch closer to deep interpretation of the language and perspective of each text. At the next class session, Jim will ask students to meet in book groups to flesh out particular interpretations of the text that have emerged in the dialogue. Thus, students have the opportunity to think about the big ideas in multiple formats: the large group setting, the small reading group, and as individuals. As a logical next step, students will be asked to choose one or two other readings from those discussed during the Socratic to support student essays they write to answer the focusing questions.

Like any kind of content, learning through dialogue must be done through practice. Especially, young adults must recognize both the promise and pitfalls of struggling with large questions in a social context where views will differ.

- Democratic classrooms publicly respect and include all voices.
- Democratic classrooms require shared leadership among students and build the capacity of each to lead.
- Democratic classrooms allow teachers to facilitate learning off center stage. Teachers take risks and trust students.
- Democratic classrooms increase the students' capacity to explore universal questions.

In a democratic high school, student engagement in dialogue and debate becomes the foundation of their engagement with the larger community.

MARY'S TEAM TAKES ON MATHEMATICS

"Geometry is not the poor stepchild!" When inquiries are made about teaming at the high school level, questions always arise about math. Our comfort level with heterogeneous grouping practices often stops at the entrance to the math department. At Noble High School and in Mary's team, integration of mathematics is still a "work in progress" for several reasons. First, many students pursue algebra and geometry in middle school. Consequently, some freshmen may end up in Kevin's sophomore geometry classes. Further, the strongest math students will have taken geometry in the eighth or ninth grade while students from Mary's team may be studying ninth grade algebra. Kevin has many "off team" students who are not included in team projects (these students would have their own freshman projects to worry about). As the entire math curriculum evolves toward a more integrated approach, Kevin sees a resolution in sight, especially with more algebra and geometry being taught in middle school. In the coming years, the integrated math program will allow all levels of learners to pursue topics in math in greater depth within their own team setting.

One large challenge is to ensure that all students have access to a rigorous math curriculum. In this school, the first course is algebra, and all students are expected to take four years of rigorous math. To succeed in this goal, the school must provide a wide variety of supports for skill-deficient learners. Kevin uses the team interact block to give students time for practice. Further, the Learning Center staff tutors students during a free block over the two-day cycle of the schedule. Students who continuously struggle with geometry may be recommended for summer school, where they will continue to work on the standards for meeting proficiency. In the junior and senior years, students who struggle in advanced algebra will be allowed to take a second year to fulfill the four-year math requirement. Because educators have generally interpreted the math curriculum as a "staircase," Mary's team struggles with the grouping practices and arrangements of courses. The school's responsibility is to ensure equity of opportunity for all students to meet rigorous standards in mathematics, in accordance with the state learning standards. It is the job of the teachers to organize the structures necessary to ensure student success, whether the learning is on-team, off-team, or year-round.

Students, parents, and teachers are meeting throughout the year to rethink the math program. A board member regularly joins the group. A parent facilitates the sessions, guided by the essential question: "What teaching structures and strategies are required to ensure that all students learn mathematics to a rigorous high standard?" Research on mathematics is provided by the local university to dispel common myths about who can learn "hard" math.

Mathematics challenges Mary's team to design practices that help each student meet standards required of all students uniformly.

- Democratic schools provide students with multiple means to achieve learning goals without penalty. Student learning needs determine the organization time and space for learning.
- Democratic classrooms allow for grouping and regrouping of students to ensure that all learners are challenged and supported in meeting the standards.
- Democratic schools include all stakeholders in important conversations about teaching and learning. They have no secrets.

In mathematics, Mary's team joins the school's community in exploring options that fit a democratic ideal.

STRUCTURES THAT SUPPORT DEMOCRATIC TEACHING AND LEARNING

Of the many factors that undercut democratic teaching and learning, three elements of high school structure play a dominant role in determining how democratic a high school can grow to be. They are:

1. How the school organizes the day for teaching and learning;
2. How the school groups students and schedules the core course requirements within a program of studies;
3. How the school reports achievement—the grade reporting system.

In a democratic school, these factors mutually adapt to improve learning for all students, slowly approximating the school's vision. "The traditional schedule is the cold hand of death," said Eve Bither, former Maine commissioner of education. Indeed, a lockstep daily schedule can prevent growth toward democratic learning and teaching, freezing practice into one uniform pattern.

Organizing the Day

Democratic schools are not "prisoners of time." They organize time to support all learners, to extend the school into the community and beyond, requiring students and teachers to make daily decisions about the use of time and space. In addition to common planning time, Mary's team has five blocks of time for work with students over a two-day period. The school schedule consists of four 80-minute blocks, with four classes held one day, four the next. Thus a student may be scheduled for eight blocks of time. On Mary's team, students have three scheduled blocks on one day and two blocks on the next day. During that time, students attend English, biology, history, and geometry class and the interact block. Because the entire team meets during these common blocks, teachers may adjust the schedule for field trips and other activities without disrupting the rest of the school.

The teams are all heterogeneously grouped, as are all courses in the school, thus the classes of about twenty students do not move as a cohort within a team. They are regrouped so that students work with the entire team during a two-day cycle. In addition to the team blocks, Mary and her colleagues teach a junior/senior seminar or AP course. This scheduling pattern is repeated for all freshman and sophomore teams. The interact block provides time for academic support and portfolio preparation, which are presented in roundtables in the freshman year and through a sophomore exhibition at the end of sophomore year. Further, students use their portfolios to demonstrate achievement of the course learning standards and to conduct student-led parent conferences.

At the junior/senior level, students choose seminars around topics of personal interest, such as women's history or scientific research. The seminars are team taught by teacher partners who share an interest and who support their students in developing final exhibitions for graduation. Students generally stay with the same seminar teacher/advisors for two years. The upper grades are organized into houses where students share the same core academic teachers. Houses are larger than teams and allow for students to attend vocational courses, internships, and other off-site programs. House teachers have common planning time during which their focus is supporting students with their personalized learning plans, senior exhibitions, and other future planning activities, such as career placement and college planning. Recently, the school has adjusted seminar time to include a greater focus on an advisory program.

Early in the development of teaming at Noble, students complained that they did not have an opportunity to interact with students on other teams unless it was during arts or other elective classes. To solve this problem, students and teachers worked out a plan for a common, forty-minute lunch period. After consulting with the cafeteria staff, the plan was launched. Faculty divided themselves up in to five "lunch squads" to supervise the school while students ate and relaxed with their friends. Teams and teachers of a content area got together to plan a duty schedule so teachers could use four of five days for lunch meetings. Students sold the idea to the school board by describing all the activities that could happen during the forty minutes, including the use of the gym, art studios, music area, library, and computer labs; and use of outdoor picnic areas and of classrooms for club meetings. Food service areas were set up in different locations around the school. This example of creative scheduling illustrates how students, teachers, and support staff can come together to solve a problem and respond to ideas presented by students.

Teams provide support for individual teachers, but also rely upon the unique contribution of each member. In Mary's school, new teachers do not teach "leftover" courses that senior faculty does not want to teach. In the first place, the core, heterogeneously grouped classes prevent such courses from existing. Secondly, new teachers become attached to teams or houses, as opposed to content-based departments that may be more territorial and exhibit professional jealousy toward any bright, enthusiastic new hire. A new English teacher on a team is the only English teacher on the team. This status alone gives each teacher key importance in shaping the future of the team and in leading learning experiences for students.

Core Requirements and Electives

"This course is open to all students who are willing to work hard," proclaims each Advanced Placement (AP) course description in the program of studies. The open enrollment policy for AP classes assures students equity of opportunity. Democratic schools open all programs to all learners. Further, they insist on an academic core that ensures that all students will meet the learning standards of the school and state. Mary's team offers the core sophomore academic courses within a required core of four years of math, science, and English and three years of history, constituting a twenty-credit requirement for graduation. The faculty and administration made sure the twenty credits of required course work were in place within a structure that allowed for elective choices beyond the essential curriculum. The program of studies represents the clear sense of purpose and desired learning outcomes for all students in the school. If students are to fully participate in a democratic society, they need the strongest literacy skills the public school can provide, whether a student is going to pursue a liberal arts degree or attend a technical school.

Many schools require students to jump through a series of hoops to "get to the next level" or to take an "honors" class. Once schools get into the business of levels, tracks, or ability groups, it is easy to go down the slippery slope of weighted grades. Mary's school does not level classes in the first place. Additionally, the courses are not weighted. No program or class is valued or "counted" more than another for the purpose of determining a student's class rank (a practice the school is phasing out). Honors designation on the report card is an option for students in any course, based upon a contract for more challenging work arranged among the student, teacher, and parent. Following the new learning standards and the move to a standards-based system, this concept is also working its way out of the system. Because democratic schools respect the diverse talents of their students, they equitably respect all course offerings and programs. Democratic schools support a "can do" mentality in which students gain confidence by working hard to "get smart."

Grading and Reporting

The traditional grading system of quarterly number averaging to achieve a "semester average," with an additional percentage calculated to account for final exams, has no place in a school with authentic teaching and learning at its center. Mary's school abandoned quarterly grades for a system of narrative progress reports over the semester. This plan was developed by a community group of teachers, board members, students, and parents who were originally charged with rethinking the traditional concept of "top ten" and other stalwart props of senior year recognition. The committee recommended adopting a philosophy of continuous progress throughout a semester, assessing students based on what each had achieved at the end of each semester, in January and in June. Further, these grades (A, B, C, N for novice, and NC for no credit) would not be averaged, nor would they represent any type of averaging process.

Standards-based assessment creates a representation of how well students met the expected learning standards of each class. Holding grades until the semester end does not hold students hostage if they get off to a slow start in a new subject area. Further, successful students cannot rest on their laurels during a second semester, expecting that a higher grade will average with a lower grade to see them through the spring. This system prevents students from being discouraged by early failure, because they know poor grades early in the term will not disappear in a mysterious average. Standards-based reporting also provides richer and more detailed information to parents throughout a term.

School Governance and Decision-Making

For many high school students, democracy stops at the schoolhouse door. In conventional high schools, freedom of speech, participation in decisions affecting their lives in school, and opportunities to learn are all determined by adults who hold the power. If democratic public schools are essential to the survival of our national democracy, the strategies we use to determine practices and policies should offer a means for students to experience democratic governance and leadership. Teachers, students, and administrators should both lead and learn as they work through their days.

In Mary's school, the faculty council, consisting of about twelve teachers, meets bimonthly with administrators to organize faculty meetings, professional development activities, and to maintain focus on the vision of the school. Two students from the student council are usually present. These students also serve as student members of the school board. The council crafts its meetings to focus time on student achievement. Teachers select the council by checking names on a ballot that contains every teacher's name in the school. The top twelve serve for one year, with everyone having the option to decline. The head secretary and custodian also participate regularly. At this time there are no parents on the council, but every important initiative affecting curriculum, instruction, or assessment has involved parents either on a task force or in public forums.

Over several years the council has evolved from a "strategic planning team" to a "leadership team" and finally into a general "council." The council's meetings are open to all who wish to attend—and many do. The principal's role is to participate as a member, with teachers taking turns facilitating the meetings. Meetings range from form-planning sessions to text-based seminars on current research. When decisions need to be made, the principal is clear about those that have to rest at her door, such as adhering to health and safety rules. Most decisions move from the council to the full faculty for endorsement, and perhaps to public forum. Decisions are made by consensus as much as possible, always guided by the best interests of students.

To support new teachers and to provide personalized professional development for all staff, nearly every teacher participates in a Critical Friends Group. These groups, initiated several years ago by the Annenberg Institute for School Reform, give teachers a place to talk about classroom practice, often using structured protocols to give and receive feedback on teacher or student work. The practice of "tuning" among teachers has now filtered into the seminars where students "tune" their senior projects with peers. Seminars are an evolving strategy, providing all students with two years to study a topic of interest in depth. By design, seminars provide students with ultimate choices. What do they want to know? What skills will they need in the future? In seminars, teachers face a continuous challenge to engage and meet the needs of all learners. The council is currently working with students to figure out ways to make seminar time more meaningful and support students in completing their graduation portfolios in the first semester of the senior year.

At Mary's school, teachers and students have a voice in every aspect of school life, from curriculum and assessment practices to hiring new staff and assessing teacher performance. On the most mundane level, teachers work on teams to determine the duty schedule for the year. Some love to walk the student parking lot. Others would rather interact in the cafeteria. Teachers construct and lead their teams or houses in the best interests of students, so all can exert power over their lives. One team's narrative progress reports may not resemble other team reports. Not all student conferences need to occur on the same day. The results may appear to be chaotic at times, but students thrive in this environment. Why? Because students also have power over their own lives. They know they will be included, consulted, and given choice, both in the classroom and beyond.

Like any democracy, Mary's school is far from perfect, experiencing daily the leadership challenges of engaging a thousand rural teens in learning. But what is more important is how the school works on its daily imperfections. In Mary's school, democracy is education, loud with the many voices eager to be heard. Engaged deeply in thoughtful, important work, democratic schools are messy and impatient to improve. They celebrate the power and uniqueness of the individual, but work together under a common purpose. They are deep and fearless communities, expecting all members to participate as teachers, leaders, and learners. They are equitable by design, and passionate about democracy in practice.

RESOURCES

Cohen, E. (1986). *Designing Group Work: Strategies for the Heterogeneous Classroom*. New York: Teachers College Press.

Darling-Hammond, L., & Ancess, J. (1994). *Graduation by Portfolio at Central Park East Secondary School*. New York: National Center for Restructuring Education, Schools, and Teaching, Teachers College, Columbia University.

Finley, M. (1984). "Teachers and Tracking in a Comprehensive High School." *Sociology of Education 57*, 233–43.

Glickman, C. (1993). *Renewing America's Schools: A Guide for School-Based Action*. San Francisco: Jossey-Bass.

Johnson, Susan Hackett. "Understanding Political Parties." *Electronic Learning Marketplace*. http://www.elm.maine.edu/assessments/teacher/, updated May 26, 2001 [accessed August 22, 2002].

Kohn, A. (1998, April). "Only for My Kid: How Privileged Parents Undermine School Reform." *Phi Delta Kappan*, 569–77.

Kohn, A. (1993). *Punished by Rewards*. Boston: Houghton Mifflin.

Lee, V., & Smith, J. (1995). *Effects of High School Restructuring and Size on Gains in Achievement and Engagement for Early Secondary School Students*. Madison: Wisconsin Center for Education Research, University of Wisconsin.

Maine Department of Education. (1990). *Maine's Common Core of Learning: An Investment in Maine's Future*. Augusta, ME: Author.

McDonald, J. (1993). "Planning Backwards from Exhibitions." *Graduation by Exhibition: Assessing Genuine Student Achievement*. Alexandria, VA: Association for Supervision and Curriculum Development.

National Association of Secondary School Principals. (1996). *Breaking Ranks: Changing an American Institution*. Reston, VA: Author.

Oakes, J. (1986, June). "Tracking in Secondary Schools: A Contextual Perspective," *Educational Psychologist 22*, 129–54.

O'Neil, J. (1993, June). *Can Separate Be Equal?* Alexandria, VA: Association for Supervision and Curriculum Development Update.

Schlechty, P. (1997). *Inventing Better Schools: An Action Plan for Educational Reform*. San Francisco: Jossey-Bass.

Schlechty, P. (1990). *Schools for the 21st Century: Leadership Imperatives for Educational Reform*. San Francisco: Jossey-Bass.

Sizer, T. (1984). *Horace's Compromise: The Dilemma of the American High School*. Boston: Houghton Mifflin.

Sizer, T. (1992). *Horace's School: Redesigning the American High School*. Boston: Houghton Mifflin.

Sizer, T. (1996). *Horace's Hope: What Works for the American High School*. Boston: Houghton Mifflin.

Slavin, R. (1990). *Achievement Effects on Ability Grouping in Secondary Schools: A Best Evidence Synthesis*. Madison: Madison National Center on Effective Secondary Schools, University of Wisconsin.

Sternberg, R. (1997, Dec. 3). "A Waste of Talent: Why We Should (and Can) Teach to All Our Students' Abilities." *Education Week 56*.

Tucker, M. (1994). *Designing the New American High School*. Washington, DC: National Alliance for Restructuring Education.

Wasley, P., Hempel, R., & Clark, R. (1997, May). "The Puzzle of Whole School Change." *Phi Delta Kappan*, 690–97.

Wasley, P., Hempel, R., & Clark, R. (1997). *Kids and School Reform*. San Francisco: Jossey-Bass.

Wheelock, A. (1992). *Crossing the Tracks: How Untracking Can Save America's Schools*. New York: The New Press.

For additional information, contact:

Pam Fisher, Superintendent of Schools, Acton, Maine

Consultant, Center for Inquiry on Secondary Education, Maine Department of Education

P.O. Box 323

North Berwick, ME 03906

(207) 676-9475

pfisher@acton.k12.me.us

CHAPTER 7

Service at the Heart of Personalized Learning
Developing Relationships between Self and Other

PATTI SMITH
Education Alliance at Brown University
(with Karin Schaefer, director of Side by Side)

This chapter will address an important aspect of personalized learning—the development of relationships between self and other through service-learning. This chapter uses the Side by Side program as an example of best practice, and makes recommendations for implementing service-learning programs and for adopting a service-learning mentality to improve the culture of an entire high school.

Nelson (age 11) said: "At Side by Side the councilors don't do everything for you. They do it with you."

Laura (age 10) said: "After working in the garden at Side by Side last year, I joined a gardening club at my school back in the city."

Tommy (age 9) wrote: "Today I worked in the garden, I drew a tall tree and went swimming. I got to cook with my councilor and started to learn the play. The last thing we did before bed was go out on a star walk. I saw a bat and lots of stars."

Ersell (age 10) wrote: "My favorite time at Side by Side is the time I spend with my own councilor. Today we went exploring the stream and climbed a big hill to feed the chickens."

Housed on the campus of Sunbridge College, surrounded by organic gardens, woods, and ponds, Side by Side is a three-week service-learning program focused on community building, mentoring, the environment, and artistic expression. Participants include students 16–22 years old from diverse academic, ethnic, and socioeconomic backgrounds; and campers, ages 9–12, from urban schools and community-based organizations.

Sunbridge College is in Spring Valley, New York, twenty miles north of New York City. The Center for Life Studies at the college instituted the program in an effort to address the growing need of high school and college students to feel a sense of accomplishment, to develop appreciation for service, to be in the presence of caring adults, and to develop community with peers of different backgrounds.

The program takes place in August. Students arrive from all over the country and often from other parts of the world. They instantly develop a strong teaching and learning community among themselves by intensely working with program staff during the first week. Staff members serve as mentors to individual students, modeling positive supportive behaviors. Staff and students share life stories, and students learn to record their experiences in journals. Students engage in artistic exercises, maintaining the household, and preparing classrooms and materials for campers.

Campers arrive from organizations in New York City the second week. Each is assigned an individual mentor. Students develop intense relationships with their campers. They cook together, work side by side in the garden, do artwork, and read before bedtime. To our surprise, we find that for many students and campers this is the first time in their lives they have received one-on-one attention for a sustained time period.

The day begins with group singing, after which students and campers work in the gardens, picking vegetables for meals they prepare. Swimming precedes lunch, washing away the soil from the fields. Solo time for quiet reflection happens in the afternoon, followed by individual and interactive journal work. Drama is the final activity before dinner, chores, and bedtime stories. The play, incorporating all the artistic activities, serves as the crowning event at the end of the campers' stay.

The program provides opportunities for students and campers to experience the benefits of the whole community, the intimacy of a mentor relationship, and the necessity of individual quiet time. Everyone learns by engaging in activities that serve others as well as themselves. Several components contribute to the overall success of the program.

CREATING A COMMUNITY OF CARE

The students live together, collectively caring for daily living arrangements and organizing household responsibilities. The tension between
self and other, each with a distinct set of boundaries, creates opportunities for lively discussion and reflection on group dynamics. Students
confront their communication skills, face biases, and assess their leadership abilities and limitations.

As one student discovered: "The most powerful part of my Side by
Side experience was the development of community among the counselors; we were all from drastically different backgrounds, able to offer
and receive different things. A beautiful community developed between
us. I think that all of us experienced an unexpected culture shock; it
was this cultural exchange which provided us with a wealth of power,
community, inquiry, and love with which to approach the children. I
was forced to face my own prejudice, ignorance, and privilege in a way
I'd never expected."

Another student discovered his snobbery: "Rooming with Danny
turned out to be a very humbling experience. It was helpful, especially
with distance from my life, to see in depth, a totally different way of
conducting oneself and interacting with others. I was able to see that
his ways were just as valid as mine were. Danny told me during the
closing ceremony that he had learned a lot from me. Danny loved
working with the kids, especially on a one on one basis, but at times
had trouble. There was one day in particular when only half of the
councilors were healthy enough to work with the kids. Under tremendous pressure I stepped up, entertaining the campers during transitions
between activities. Danny told me that he admired the way I handled
the pressure."

One student even decided to practice newfound capacities: "Side by
Side gave me constant pointed practice in community living—trying to
observe any group I was a part of from an objective standpoint, determining what role I could best fill, finding the best way to let my individual needs and gifts interact with the group's needs and potentialities.
I continue to practice these interpersonal skills daily in various situations, whether it's in my co-operative housing situation, in classes, with

friends, engaging in community projects or in designing future educational and activist communities."

Breaking bread is essential for community development. During the school year, too many students eat alone and miss the opportunity to engage in meaningful conversation, meal preparation, and assisting with after-dinner chores. The gardening program is an antidote to these conditions. Harvesting vegetables, students learn firsthand where food comes from, how much energy goes into preparing it, and that the simple activity of eating together proves to be more than physically nurturing.

Singing grows on students and campers, just like foliage on the garden. By the middle of the week, everyone sings at mealtime, during the evening nature hikes, and on midnight star gazing walks. Students experience music's lure as a common language.

Celebrating accomplishments is at the heart of any healthy community. Producing a play, from memorizing lines, to coaching each other, to creating costumes and sets is reason for celebration. Students learn that acknowledging the fruits of hard work nurtures feelings of pride and accomplishment. Parents come from the city to share in the culminating event before packing their children up and taking them home.

Building a community of care has a ripple effect and, from our experience, appears to be a genuine way to involve parents. Parents witness the program benefiting their children and intuit that more exposure to the program might be advantageous for them as well.

Over the years, some families have had a child participate one year, and a second child in a different year. These families have developed a trusting relationship with the staff, exemplified by the fact they requested midyear gatherings at the college for the families to revisit the program experiences. The Center for Life Studies now sponsors an autumn nature walk for these families. Happily, the students sing songs from the summer as the group hikes the leaf-laden trails, observes the sleeping garden, makes centerpieces for Thanksgiving and ornaments for Christmas. A spring walk also occurs when several Side by Side students join the group during their college break. Waking up the garden, families plant seeds, the fruits of which they will eat at the summer dramatic performance, and help the farmer with other chores. Seeing this made me realize that when families discover that you are making their children happy, they are more likely to become involved in the program.

EXPLORING IDENTITY THROUGH STORIES

Of course, before the campers arrive, students take initial steps toward working together. We find sharing life stories to be particularly useful in recognizing that we are all on a common journey, although story sharing is not limited to the opening day. The first exercise is "What experiences led you to Side by Side?" The program staff begins the exercise by explaining what led them to Side by Side. One staff member describes a needle exchange program he instituted at the mental heath center where he works. The program, consumed by political debate, was terminated in spite of the number of addicts it served. The closing of the program was a grave disappointment. His desire to work with a community, however, led him to Side by Side. Another staff member shared an intense sense of loss she experienced over the suicide of her daughter's friend. The event refocused her attention on the needs of high school students, leading her to Side by Side. These examples of vulnerability make it safe for students to share similar events.

Latisha described herself as a tough young black woman suspicious of white students and teachers. She loves painting and wants to learn how to paint with young children. She met one of the Side by Side staff at the community center teaching a painting course. Latisha likes her, even though she is white, because she is a great painting teacher. The director of the center asked Latisha to participate in the program. She agreed because it is an opportunity for urban students to get out of the city and develop painting skills. She is apprehensive about living with white students.

Paul described himself as a white male scared by women like Latisha on the subway. Paul shared his apprehension to ride the subway above 96th Street in New York City. He is anxious to work with students from diverse backgrounds in hopes of overcoming his fears. He heard about Side by Side at his school and is attracted to the idea of forming a community with ethnically diverse students.

Daniella described herself as culturally naïve, attending a private school where there is no diversity. She wants to teach in an urban environment and has no experience with urban children. She chose the program because of her interest in forming diverse communities through artistic expression.

Danny described himself as an unmotivated student looking for direction. His counselor suggested the program because it focused on outdoor activities that Danny loves. Danny explained that since the focus of the program is on creating a diverse community, he had something to offer, since he is physically disabled. He wants to show children they can participate in outdoor activities even when disabled.

Choosing to attend the program is the common thread binding members of the newly constituted community. Students express aspirations and share vulnerabilities they hope the program will help them address. The motivations for choosing the program are unique and sometimes contradictory. The stories make common threads explicit and differences apparent. They are surprisingly honest and heartwarming. The substance for our work together lives among us in the pictures created from the stories.

One student observed: "Hearing the other students' stories, I began to realize that they had things to extend to me which I had never expected, things I did not necessarily want to accept. I saw that we were all ignorant in a lot of ways; others were awake to things I would never be awake to, and vice versa. I began to soak it up, accepting the two way exchange of culture and knowledge and innocence."

Another student stated: "I thought I would just work here with the others, but because of the stories we have told each other we are so tight now, I see 'me' in everyone. The story that struck me most involved one of his school aids. Embarrassing as it was, Danny needed others to carry his books, move chairs for him and to be present in case he fell. In high school one of his aids made blatantly racist remarks about Hispanics, not knowing that Danny was Puerto Rican. Danny let this woman jabber on and just listened to her for years. They developed a relationship in which the woman found immense respect for Danny. Finally, one day Danny told her that he was Puerto Rican. The woman is now permanently changed. I admire the strength and patience that Danny utilized in making this woman deal with her racism. I know that

I would have immediately challenged this woman, and that she never would have learned the lesson."

Yet another student resolved to change her perspective about life: "Since Side by Side, I've grown more than I ever thought I could. I feel as if I've been awakened, and I see the world I live in as a wealth of experience and knowledge, as opposed to a dark and frightening mystery. I am now fascinated with the idea of diversity and exchange, and I see this interest reflected in my academic, artistic, spiritual, and social lives. A bit of exposure has awakened me to incomparable beauty in the world, and I refuse to stop seeking it out and spreading it."

MENTORING AND ADULT INTERACTIONS

To enhance the mentor relationships between the staff and students and students and campers, Side by Side provides sessions with "workers in the field." The purpose of these sessions with professionals from various fields is twofold. The primary goal is to provide an experience of collegial rapport with adults. Secondarily, students learn about mentoring and the power of life stories from yet another lens.

Prior to participating in Side by Side, students' predominant mode of adult encounter is being yelled at by parents and talked at by teachers. Side by Side revived the obsolete dinnertime chat to allow informal exchanges between adults and students to occur. During dinner conversations guests tell life stories, paralleling staff/student sessions, emphasizing struggles, failures, time of doubt, and descriptions of individuals who provided support and direction during times of need. Students are grateful for the frank exchanges. Some even said the dinner chats revitalized their faith in adults. Students learned the value of conversation in building relationships.

Guests' positive impact on students is evidenced in journal writings: "I wonder if my father struggles like this man? Hearing our guest yesterday made me think of him for the first time in years. I will never know, but I am glad to know that there is hope for me as I struggle along to find my interest."

Another student describes her learning: "I get it! This week I get what it means to be a mentor to the children, and I have been having so much fun being with the campers now. I loved watching and observing the amazing transformation and growth of children. They grew, I grew, and the plants grew!"

Yet another student learned how to internalize the process: "I watched the staff, how they worked together and how they drew upon each other's skills. I realized that I had to do that with my fellow side by siders so my camper could have the best experience."

JOURNALING: REFLECTING ON SELF AND OTHER

Side by Side, premised on the idea that artist expression is a fundamental medium for human communication, teaches students a journaling technique using painting, photography, drawing, and collage. The word *journal* suggests a journey. Students keep a carefully illustrated daily record of experiences and reflections, a habit we hope they will continue after the program. The journal is a lively self-assessment and precious reminder of the summer journey they embarked on with other students and campers. For many students it represents their first beautiful handmade creation—supplying motivation for future self-expression.

Students demonstrate the technique to campers, who also record their experiences in words and pictures, with visual illustrations and prose. Students learn that artistic exercises inspire other forms of self-expression and are effective in teaching young children to read and write.

One student observed: "I think that the journaling component of side by side is a very valuable elemental of the program. Personally, I felt that the time journaling was a time to connect with and get to know my child, but through the veil of drawing and writing. We were able to communicate best through our artistic activities, and my camper's most engaged writing came when inspired by an artistic activity."

Another student wrote about the value of the journal: "During the camp weeks, I realized that children are our best teachers. In my weeks with the campers, I learned how to braid cornrows, the lyrics to a multitude of rap songs, and heard a few of the painful stories I would have expected, as well as many beautifully surprising ones. In the garden a kid taught me how to pick up a worm, and another told me stories about the Greek Gods as we gazed at the stars together. I'll remember everything because it is recorded in my journal."

Yet another student describes how she integrated the experience into her life after the program: "Because we worked so hard on our journal communications, I keep in contact with my camper who now writes to me from her home in the projects, telling me that she misses walking with me, and that she loved drawing leaves with me. I write back and say, 'me too.' I think that the best exercise is the 'Conversation in Color,' where a student and camper have a conversation together using not words but colors. What I like about this exercise is that beautiful drawings emerge, the creation of which is an even interchange of ideas, just like a word conversation. After the conversation is complete, when asked to describe the conversation, even typically silent kids recount elaborate, rolling stories full of laughter and tears; they can see the conversation alive in the colors on the paper. To me, this is success; real communication happens, when it might not otherwise. I have brought this 'Conversation in Color' exercise away from Side by Side and into my own life. Once back at school, I brought this exercise into my drama class, in addition to sharing it with my friends."

Students invariably report Side by Side to be a life-changing event. Program staff contacts alumni each December as part of a long-term evaluation process. We are still in touch with the majority of the students who have participated in the five years of operation. During our most recent conversations with alumni, six discussed using the journaling technique in community-based organizations last year, twenty-two are in college using the exercises whenever possible, several are participating in internship programs, and others are working. All speak about Side by Side as a pivotal experience and attribute the lasting impact to the duration of the program, the ethnic diversity of their peers, and working with the children (many still keep in touch with their campers).

Chloe Junge, Side by Side participant from 1998, shared: "Side by Side was a very meaningful experience and is still very alive for me. Last year I worked a lot with a kid who grew up in the projects right near Stand-Up Harlem [Stand-Up Harlem was a program site during the year she attended Side by Side]. It meant a lot to me that I had experienced, however briefly, his neighborhood. I would definitely recommend Side by Side to others and would be happy to distribute fliers. Perhaps some of the people who volunteer for the agency where I work would be interested. The work I do is mostly helping people maintain their connections to the community during their incarceration. I go to the jail at least three times per week and visit each housing unit, taking requests to mail letters, make calls to family members, employers, other helping agencies, giving out writing supplies, etc. Then from my office I make calls and do all the other follow-up. In some cases I get to know clients quite well, and am able to continue to serve them during their transition back into the community, or by correspondence after they have been transferred to prison. My favorite part about the work is knowing the people; in some cases I get to know other family members as well. The advocacy I do within the jail is one of the hardest things. The jail staff for the most part is not terribly respectful, and can be uncooperative to say the least. There is very little outside monitoring of conditions in the jail except for my coworkers and me. Being denied medical treatment or being beaten by guards are the most disturbing violations, but there are many more minor that we try to address. It can be hard to see so much misery and a justice system that is so arbitrary and unjust."

WHAT EDUCATORS CAN LEARN FROM STUDENTS' EXPERIENCE AT SIDE BY SIDE

Why should a three-week supplementary educational experience have such an impact on students? I believe it is the sincere sense of responsibility that all members of the community are expected to take for the success of the experience that makes it remarkable. Coupled with a comprehensive effort to nurture the students artistically, socially, and spiritually, the notion of honestly relying on students changes them.

After implementing Side by Side for five years, I know that students have an unacknowledged and incredibly rich threshold for challenge that high schools do not exploit. High school students thrive on personal attention; it nurtures them. Properly channeled, this attention can be harnessed for the sake of nurturing others. Service learning exploits that attention and directs the impulse for discovery.

SIDE BY SIDE AND THE *BREAKING RANKS* RECOMMENDATIONS

The National Association of Secondary School Principals, in partnership with the Carnegie Foundation for the Advancement of Teaching, developed *Breaking Ranks: Changing an American Institution* (1996), offering a series of recommendations that provide a powerful and challenging vision for high schools of the future. These recommendations promote a personalized and caring environment for students, confirming what was discovered and predicted in Side by Side.

HOW DO WE NURTURE HIGH SCHOOL STUDENTS?

1. Creating a Community of Care

Breaking Ranks says:
"The physical setting of a high school should nurture a student in much the same way that the clear, safe, interior of a home makes the youngster feel safe and comfortable."

Side by Side uses space to create a healthy atmosphere. The physical space is beautiful. Campers and students are taught to respect the space, to keep it clean, and to enhance the space with artwork and items from nature whenever possible. The program is designed for interdependence to occur, the healthy kind of support that keeps families together.

The staff strives to be archetypal parents, worthy of imitation. The students, like older siblings, look to the staff for advice and skills while being given responsibility for the younger children. Sharing life stories, a safe atmosphere grows while students identify similarities and differences among the group. The process succeeds because everyone is respected—the first step in creating a community of care.

2. The Need for Personalized Learning

Breaking Ranks says:
"Each high school teacher involved in the instructional program on a

full-time basis will be responsible for contact time with no more than 90 students during a given term so that the teacher can give greater attention to the needs of every student."

Unique to Side by Side is the student-to-camper ratio and the small size of the program. The intimacy afforded by one-on-one relationships is daunting and unfamiliar at first, but because of the trust-building components, it soon becomes the hallmark of the program. It is striking to note that foundations, our primary source of financial support, are generally interested in programs that can potentially be "scaled up" to serve large numbers of students. Side by Side, however, champions the need for small, intimate programs providing personalized attention to participants. We believe that students receive far too little individual attention and that the gift of time is the greatest opportunity we can provide them. Perhaps the *Breaking Ranks* document will influence foundations to change their emphasis from scaling up to focusing in.

Breaking Ranks says:
"Schools must unabashedly teach students about such key virtues as honesty, dependability, trust, responsibility, tolerance, respect, and other commonly held values important to Americans."

Trust-building is the first ingredient for creating a community of care at Side by Side. The staff is responsible for initiating the expectations of the caring community through the behaviors they demonstrate. These attitudes of care and respect are models for the students in developing relationships with each other. Students literally work side by side with the staff, learning together, making mistakes, reflecting on the success and failures of the day, and taking joint responsibility for the experience. Students perform because they appreciate the trust bestowed on them. They produce because they are challenged to meet high expectations on a minute-to-minute basis.

3. Students Want to Know Their Peers

Breaking Ranks says:
"High schools should, if necessary, be islands of tolerance where those customs and traditions and ideas that might be subjected to derision elsewhere can find refuge."

The essay section of the Side by Side applications illustrates that students are longing to spend time with peers who are very different from them. As some students stated in their opening stories in this chapter, they are interested in participating in discourse to address these differences. They are attracted to the idea of living with students from diverse ethnic and social backgrounds. During the school day, however, such meetings are seldom possible. Students generally find more similarity than difference among their classmates. Schools provide few opportunities for students to commingle with students of different levels of apparent academic proficiency.

Eyler and Giles (1999) report that service-learning activities are more likely to be attended by a diverse group of students since involvement is not dependent on academic standing and is usually voluntary. Students in their study report that a primary advantage to program participation is interaction with students they usually have little contact with in other capacities at school.

4. The Importance of Advocate and Mentor Relationships

Breaking Ranks says:
"Every high school student will have a Personal Adult Advocate to help him or her personalize the educational experience. . . . Having someone on his or her side can help a young person feel a part of the school community."

At Side by Side, capacities and relationships are reviewed during reflection sessions. Reflection time is pertinent to the success of the program. At school, on the other hand, students generally have no time to reflect on their learning. Moving from class to class, there is no thread holding the experiences of the day together, nothing connects the content learning throughout the day, and there is no time allotted for assimilating experiences and ideas. When and how do students share their thoughts about the learning and the social encounters of the day?

Just as the body needs time to digest food, students need time to digest their school day. Indigestion results from overeating and eating too fast; similarly, burnout and lack of motivation result from students' inability to digest the school day. A personal advocate serves as an antidote to this problem, meeting with the student on a daily basis, reviewing highs and lows, and helping to provide a context for the experiences accompanied by encouragement and advice.

At Side by Side, we find that the program activities are enhanced as a result of these daily reflection sessions. Not only do students meet individually with their staff mentor, but also the group meets together to review the day. Students are able to debrief their interactions with the campers, providing helpful tips for each other. Students also know there is safe time each day for commiserating, for sharing frustrations with each other or with a staff member. The well-facilitated reflection period allows each member of the community to grow as an individual, and the community as a whole is enriched.

Side by Side profits from this activity; program enhancement is ongoing. We credit the high level of exchange around program content for the improvement. The staff agrees that they learn as much from the mentor/advocate experience as do the students.

5. Older Students Assist Younger Students

Breaking Ranks says:
"High schools should foster experiences that lead to genuine success for students, experiences upon which youngsters can build confidence."

Coaching younger students provides another natural and meaningful way for "digestion" to occur. Recently, I worked with high school students who were inadequate readers in an after-school program using Side by Side program techniques. We trained them to read, draw, and journal with elementary school students. Simple picture books were chosen as content. Students practiced reading one afternoon, drawing a picture from the story, and writing a sentence about the story in a journal. The following day, the students read books to the little children, draw pictures, and write a sentence about their favorite part of the story. On the third day, the high school students share the experience with each other and write about the experience with the children. The students experienced themselves as readers rather than nonreaders. As time progressed, students began to know the children and took responsibility for finding appropriate stories for each of them. The little children loved reading with their high school tutors.

The high school students were excited to be involved in something useful. Practicing, playing, and deepening their work in a nonthreatening atmosphere was a key to their own improvement as readers. High school students can serve as athletic coaches for children in elementary and middle schools as well.

6. The Importance of Creative Opportunities

Breaking Ranks says:
"A problem plaguing high schools has been that too many teachers teach in only one way; that is by the lecture method—the same way they were taught. They often feel that lecturing is the most expeditious method for covering a large volume of material. Too often this approach leaves students unengaged, not caught up in the lesson, which is centered more on the teacher than the students."

My one disappointment with the *Breaking Ranks* document is that the arts are not highlighted as a means for improving teaching, accommodating learning styles, and engaging students. Side by Side students experience the arts as a tremendous friend both in supporting their expression and in embellishing the work with campers.

With the recent frenzy about standards and academic improvement, the creative impulses of students remain an untapped reservoir of opportunity. During Side by Side students learn to use the visual arts to spark self-expression. It is less threatening for them to draw a picture, take a photograph, or create a collage to express their ideas. The play production served up a smorgasbord of opportunities to engage in multidisciplinary learning as it provided a festive mode of performance assessment.

Several students communicate with their campers to this day, exchanging poems and short stories on the Internet. Reviving the Art of Letter Writing is a program developed by Side by Side graduates to encourage writing between young students and college students.

7. Creating Community Connections

Breaking Ranks says:
"High schools will form partnerships with agencies for youths that support and supplement the regular programs in the school. The health

of our democracy depends on students gaining a sense of their connection to the larger community."

One of the best ways to create such ties is through service-learning, which enables young people to contribute their efforts to activities that are useful to the community and helps them reflect on what they learn from their participation.

Service-learning is a relatively new concept lacking a universal definition. Some proponents describe service-learning as an educational philosophy traced to John Dewey. Others consider it an instructional model, while still others consider it simply a curricular tool. Sigmon (1994) distinguishs service-learning from other experiential learning and community service activities. This researcher states, "service-learning is intentionally designed to equally benefit the provider and the recipient of the service as well as to ensure equal focus on both the service being provided and the learning that is occurring."

Furco (1996) characterizes "true service-learning" as symbiotic, and points to an important distinction that's easy to miss. Not enamored of the "do-gooder" mentality traditionally connected with community service, he describes service-learning as a mutually beneficial experience. A student is not expected to simply do the good deed of visiting an elderly person, but rather to develop an interdependent relationship with that person, the benefits of which serve both parties. To be an authentic service-learning experience in his view, the student and elder engage actively together in the learning process.

Cousins and Mednick (1999) provided a real example of this notion in their description of a service-learning project in a middle school in Brooklyn. Students, as part of a learning expedition, visited elderly people in a retirement home over the course of a school year to learn the history of their community. During that time the students painted portraits and documented biographies of the elderly. At the end of the year, students prepared a gallery in the foyer of the school for the entire community to view in honor of their subjects. The students and the elderly were enriched; both felt they contributed to the learning of the other. The experience also enriched the entire school community. Parents, other students, and teachers were proud that their school participated in this kind of learning exchange.

Certainly, the learning and the giving are clearly evident in the examples of student writing provided herein. The meaningfulness of learning re-enlivens the students to return to school with newfound capacity to work with others and to share their summer learning with other students in their communities. This motivation is generated by relying on the students, trusting them with the success of the program. Imagine if we trusted students enough to make them responsible for some aspects of their school program?

Listed below are compiled findings from studies of existing service-learning programs. The results of Side by Side are echoed in these findings:

- Middle and high school students who engage in high-quality service-learning programs showed increases in measures of personal and social responsibility, communication, and sense of educational competence (Weiler, LaGoy, Crane, & Rovner, 1998).
- Students who engaged in service-learning were more likely to treat one another kindly, help one another, and care about doing their best (Berkas, 1997).
- High school students were more likely to develop bonds with more adults, to agree that they could learn from and work with the elderly and disabled, and to feel that they trusted others (besides parents and teachers) to whom they could turn for help (Morgan & Streb, 1999).
- Students showed increases over time in their awareness of cultural differences and in their attitudes toward helping others (Stephens, 1995).
- Students enjoyed helping others with projects, became more dependable, and felt more comfortable communicating with ethnically diverse groups (Loesch-Griffin, Petrides, & Pratt, 1995).
- Students showed an increase in awareness of community needs, believed they could make a difference, and were committed to service now and later in life (Melchior, 1999; Westheimer & Kahne, 2000).
- High school students developed more sophisticated understandings of sociohistorical contexts, were likely to think about politics

and morality in society, and were likely to consider how to effect social change (Yates & Youniss, 1996; Morgan & Streb, 1999).

- Teachers and students reported increased mutual respect (Weiler et al., 1998; Berkas, 1997).
- Educators and students reported a more positive school climate as a result of a feeling of greater connectedness to the school (Weiler, D., LaGoy, A., Crane, E., & Rovner, A., 1998).
- Educators involved in service-learning engage in ongoing reflection and analysis to determine how to improve educational services to students (Billig & Conrad, 1997).

SERVICE-LEARNING PROGRAMS

Is there a way to structure the school day to maximize the eagerness and excitement that students described here? Looking to Quest High School in Humble, Texas, the answer is yes. The school is divided into family groups, each consisting of twenty-five students and one or two family heads. The family stays together over the course of a student's high school years. On occasion, the family engages in building community skills through ropes courses and trust-building exercises, not dissimilar to Side by Side. Whereas students reported an impact from the three-week intensive experience, students at Quest speak favorably about their experience over years.

One student reported: "A families [sic] purpose should be to, set us apart, prevent us from falling through the cracks; have people to turn to, talk to, and support, to get to know people and not feel like you're forgotten, to bond and really get to know others; to have direction in finding out who you are."

The school community engages in service-learning every Tuesday morning for two hours. The program is viewed as one of the most powerful drives of the school culture.

A student reflects on his service-learning work: "You know you've learned something when you teach it. Before Quest I wasn't really reading. I did all my learning from my friends—I learned about cops, girls, and about how to run from what is facing me. Quest expects you to meet more than that. Like when I was tutoring second graders in reading. I could understand a lot of their difficulties, the ADHD or what you call it because I have auditory and visual dyslexia."

SERVICE-LEARNING CULTURE WITHIN THE HIGH SCHOOL

The work of service-learning programs, although organized at school, usually occurs outside the walls of the classroom. Schools themselves, however, when operating in the context of personalized learning communities, can engage in service-learning programs within the walls of the school, enriching the school community with the same potency that is reported by successful programs outside the school. Imagine projects at school that increase mutual respect between teachers and students, that make all students' feel greater connectedness to the school, and that increase students' sense of self-confidence. Perhaps the content and context of programs similar to Side by Side hold clues for helping schools to successfully engage all students.

Breaking Ranks suggests that high school require students to participate in a service program in the community or in the school itself that has educational value. Why should students need to leave the school to have service-learning experiences? Are there not a plethora of opportunities to engage in service-learning on campus? My contention is that school is *a real-life situation* that can be maximized to provide meaningful, nurturing, collaborative, authentic, reflective learning on campus as well as off site. High schools can feel free to steal from service-learning program content to enhance the learning modalities and culture of the entire campus.

Ultimately, school is the quintessential service-learning community. Teachers provide a service to students. Students learn as a result of the service. But can this interaction hold up under Furco's (1996) definition that service-learning "is intentionally designed to equally benefit the recipient of the service as well as to ensure equal focus on both the service being provided and the learning that is occurring" (p. 5)? Do teachers feel they are benefiting from the service? Are students really learning from the provider? Do teachers and students feel a reciprocal process occurring in classrooms, mutually benefiting from the experience? Has education moved so far from schooling as service toward schooling as enterprise that such an idea is outdated?

Relationships within the school community need serious rethinking for high schools to engage in the types of personalized learning opportunities demonstrated in Side by Side and suggested by experts in the field. Service-learning programs provide clues for deepening student–teacher interactions and for creating a more nurturing learning environment. In such an environment, teachers view themselves as expert mentors, and students see themselves as novices in the learning experiences. Students are also seen as experts mentoring novice student learners. The *real-lifeness* of school can be exemplified though personal stories, portraits that personalize the classroom and school climate and link learning in a subject area to the real lives of students and teachers.

Another way to strengthen the relationships within a school is to develop daily activities bringing the community together. As students learned at Side by Side, mealtime can nurture productive conversations and provide opportunities for students to be physically and socially nurtured. Teachers and students share this respite together as members of the same community where learning is occurring all the time.

Celebrating accomplishments builds trust and familiarity in a community. Again, Side by Side students learned that acknowledging the fruits of hard work nurtures feelings of pride. In schools where there are weekly gatherings among groups of teachers and students to share work, it is reported that a culture of trust is strengthened. At the Met School in Providence, Rhode Island, students have daily sharing time during which they report the activities of the day and accomplishments of individual students. Members of the local community are invited to share information about upcoming events such as craft shows, artistic performances, and political events, enhancing the notion that there is a larger community of which the students are also members.

This requires the attention and participation of all members of the community. All adult members of the school team must experience "buy-in." Can you imagine Side by Side, Quest High School, or the Met without the involvement of everyone? A service-learning mentality needs to be developed within the entire school community. It should *be* the culture operating in a school. Side by Side is successful because every facet of the program is steeped in a culture of care. It is not fair to ask students to engage in meaningful reciprocal learning for a portion of time and then return to a mediocre, less nurturing climate. Students at Quest only spent two hours each week doing off site service-learning, but the culture of service permeated the school.

Personalized learning divorced from an engaged, caring community will lead to students seated in cubicles doing individual work that interests them. Isolation is not the goal of service-learning; luckily, it cannot occur in a vacuum. It relies on positive human exchange as a measure of success, thus serving as a healthy model of personalization.

RESOURCES

Cousins, E., & Mednick, A. (eds.). (1999). *Service at the Heart of Learning: Teachers' Writings.* Dubuque, IA: Kendall/Hunt.

Eyler, J., & Giles, D. (1999). *Where's the Learning in Service-Learning?* San Francisco, CA: Jossey-Bass.

Furco, A. (1996). Service-Learning: A Balanced Approach to Experiential Education. In B. Taylor (Ed.), *Expanding Boundaries: Service and Learning.* Washington, DC: Corporation for National Service.

Loesch-Griffin, D., Petrides, L.A., and Pratt, C. (1995). *A Comprehensive Study of Project YES—Rethinking Classrooms and Community: Service-Learning as Educational Reform.* San Francisco: East Bay Conservation Corps.

Melchior, A. (1999). *Summary Report: National Evaluation of Learn and Serve America.* Waltham, MA: Center for Human Resources, Brandeis University.

Morgan, W., & Streb, M. (1999). "How Quality Service-Learning Develops Civic Values." Unpublished paper, Indiana University, Bloomington.

Sigmon, R. (1994). *Linking Service with Learning.* Washington, DC: Council for Independent Colleges.

Stanton, T.K., Dwight, E.G., Jr., & Cruz, N.I. (1999). *Service-Learning: A Movement's Pioneers Reflect on Its Origins, Practice, and Future.* San Francisco, CA: Jossey-Bass.

Stephens, L. (1995). *The Complete Guide to Learning through Community Service, Grades K–9.* Boston: Allyn & Bacon.

Thomas, B. (1997, February). *Strategic Review of the W.K. Kellogg Foundation's Service-Learning Projects, 1990–1996.* Battle Creek, MI: W.K. Kellogg Foundation.

Wade, R.C. (ed.). (1997). *Community Service-Learning: A Guide to Including Service in the Public School Curriculum.* Albany, NY: State University of New York Press.

Weiler, D., LaGoy, A., Crane, E., and Rovner, A. (1998). *An Evaluation of K–12 Service-Learning in California: Phase II Final Report.* Emeryville, CA: RPP International and the Search Institute.

Westheimer, J., & Kahne, J. (2000). *Report to the Surdna Board—D.V.I.* New York: Surdna Foundation.

Yates, M., & Youniss, J. (1996). "Community Service and Political–Moral Identity in Adolescents," *Journal of Research in Adolescence 6,* 271–84; cited in Perry, James. (1999). *The Grantmakers' Forum Community and National Service Research Task Force Report.* Bloomington: Indiana University.

CHAPTER 8

Community-Connected Learning

Personalization as a Vehicle for Reform

ADRIA STEINBERG
(with Jane Milley and Marty Liebowitz)

Although young people are not always articulate about what they want and need from high school, their criticisms and wish lists often come down to a desire for more connection, choice, and challenge—what we term the "three C's." They tell us they want "teachers who care," peers they can trust, and chances to "do something real" and about which they care. Yet only a small percentage of high school students can count on finding these three C's. The lucky few are connected in positive ways to teachers and peers and find both choice and challenge in honors or advanced placement courses, interest-based electives, school leadership positions, and extracurricular activities.

For many other young people, high school is a vastly different experience. As they will freely tell you, they do not work very hard in school; in fact, they find it boring. With graduation requirements increasing, they have less choice of electives, and they believe that their teachers either do not know or do not care about them. One large-scale survey indicates that 40 percent of high school students are simply "going through the motions" (Steinberg, Brown, & Dornbusch, 1996). As a result, they leave high school inadequately prepared for college or careers.

Although most graduates head to some form of postsecondary education (the national average is approaching 70 percent), at least half leave before getting a degree or other credential, and many spend the next five to ten years in some way combining course work with jobs that are temporary or in the youth labor market. For many young people, this floundering can last into their late twenties. They enter adulthood lacking either the credentials or the critical thinking, problem-solving skills, and habits of mind and work that form the basic currency of the emerging economy.

GUIDING PRINCIPLES

Over the past ten years, Jobs for the Future has engaged in extensive work with schools, districts, and communities that are committed to addressing these challenges and giving students more help in making the transition into adulthood. In these communities across the United States, education reform is directed not only at providing more challenging, relevant, and personalized experiences in school but also at strengthening student engagement with and connection to productive activities and adults.

Jobs for the Future uses the term "community-connected learning" to describe these educational strategies. Community-connected learning demands that schools enter into new relationships with a variety of community partners and build with those partners a system of opportunities and supports for youth. As figure 8.1 illustrates, four key principles, as well as a set of enabling conditions, characterize this approach to high school reform.

In partnership with schools and districts throughout the country, Jobs for the Future has defined each of these principles as follows:

Rigor and Relevance

When students ask—as they frequently do—"why do I need to know this?" they are searching for a more apparent connection between what they are learning in school and the potential uses of that knowledge in the world beyond school. Research in cognitive science confirms that these connections motivate students *and* provide rich contexts for deepening their understanding of key concepts and sharpening their skills. While the focus in many schools and districts on setting and measuring high academic standards is a necessary step to educational improvement, it is also necessary to focus on innovations in teaching

Enabling Conditions

- Schools as professional communities
- Data-based reform
- Supportive district and state policies
- Community-wide support for reform

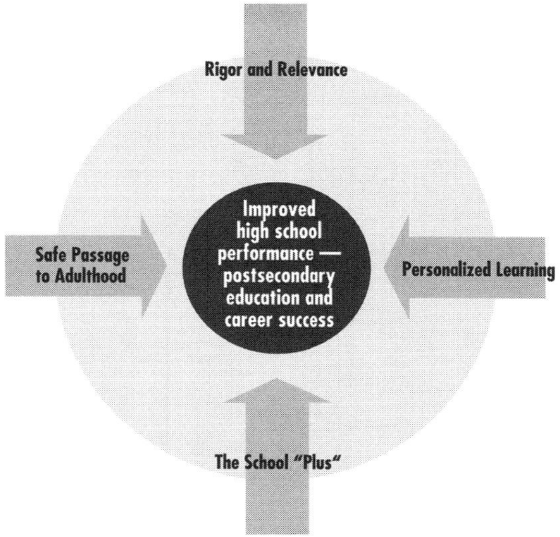

Figure 8.1. Guiding principles and enabling conditions for community-connected learning.

and learning that will enlist young people in meeting those standards—particularly at the high school level, where students are passive recipients of a steady diet of lecture, classwide discussion, and drill.

Personalized Learning

In a very real sense, all kids go to small schools. Deborah Meier, the founder of several small schools, often points out that young people deal with the anonymity of large schools by identifying with a group of friends and, often, a subpopulation of students (the jocks, the burnouts, the artsy ones). But, as Meier also emphasizes, most of these "small schools" lack adult presence and are unacademic in focus (Meier, 1996). The size of the learning community appears to be particularly important for those students who are traditionally least successful in school. Smaller, more personal schooling environments make it possible for a student to form relationships with adults who know the student well enough to build on his or her strengths and interests. These learning communities also encourage conversation and collaboration among teachers as they work toward more student-centered, active learning in the classroom.

The School "Plus": Productive Learning in Workplace and Community

Even with more active and more engaged forms of teaching and learning, the high school classroom is not the only setting for learning, or, for some students, even the best one. It is important to look beyond the box of the insular, self-contained high school to a broader conception of secondary education that makes use of the rich variety of learning contexts, teachers, and resources a community has to offer. In this vision of high school reform, the student experience encompasses not only rigor and relevance in school but also high-quality learning opportunities in workplace and community settings, where adults support and push them to do their best.

Safe Passage to Adulthood

Young people in the United States come of age in a society that lacks a well-developed set of policies and institutional connections to help them make the transition to adulthood. Between the critical ages of 16 and 24, a disturbing number of young adults spend significant portions of time detached from school, the labor force, and family. Such isolation can be toxic in multiple doses, showing up in lower incomes by ages 25 to 28, as well as in a greater chance of incarceration for men and a higher rate of poverty among women. Implemented well, community-connected learning not only helps students attain the learning goals of school; it also helps them acquire the intellectual competencies, personal attributes, relationships, and networks they need to make a successful transition to higher education and careers.

THE CASE FOR MAKING SCHOOLS SMALLER

In translating these principles into action, many schools and school districts are creating smaller, more personalized learning communities within larger, bureaucratically organized high schools. Some districts and states have also begun to experiment with organizational arrangements and choice plans that encourage and support the formation of new small high schools.

The move toward small learning communities and small schools is grounded in a robust body of research. A significant number of studies have found a connection among school size, student engagement, student achievement, and other indicators of student well-being. Findings suggest that students in small schools, or small learning communities within schools, are:

- More satisfied with their schooling (Lindsay, 1982; Burke, 1987; Fouts, 1994; Gordon, 1992)
- More academically productive and better performing than comparison groups in comprehensive high schools with respect to percentage passing and credits earned (Lee & Smith, 1993, 1994; Lee, Smith, & Croninger, 1995; Robinson-Lewis, 1991; McMullen, Sipe, & Wolf, 1994; Crain, Heebner, & Si, 1992)
- Less likely to drop out (D'Amico & Adelman, 1986; Dayton, 1987; Gordon, 1992; Pittman & Haughwout, 1987)
- More positive about themselves and their abilities (Lee & Smith, 1993, 1994; Robinson-Lewis, 1991)

As smaller learning communities have gained recognition and credibility as a propitious reform strategy, entire districts, especially in large urban systems, have moved to implement them in their high schools. In fact, the U.S. Department of Education launched an initiative to support such activity in school districts across the country.

Within the context of "scaling up" this strategy, Jobs for the Future is working to identify the vital characteristics of those small schools or learning communities that are having a positive impact on young people, especially young people who have been least well served by their high schools. Small size may be a necessary condition for powerful, personalized learning, but that alone does not guarantee success. Certainly, students do not derive the benefits of smallness if the school continues to "act big" in its daily routines and rituals.

Small schools and small learning communities within large schools are effective when faculty build on this structural foundation to address the anonymity and alienation that are a prime obstacle to engagement and learning in large impersonal high schools, particularly for students who have traditionally been least successful in school. Smaller schooling environments work when they are organized to make it possible for teachers and counselors to know students well enough to build on their particular strengths and interests.

These learning communities also need to be organized in ways that encourage conversation and collaboration among teachers, enabling them to work together to achieve more student-centered, active learning in the classroom. These conversations provide the foundation for developing a coherent sense of instructional focus—a key factor in improving student performance. Small learning communities, many of which use a broad theme as a context for learning, have been especially successful with urban, traditionally low-achieving students.

COMMUNITY-CONNECTED LEARNING IN PRACTICE

Jobs for the Future has documented and collaborated with a range of schools, from small schools that have gained a significant degree of autonomy from the usual bureaucratic restrictions to large high schools that are reinventing themselves into smaller learning communities. The two school environments described below exemplify this range. The Metropolitan Career and Technical Center in Providence, Rhode Island—the Met—is part of a growing system of small schools in which each student meets regularly with a personalized learning team to fashion and monitor a personalized learning plan directed at achieving schoolwide learning goals. Just north of San Francisco, Sir Francis Drake High School, a comprehensive high school in San Anselmo, California, is reinventing itself around student-centered, project-based learning, both within and outside small learning clusters and academies.

Different approaches and different environments, yet both schools personalize learning. By enhancing connections, choices, and challenges for all students, both the Met and Drake High School demonstrate the power of personalized learning to combat student apathy and heighten student achievement.

The Metropolitan Career and Technical Center

On June 9, 2000, forty-three young people received their high school diplomas from the Metropolitan Career and Technical Center—the first graduating class of this unique, state-funded high school in Providence, Rhode Island. Every Met graduate applied and was accepted to at least one college, many receiving substantial financial aid packages—an unusual circumstance for an urban school in which 70 percent of the students are children of parents whose education did not go beyond high school.

Upon entering the Met, the class of 2000 looked very much like their peers in the Providence school system. In fact, the composition of the graduating class is an almost perfect mirror of the Providence schools: 52 percent of the students qualify for free lunch; 22 percent are African American, 38 percent Hispanic, and 38 percent white. The first cohort included a substantial number of students who entered the Met two or three years behind grade level in skills. The group ranged from students who had repeated or were about to repeat a grade to students assessed as gifted and talented, with most clustering at the lower end of the achievement scale—getting by and receiving passing grades, yet not developing the skills necessary to succeed in college and careers.

After many years running a middle school and then a high school where they tried to make room for both the traditional curriculum and the central developmental tasks of adolescence, the two founders of the Met decided to try a very different approach. Dennis Littkey and Elliot Washor wanted to give each student the support and opportunity only the most privileged get at home. To do so, they opened up the school day and the school building, creating time and opportunities for each student to develop a web of adult relationships, both inside and outside the school. Their goal has been to guarantee all students an opportunity to gain the skills, life lessons, and connections they will need in their transition to adulthood.

At the Met, students find themselves in a school unlike any they have ever attended—or probably even imagined. As one Met student explained, the school is never boring because every day is different. There is no such thing as a "typical day." Unlike most schools that pride themselves on setting a schedule in April or May that determines what will happen each hour of the day, every day of the following school year, the Met's schedule differs from day to day, week to week, and student to student.

Instead of being handed a schedule of classes, each quarter every student meets with a team, including a teacher-advisor and a parent, to plot how she or he will make progress toward the school's learning goals. Instead of spending the school day in classes, students fashion independent, personalized projects through which to explore their interests and meet their learning goals. Instead of tests, they create quarterly exhibitions of their work and accumulate a four-year portfolio. Instead of seeing six or seven different teachers and groups of peers each day, they spend intensive time with one advisor, an advisory group of thirteen or fourteen peers, and with adults in the community who mentor them in an interest area.

The most successful teachers in most high schools find ways to make the required curriculum interesting and relevant to students. At the Met, the road to effective teaching proceeds in a very different direction. Teachers, students, and parents are collectively responsible for developing a learning plan—and revising it four times a year—laying out how each student will meet the Met's learning goals and listing the knowledge, competencies, and personal qualities the Met believes to be essential to a successful transition to college and careers. Starting from what students find interesting and relevant, teachers look for ways to help the student articulate and pursue these interests through projects and activities that are rich with opportunities for reaching the learning goals laid out in the plan.

Unlike most high schools, the Met does not require all students to proceed through a preordained curriculum or set of classes. Fourteen-year-old ninth graders spend their days carrying out independent projects and internships—activities that in most schools happen, if at all, in the second semester of senior year after students have met all course requirements. In their senior year, when their peers in "regular schools" are likely to be slacking off, Met students spend much of their day in classes—on nearby college campuses.

In fact, from the moment Met students meet the requirements for entrance into the Senior Institute, which for most students occurs at the completion of their second year, they are encouraged to focus on preparing for college. This may seem a surprising choice, especially given the Met's emphasis on project-based and work-based learning, as well as its origins as a career and technical school. But the students see the Met's focus on college as consistent with its insistence that the purpose of an internship is not to train for a specific job but rather to help students achieve the Met Learning Goals and fulfill their personalized learning plan.

Through the Senior Institute, the Met is trying to redefine "college preparatory" in a way that not only ensures access to college and high-skill careers but also helps students to build the skills, habits of mind and work, and personal qualities that will allow them to survive and thrive in a high-performance environment—whether it is school or the work world. One of the surprises for Met juniors and seniors taking their first college course is the realization that the Met is "a lot like college." They point to the ways they have learned to take responsibility for their own learning, a posture that they can see is necessary in college.

Student Voices from the Met

Students attest to the effectiveness of personalized learning at the Met. In describing her first project, Nadia had this to say:

In the traditional schools, you go in, you do a worksheet, you're out. But how do I use the equation I learned and apply it to my real life? I never figured that out. Here at the Met I'm working on that. It's actually harder to look at math and use it in a real situation than to just do a worksheet.

Nadia, who did well in her previous school, explains how personalized learning at the Met has given her confidence in her ability to do even higher-level academic work:

Now that I've done all I've done I think next year I can take on more challenging things. . . . My writing I feel like I should keep improving because I know it's not something you learn and then you learned it. It's something you keep improving at. It has improved a lot, just the way I approach different tasks and the way that I reflect on what I do.

Students repeatedly bring up mentors as important adults whom the Met has brought into their lives, attesting to the importance of connections with adults. It is common to hear students say that they can "talk about everything" with their mentor, that their mentor is someone to whom they look up, a great role model. As Freddie explained:

Manny is like another advisor, someone who coaches me to do what I need to do, shows me the ropes, how to present myself to people. He shows me the grown-up world, the business world. I can tell he's not a teacher, but I learn a lot from him. He has very good advice, so I take that and that helps me out.

Students are very clear on how much support—and pushing—they get from the school, and especially from their advisors. Maya explains why:

It's because of the motivation. They won't let you slide. . . . You've got even the principal in your face: "Did you apply yet?" People want you to go to college, and you see a future for yourself.

As the students point out repeatedly, the Met is more like a family or community than it is like a traditional school. What makes it that way is the range and quality of interactions taking place among adults and young people. The depth of the alliance that students feel with their advisors is evident during students' final exhibitions, when virtually every student described his or her advisor as being "the best." As Nadia said, "She has won a place in my heart. I'll never forget her and all the great things she has done for me."

Over and over again, students indicate how critical conversations with advisors have been to their ability to focus and get down to work at the Met—and perhaps most important, to their ability to understand, accept, and feel good about themselves. The Met has turned the curriculum of high school inside out, pulling to the center the experiences, conversations, ethical dilemmas, life lessons, personal qualities, and work habits that are usually left to the student to learn at home or in the community.

Sir Francis Drake High School

While it is a less radical departure from high school as we know it, Sir Francis Drake provides a powerful demonstration of how a traditional suburban high school can reinvent itself. Drake offers its students choice among learning contexts and learning communities with different themes. It is an environment where students and teachers know each other well and in which project-based learning and opportunities to learn beyond the classroom foster personalized learning that builds upon students' interests and passions.

Drake's student body of about 1,000 students is the most economically diverse of the three schools in the Tamalpais Union High School District. A decade ago, Drake was also the lowest achieving of the district's high schools. Although most of Drake's students were going on to college, there was a growing feeling among parents and district administrators that the school could and should be doing better.

The Spark for Schoolwide Change

The inception of Drake's restructuring initiative dates back to the 1989–90 school year, when the school district targeted the campus as the site for the Marin School for Integrated Studies (MSIS), a new, integrated studies school within a school. Their hope was that this new program would spark a turnaround at Drake, and they envisioned that MSIS would combine technology with cross-disciplinary, project-based instruction. The program's initiation was bolstered by funding and in-kind and technical support from the AutoDesk Foundation, a newly created charitable spin-off from a computer software developer located near the school.

However, with funding and faculty brought in from outside, MSIS, like many school-within-a-school models, touched off negative feelings among veteran faculty, who felt unrecognized for their efforts and inadequately consulted in the formation of the new program. The situation came to a head by the end of MSIS's second year, when all but one of the faculty members associated with the program quit. At this point, though, encouraged by district and AutoDesk Foundation personnel to redesign MSIS, Michelle Swanson, the one remaining teacher, began recruiting Drake teachers to join with her in revamping the program.

Renamed the Drake Integrated Studies Curricula (DISC), the program went from being a school within a school to an incubator for integrated programs of study. In its first year, DISC launched three new programs: two eleventh- and twelfth-grade academies with a broad career focus (the Communications Academy and the Survey of Engineering) and one ninth-/tenth-grade cluster (called the Revolution of Core Knowledge) in which students could build the skills, knowledge, and behaviors necessary for successful participation in the academies.

While a particular set of circumstances and external pressures and supports led to the launching of these programs, it was the determination of the principal and the DISC staff not to let these programs become isolated from the rest of the faculty that laid the groundwork for a schoolwide focus on issues of personalization, engagement, and the conditions necessary for high-quality learning. By 1993–94, all of the staff agreed to serve on committees corresponding to identified areas for reform. As a result, a number of veteran teachers became deeply involved in exploring how students' and teachers' days could be better organized to promote student learning, and a schoolwide student advisory structure was created.

Reform efforts at Drake were given a further boost when a few faculty members agreed to act on a suggestion by Theodore Sizer (reported in the February 24, 1999, *Education Week*) that high school teachers try shadowing a student through a day at school. The veteran faculty who volunteered had assumed that the students' educational experiences were at least reasonably coherent and challenging. Instead, they witnessed learning that often seemed superficial and a day that was disjointed and frequently disrupted. Yet they recognized that there were times when students truly appeared engaged in learning, and these times tended *not* to occur in the core disciplines but rather in the integrated studies academies and in extracurricular activities. What all these learning environments had in common was an emphasis on personalization, performance, and well-defined criteria for excellence.

Through regular student exhibitions, the high level of student performance in the DISC programs was becoming increasingly evident to the whole faculty. Impressed by the exhibitions of student work coming out of the first three models, several Drake faculty members began developing plans for new academies: Academy X, launched in 1995–96 to focus on leadership and public service, and Studies of the Environment Academy, launched in 1996–97. Students who elect to spend their junior and senior years in an academy take half of their course work in the academy, including some core academic subjects. An outgrowth of staff interest rather than a top-down mandate, these academies continue to engage students through project-based learning and an emphasis on high-performance skills.

Drake Integrated Studies Curricula

The *Communications Academy* (COMACAD) integrates social studies, English, advanced video productions, and advanced drama to provide opportunities for students to combine their academic and artistic interests. Students use drama skills and cutting-edge digital video technology to produce public exhibitions of their learning.

The *Revolution of Core Knowledge* (ROCK) integrates science, English, history, social issues, art, and technology into a coherent curriculum and offers students the opportunity to improve time management and higher-order thinking skills while developing interpersonal competencies. While working on challenging projects in teams, students learn and apply high-performance skills, such as gathering and sorting information, thinking critically, speaking publicly, organizing people and events, writing effectively, and communicating visually and dramatically.

The *Engineering Academy* integrates physics, sculpture, electronics, and an engineering-projects class. The program introduces students to different areas of engineering and computer-aided design and requires them to apply academic concepts from physics and mathematics to solve real-world engineering problems.

Academy X prepares eleventh and twelfth graders for leadership in community, business, and government organizations. Students take an integrated core curriculum of social studies, English, and advanced leadership classes and complete internships at local businesses and public institutions.

Studies of the Environment (SEA-DISC) integrates environmental science, chemistry, algebra, probability/statistics, economics, government, and internships as eleventh and twelfth graders study complex environmental problems through extensive projects involving field studies, laboratory experiments, mentorships, and research-level technology.

Expansion and Acceptance

Evolution in the faculty's beliefs about what students could do was put to the test in a vote of the faculty on a new schedule, as was the faculty's appreciation for the conditions under which high-quality learning emerged. When the scheduling committee proposed a block schedule that included much longer class periods and twice-weekly periods for student advisement and club activities, the measure passed by an overwhelming majority.

Work continued on the development of a broad vision for the school. Ongoing discussions among staff led to the identification of four key elements: learning that is more personalized, instructional design that engages student learning, a broader range of academic and emotional support systems for students, and a school culture that encourages a common vision for the future. The challenge, of course, was to ensure that the vision was widely held and put into practice.

Two primary vehicles for doing that have been the Drake Plan, which encapsulates the school's strategy for reform, and the Forum, a group of twenty teachers, parents, and students, including four teachers with reduced teaching responsibilities, two others who receive stipends, and two stipended parents. The Drake Plan called for all staff to engage in action research teams, each of which designs, implements, and measures the effectiveness of a classroom intervention that addresses student engagement and achievement.

The Drake Plan also set out a number of initiatives to build systems and structures supporting the four critical elements, chief among them a "cluster" model for all ninth and tenth graders. Concern for the academic difficulties encountered by younger students has led the school to personalize their instruction by clustering all freshmen and sophomores, not just those signing up for ROCK. Students in these smaller learning communities share the same three classes and the same teachers during each of their first two years of high school.

In-depth faculty collaboration to improve practice—another DISC hallmark——has become more common, as faculty with increasing frequency form teaching and learning action research groups, use department meetings to focus on student outcomes, and create informal teaching teams. As a result of this cross-fertilization, non-DISC staff have become interested in project-based learning. Even in the non-academy part of the eleventh and twelfth grade, some courses are now being offered in an integrated fashion, another example of how the personalized, integrated studies approach continues to color and give shape to Drake's reforms.

Student Voices from Drake

As with the Met, the students themselves are perhaps the best spokespeople for the reforms at Drake. Now a nationally recognized model high school, Drake frequently hosts visitors from other schools. Student guides skillfully articulate what they are learning and why.

For example, Amelia, a Communications Academy student, stresses the educational power of combining rigor with relevance and providing opportunities for public exhibitions of student work:

I might be disappointed with the technology and theatre programs at other places, colleges, because it won't be like ComAcad—learning to work in a group and take initiative. And the academic things that we do—if you don't take time to learn things, like economics, for example, you feel stupid. You're showing a lack of knowledge to more people than just your teacher.

Jessica, an Academy X student, attests to the importance of having opportunities to learn and apply high-performance skills as well as rigorous academics:

Academy X has prepared me for after high school. Public speaking skills, budgeting time. Already I've applied them outside of school to my internship. I look forward to using these skills outside of school. I would never have expected to do a resume in high school.

Jessica and Morgan, students in the SEA-DISC Academy, discuss their work on a project to develop a PowerPoint presentation on alternative forms of energy:

The difference between our previous school experience and the academy is that the work is much more personalized. We are interested and engaged in our project and work with other interested students. Teachers serve as coaches as we develop research, Web-based skills, and Power-Point presentations for public viewing.

As Justin, another Communications Academy student, points out, opportunities to exhibit meaningful work before meaningful audiences create high stakes that promote rigorous learning:

You have to know it, and you have to know it solid. And you have to be able to show how you knew it effectively, without any confusion—you can't make mistakes. It's all got to be researched over and over again to make sure it's correct.

These Drake students take pride in both the rigor and the relevance of the work they do in high school. While they don't use the same family imagery used by students at the Met, they clearly appreciate the powerful opportunities to develop the sense of affiliation with peers that comes from collaborative effort, to experience a teacher as a facilitator and an ally rather than a judge, and to discover something about their own passions, interests, and capabilities.

THE ANTIDOTE TO APATHY

These two very different examples of school reform illustrate the power of personalized, community-connected learning. In each, students are at the center of the learning process, and teachers engage them by using project-based learning, authentic tasks, adult mentors, and performance-based assessment. Both seek to develop content knowledge as well as high-performance skills that enable young people to make successful transitions to postsecondary education, good careers, and productive adulthood and citizenship. Small learning communities, individualized learning, authentic teaching and learning, and powerful learning beyond the classroom—together, these provide students with challenges that are relevant, choices that are meaningful, and connections that make a difference.

In both schools, students experience strong connections to other students and adults in school, while learning opportunities beyond the school walls foster connections to adults in the community. Building on students' interests, passions, and learning styles, faculty members offer students choices about what they learn, how they learn, and where they learn. Working on rigorous projects, public exhibitions of work, and meeting real-world standards of quality provides a very high level of challenge that students meet because it has meaning for them.

Personalized learning that is community connected is an effective antidote to the apathy endemic to most high schools in America. It transforms a culture of getting by, typical of far too many schools, into a culture of engagement and quality. It improves student performance, and it helps ensure that more students graduate with the rigorous academic knowledge and competencies and high-performance skills necessary for success in postsecondary education and beyond.

CONTACT INFORMATION

The Metropolitan Career and Technical Center
80 Washington Street
Providence, RI 02903
(401) 277-5049
www.metcenter.org

Sir Francis Drake High School
Sir Francis Drake Boulevard
San Anselmo, CA 94960
(415) 453-8770
http://drake.marin.k12.ca.us/

For information about Jobs for the Future's work on high school reform, contact JFF at 88 Broad Street, 8th Floor, Boston, MA 02110, (617) 728-4446, info@jff.org (www.jff.org).

RESOURCES

Allen, L., Almeida, C., & Steinberg, A. (2000). *Wall to Wall: Implementing Small Learning Communities in Five Boston High Schools.* Providence, RI: Northeast and Islands Regional Laboratory at Brown University.

Burke, A.M. (1987, May). *Making a Big School Smaller: The School-within-a-School Arrangement for Middle Level Schools.* ED 303 890.

Jobs for the Future et al. (2000). *Connected Learning Communities: A Tool-Kit for Reinventing High School.* Boston, MA: Jobs for the Future.

Crain, R.L., Heebner, A.L., & Si, Y. (1992). *The Effectiveness of New York City's Career Magnet Schools: An Evaluation of Ninth Grade Performance Using an Experimental Design.* Berkeley, CA: National Center for Research in Vocational Education.

D'Amico, J.J., & Adelman, S.P. (1986, April). *Throwing the Baby out with the Bathwater: The Impact of Curriculum and Promotion Requirements on a Successful Business Education Program.* Paper presented at the annual meeting of the American Educational Research Association, San Francisco.

Darling-Hammond, L., et al. (1998). *Inching toward Systemic Change in New York City: How the Coalition Campus Schools Are Reinventing High*

School. New York: National Center for Restructuring Education, Schools, and Teaching, Teachers College, Columbia University.

Dayton, C. (1987). *Peninsula Academy Replications: 1985–86 Evaluation Report.* Berkeley, CA: Policy Analysis for California Education.

DeSalvatore, L. (2000). "Staying the Course with a Reform Agenda: A Case Study of Sir Francis Drake High School." In *Reinventing High Schools: Six Journeys of Change.* Boston, MA: Jobs for the Future.

Fouts, J.A. (1994). *School within a School: Evaluation Results of the First Year of a Restructuring Effort.* Seattle: Seattle Pacific University, School of Education.

Gordon, R. (1992). *School within a School, Grades 7, 8, 9, 10: Focus on Program Evaluation.* Des Moines, IA: Des Moines Public Schools.

Greenleaf, C.L. (1995, April). *You Feel Like You Belong: Student Perspectives on Becoming a Community of Learners.* Paper presented at the annual meeting of the American Educational Research Association, San Francisco.

Lee, V.E., & Smith, J.B. (1993). "Effects of School Restructuring on the Achievement and Engagement of Middle-Grade Students." *Sociology of Education 66,* 164–87.

Lee, V.E., & Smith, J.B. (1994). *Effects of High School Restructuring and Size on Gains in Achievement and Engagement for Early Secondary School Students.* Madison, WI: University of Wisconsin, Center on Organization and Restructuring of Schools.

Lee, V.E., & Smith, J.B. (1995). *Collective Responsibility for Learning and Its Effects on Gains in Achievement for Early Secondary School Students.* Madison, WI: University of Wisconsin, Center on Organization and Restructuring of Schools.

Lee, V.E., Smith, J.B., & Croninger, R.G. (1995). *Understanding High School Restructuring Effects on the Equitable Distribution of Learning in Mathematics and Science.* Madison, WI: University of Wisconsin, Center on Organization and Restructuring of Schools.

Lindsay, P. (1982). "The Effect of High School Size on Student Participation, Satisfaction, and Attendance." *Educational Evaluation and Policy Analysis 4* (1): 57–65.

McMullen, B.J., Sipe, C.L., & Wolf, W.C. (1994). *Charter and Student Achievement: Early Evidence from School Restructuring in Philadelphia.* Philadelphia: Center for Assessment and Policy Development.

Meier, D. (1996). *The Power of Their Ideas: Lessons for America from a Small School in Harlem.* Boston: Beacon Press.

Oxley, D., et al. (1989, January). *Making Big High Schools Smaller: A Review of the Implementation of the House Plan in New York City's Most Troubled High Schools.* Public Education Association.

Pittman, R.B., & Haughwout, P. (1987). "Influence of High School Size on Dropout Rate." *Educational Evaluation and Policy Analysis* 9 (4): 337–43.

Raywid, M. (1996). *Taking Stock: The Movement to Create Mini-Schools, Schools-within-Schools, and Separate Small Schools.* Madison, WI: Center for the Organization and Restructuring of Schools; New York: ERIC Clearinghouse on Urban Education.

Robinson-Lewis, G. (1991). *Summative Evaluation of the School-within-a-School (SWAS) Program: 1988–1989, 1989–1990, and 1990–1991.* Kansas City, MO: Kansas City School District.

Steinberg, A. (n.d.). *Forty-Three Valedictorians: Graduates of the Met Talk about Their Learning.* Providence, RI: Brown University, Regional Laboratory. Available at www.jff.org.

Steinberg, L., Brown, B.B., & Dornbusch, S.M. (1996). *Beyond the Classroom: Why School Reform Has Failed and What Parents Need to Do.* New York: Simon and Schuster.

CHAPTER 9

Preparing Teachers for Personalized Student Learning through Teacher Training

A. THOMAS BILLINGS, Ed.D.
Salem State College, Salem, MA

Prior to college teaching, I had spent more than twenty years teaching in both private and public high school settings. I have taught, at different times, grades three through high school senior. I have spent nearly a decade of teaching courses at Salem State College that help prepare the teachers of the next generation and help support and further develop present teachers. A particular focus for me has been the preparation of secondary school teachers, both undergraduate and graduate.

I have learned a great deal from my studies, research, projects, teaching, and most importantly from my students. Whether you are studying to be a teacher, are a new teacher, or are a veteran teacher, I have discovered that we have a lot in common. I am asking you to think about the essence of your teaching. My experiences and communication from students and teachers alike suggest that we want every person that we teach: 1) to become the best person that he or she can be; 2) to learn to her or his highest level; and 3) to develop skills that emphasize his or her own unique strengths so she or he can contribute confidently to society. If you agree in general with this, then it is important to get back to the theoretical basis of these ideas. If you are studying to be a teacher or are a new teacher, I hope you find this discussion demystifying and helpful. If you are a veteran teacher, I hope you find the discussion hopeful and reflective. In either case, I remind my students that it is essential in striving to be an excellent teacher that you have a strong, thoughtful basis for your teaching and are able to articulate it and use it. I will offer you a theoretical basis to excellent teaching using Abraham Maslowe, Benjamin S. Bloom, and Howard Gardner. You might use other theorists, and that's okay. I would like you to understand mine and reflect on yours. From this base, I can further share some ideas, strategies, and practices for you to consider and develop further to create more personalized learning opportunities for your pupils.

American education for quite some time has dictated or held schools responsible for children's social development, especially along the lines of becoming a caring, civic-minded, and responsible adult. In fact, this notion of creating a "knowledgeable and responsible citizen" is often cited as the defense for using public tax dollars on education. For me, Abraham Maslowe is still timely, because that is his desired end product. But he reminds us as teachers working with children that this just doesn't happen overnight and that we must take care of and help children through a continuum of needs in order to become a fully responsible individual.

Abraham Maslowe developed a classification or hierarchy of needs that motivates human beings. These needs are grouped together into five separate areas: (a) physiological needs, (b) safety needs, (c) social or belongingness needs, (d) self-esteem needs, and (e) self-actualization needs. (Remember, Maslowe suggests that there is a hierarchy to these needs, from the most basic [physiological] to most complex [self-actualization].)

I always felt that this was a great first step in terms of personalizing learning. Maslowe gets us to wrestle with our own humanity and our greater humanity (thinking and caring about others). This is most obvious in the first two categories (taking care of our students' physiological needs and safety needs). For many veteran teachers, the danger is that this may become a mundane habit or unthinking routine that leads to an orderly classroom but an impersonal one. The teacher disengages himself or herself from individual students' needs by constructing a classroom that is equitable for all by addressing needs collectively. The litmus test for personalized learning and growth is asking the question, "I have taken care to allow for the safety and physiological needs of all my students as a group, but have I taken care of everyone's individual safety and physiological needs? Does someone need something else or need more?" This allows a teacher to keep her or his sanity and an orderly routine, but at the same time allows for an opportunity to make a close personal connection with a student at a basic human level by fulfilling a specific need. With the next two categories (social and self-esteem needs), if a teacher is to do this well, it requires the personal touch. To reflect, evaluate, and help children along a continuum of personal self-esteem growth and to have them socially interact well requires the personal touch. It requires modeling, and the teacher is the chief model in the classroom. Ted Sizer and others remind us that unless we model what we teach, then we are teaching something else. Our body language, our speaking voice, our words and our presentation consciously or subconsciously send a message. The one message we want, of course, is one of personal interest in the child's self-esteem and personal growth. These two hierarchies require us to be reflective and thoughtful in our deeds and interactions with students and they with each other. The ultimate goal is to create the self-actualized student who can take care of his or her own physiological and safety needs while having a strong sense of self and interfacing well with others.

When we want to create, in our teaching, opportunities for each student to learn at her or his highest level and develop skills for future learning, I think classically of Benjamin Bloom's taxonomy—six levels of thinking. If social development is the first critical part of our American education, then the second part involves a mastery of the four Rs—Reading, (W)riting, (A)rithmetic, and Reasoning. I believe Bloom becomes timeless when you add reasoning to the traditional three Rs. Bloom's theory can easily accommodate this.

Bloom believed that: Level 1 (Knowledge) skills were the basics of learning a new idea and this included remembering previously learned materials such as principles and definitions. Level 2 (Comprehension) skills involve students being able to show an understanding of what they remembered by being able to use examples or restate the main ideas. Level 3 (Application) skills involve students being able to apply what they have learned by answering questions, performing tasks, or solving problems. These three levels are referred to as the basic or lower-level thinking skills. What we forget sometimes, especially as secondary school educators, is that what is a basic level for many students in our classes may be a higher level for an individual student. I suggest to my beginning or "budding" teachers that ideally you would like to take each student in your class to level three. This application requires us to make both formal and informal assessments of each student in order to measure the individual growth of each student. We set class expectations, but we can only achieve them one student at a time.

Level 4 (Analytic) skills require a student to be able to take an idea and break it into smaller parts. The ability to separate fact from myth and to be able to strip away the glitter from the core concept is part of this level. Level 5 (Synthesis) skills require ingenuity and creativity in the ability to take previous knowledge and add it to new knowledge to formulate a new idea or truth for the student. Level 6 (Evaluation) skills involve a student using a set of rules or rubrics to arrive at a well thought-out judgment or value. Understanding these last three levels as higher-order thinking makes sense when we look at them as requirements for us to know better how each student thinks. Hence, a need for more personalized teaching and, more importantly, personalized assessment is required to truly measure each student's growth in these levels. Reasoning skills development and solid evaluation techniques mean that students, particularly high school students, are in need of personal reflection, teacher interest and encouragement, and teacher understanding in order to have each student stay motivated and on task.

When I think of a student becoming aware of his or her unique strengths so she or he can contribute more confidently to society, I think of Howard Gardner and his multiple intelligence (MI) theory. Howard Gardner talks about providing a way of thinking about the broad range of abilities that students possess. He grouped these capabilities into seven intelligences.

I agree with Gardner and many authors that there may be more than seven, but the point is that this theory causes us to look at each student differently and more uniquely. It helps each student to better find her or his own "intelligence," or special ability, so that each student can play off his or her strengths. The seven intelligences are:

1. Linguistic Intelligence: The capacity to use words effectively, whether orally or in writing.
2. Logical/Mathematical Intelligence: The capacity to use numbers effectively and reason well.
3. Spatial Intelligence: The ability to perceive the visual–spatial world accurately and to perform transformations upon those perceptions.

4. Bodily/Kinesthetic Intelligence: Expertise in using one's body to express ideas and feelings and facility in using one's hands to produce or transform things.
5. Musical Intelligence: The capacity to perceive, discriminate, transform, and express musical forms.
6. Interpersonal Intelligence: The ability to perceive and make distinctions in the moods, intentions, motivations, and feelings of other people.
7. Intrapersonal Intelligence: Self-knowledge and the ability to act adaptively on the basis of that knowledge.

Teachers need to give students opportunities to experiment with and experience all of these intelligences. The personalized learning part is to give each student positive feedback when he or she truly excels in an area. Further, there are two other direct benefits from teaching MI theory. The first is that when we as educators subscribe to there being multiple intelligences, we give credence to multiple assessments—or to state it negatively, there is no one right way to assess learning and achievement. The second is that it causes each student to appreciate others for special abilities and intelligences that he or she doesn't possess, and it plants the seeds to appreciate the need to cooperate with others for maximum results.

I suggest to my undergraduate and graduate students that all three theories together form a synergy that can only help each teacher think of students individually, while working in a collective context. It guarantees that a teacher to some degree personalizes the learning experience for each and every student. I further suggest in the diagram (see figure 9.1) that each theory overlaps, and where the three overlap (the blackened area of the diagram), you have master teaching taking place. Finally, and most importantly, through thinking as Maslowe does we can produce a person that becomes self-actualized and the best that she or he can be. By thinking as Bloom does, we can help a student attain learning at his or her highest level and develop skills for lifelong and future learning. By thinking as Gardner does, we help each student become aware of her or his unique strengths so that he or she can contribute more confidently to society. This, after all, fits well with the common goals of excellent teaching that students and teachers have articulated to me.

Before I share with you some further ideas to personalize learning and ways to sustain it, I would like to share with you three experiences. These experiences were generated from my teaching of this integration of three major theorists. The first took place in one of my undergraduate education courses, which had as a culminating activity a requirement that each student must produce his or her own philosophy of education. One particular student was a true star, the kind of student that hangs on every word, does every reading assignment, and throws himself into group work, discussions, and open-ended questions. I saved him until last to present orally his philosophy of education because he was such a star and a 4.0 English major. I knew it would be great, and I didn't want his presentation to hinder or intimidate the others. He delivered a strong, caring, and well thought-out one-page succinct philosophy. The best word to describe it is memorable. A magic moment occurs when you connect with a student and see a glimpse of his soul and the wonderful teacher he'll become. He was a definite can't-miss prospective teacher. The cornerstone of his philosophy and belief system was this integration and intersection of Maslowe, Bloom, and Gardner. When he finished, there was a hush, then some smiles and tears that gave way to spontaneous applause of appreciation from his fellow students. The story doesn't end there. He asked for an addi-

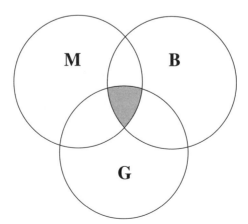

Figure 9.1.   Integration and intersection of Maslowe, Bloom, and Gardner theories.

tional minute to address everyone. He thanked us all and was very pleased that everyone agreed with his espoused philosophy. He then in turn gave me thanks for my teaching and inspiration. He paused and told us that he believed strongly that a teacher should be what he philosophized, because that's what every student deserves. He believed this so strongly that this was the precise reason he was not going to become a teacher. He assured me that he would be a strong advocate and supporter of education throughout his life. He assured me that I had made a personal connection with him and was grateful that he discovered now, in this introductory class, that he understood that he was not cut out to be a teacher. The moral of the story for me was sometimes the personal connections we make with students do not always produce the results we would hope for. Through personalized learning, we are forced to honor the choices our students make, knowing that it is well thought-out and best for them.

In one of my graduate classes, I recently had a teacher that was entering her second or third year of teaching. After going through the three theorists and engaging the students in a discussion of the overlap, integration, and intersection of these theories, I assigned a brief reflection paper for each student to write for the following class. At the next class, before collecting the papers, I asked if anyone would like to share any reflection publicly. Instantly, this second or third year teacher raised her hand. She exclaimed that prior to the last class, she thought she knew how to teach; but now she realized she had a lot to learn. She is a high school math teacher. Her S.A.T. score in math was 800. Her A.P. score in math was 5. Her undergraduate college G.P.A. in math was 4.0. She had never thought about how others learn. Math was easy, and there was only one right way to teach, namely lecture and textbook. She stated she knew her math but she did not know how to teach well. She further stated that she was willing to learn and was looking forward to the rest of her master's degree program in education. This was her first education course as well as first graduate class. I am happy to report that with this start and her motivation to learn and her high standard of excellence, today she is considered to be one of the best, brightest, and most innovative math teachers on the North Shore of Massachusetts. She earned her M.Ed., and she knows how to teach and personalize the learning experience for her students very well.

The third anecdote I would like to share involves two veteran teachers, each having more than twenty years teaching experience. One is an English teacher and the other is a science teacher. Both of these teachers were taking one of my graduate courses for professional development. Recently, Massachusetts has legislated a new license requirement for teachers to fulfill in order to be recertified. One of the recertification/professional development criteria is to take graduate courses; hence these two teachers were taking their first graduate class. I remember them both being as passive/resistant learners initially. Both did not want to be there. They were feeling put upon, especially by the state for not honoring twenty-plus years of teaching. From their perspective, they were being forced under duress to take my course. I presented my thoughts on the characteristics of an excellent teacher, using the intersecting diagram and the three theorists. Both teachers described to me at different times how this presentation was a catharsis for them. Each felt that this trilogy of theorists together honored their own experience; explained clearly what each had known intuitively; and provided them a motivation to do well in this graduate class so that by learning more, they could teach even more effectively. Needless to say, both became "A" students, but more importantly, each enrolled in the full master's degree program and eventually graduated. These two veteran teachers reminded me that we all need to keep learning and stay current for our students' sake. It reminded me that good, reflective professional development constantly brings us back to our basic motivation as to why we teach. Excellent teachers by nature want to do what's best for each and every student. That can best be achieved by personalizing learning.

In this last section of the chapter (including a resource bibliography), I was asked to share some topics and ideas that are parts of courses or, oftentimes, are professional development workshop themes in their own right. In my opinion, all of these concepts relate directly or indirectly to the overriding theme of personalized learning.

My doctoral applied research project (1992) dealt with a three-year study to significantly lower the dropout rate at a local high school. The project was successful in lowering the rate from more than 18 percent to less than 3 percent. The most significant finding for me dealt with the research and study that concluded that the number-one reason students dropped out was because of perceived impersonalization. In my project, "at-risk" students wrote words such as: "Cold," "Uncaring," "No one knows me," "Teachers don't even know my name," and "Prison" in their description of school climate.

Personalizing students' learning can make a big difference. In addition to the strategies and "how to's" found elsewhere in this book, and in hopes of not being repetitive, I present to you my top ten list, with a brief sentence or two of explanation for each item.

BILLINGS' ADDITIONAL SUPPORT FINDINGS AND IDEAS FOR INDIVIDUAL STUDENT LEARNING PERSONALIZATION

1. Every student should have a learning plan. Can you imagine if every student, particularly in high school, knew his or her learning strengths and weaknesses? If every teacher knew best how to approach his or her teaching so each student learned best or at least had some workable strategies to address weaknesses, how much more learning could take place? Each school classroom and teacher would then have the necessary materials and supports for each student to excel as a required legal right with full parent support and approval.

2. Celebrate diversity. Welcome it. Use it to enrich your school and classroom. It gives honor to each student's heritage and requires an "ethos" of collaboration and mutual respect.

3. Less is truly more. Require students to learn the basic four Rs (Reading, Writing, Arithmetic, and Reasoning). Make sure each student learns skills to deal with the subject or concept on his or her own. We can't teach everything; but we can teach skills, so that in the future, students can learn anything.

4. There is no one right way to learn. The opposite is depersonalization of education and has not worked for all students in the past or present.

5. Genius comes in many forms. Once we accept this, multiple intelligence theory can come to life.

6. Multiple assessments. There is a great deal of research that sug-

gests that standardization of testing lowers expectations of student learning. I concur. My colleagues offer many suggestions as to how to assess differently.

7. The American ideal of rugged individualism and self-reliance is alive and well. Each student's taking personal responsibility for his or her own learning is the foundation of personalized learning. When students are engaged and motivated in their own learning, they learn more.

8. I-Thou teaching unlocks doors. On the road to making students self-actualized, they need to deal with self-esteem and socialization issues. The key to self-esteem is respect. Teachers show respect, get respect, and model respect through I-Thou teaching.

9. More successful socialization with thou based on a stronger I. Once the student's self-esteem is in place, he or she can better take her or his place in society. Personalized learning creates a stronger I so that when a student interacts with another, the interaction becomes better, deeper, and more equitable.

10. This new millennium needs to create an independent, self-starting, caring, and self-motivated lifelong learner.

Personalized learning is the key to the future. Our society can no longer afford to waste our most precious resource—each and every student.

RESOURCES

Airasian, P.W. (1994). *Classroom Assessment*. New York: McGraw-Hill.

Arends, R.I. (1994). *Learning to Teach*. New York: McGraw-Hill.

Armstrong, T. (1994). *Multiple Intelligences in the Classroom*. Alexandria, VA: ASCD.

Baloche, L. (1997). *The Cooperative Classroom*. New York: Prentice Hall.

Banks, J., & McGee, C.A. (1997). *Multicultural Education: Issues and Perspectives*. Needham Heights, MA: Allyn & Bacon.

Barth. (1997). *Improving Schools from Within*. San Francisco: Jossey-Bass.

Buber, M. (1958). *I and Thou*. Translated by Ronald G. Smith. New York: Charles Scribner's.

Calhoun, E., & Calhoun, Joyce B. (1998). *Learning to Teach Inductively*. Needham Heights, MA: Allyn & Bacon.

Carnegie Council on Adolescent Development, Task Force on Education of Young Adolescents. (1990). *Turning Points: Preparing American Youth for the 21st Century: Recommendations for Transforming Middle Grade Schools*. Washington, DC: Carnegie Council on Adolescent Development.

Cooper, J. (1995). *Teacher's Problem Solving*. Needham Heights, MA: Allyn & Bacon.

Damn, K., & Damn, R. (1993). *Teaching Secondary Students through Their Individual Learning Styles*. Needham Heights, MA: Allyn & Bacon.

Davis, B.G. (1993). *Tools for Teaching*. San Francisco: Jossey-Bass.

Duckworth, E. (1996). *The Having of Wonderful Ideas*. New York: Teachers College Press, Columbia University.

Evan, R. (1996). *The Human Side of School Change*. San Francisco: Jossey-Bass.

Freedman, S.G. (1990). *Small Victories: The Real World of a Teacher, Her Students, and Their School*. New York: Harper & Row.

Gardner, H. (1993). *Multiple Intelligence: The Theories in Practice*. New York: Basic Books.

Gelfke, N. (1987). *On Being a Teacher*. Kappa Delta Pi Publication.

Glassner, W. (1993). *Schools without Failure*. New York: Harper & Row.

Goodlad, J.I. (1984). *A Place Called School: Prospects for the Future*. New York: McGraw-Hill.

Grant, Gerald. (1996). *The World We Created at Hamilton High*. Cambridge, MA: Harvard University Press.

Henson, K.T. (1993). *Methods and Strategies for Teaching in Secondary and Middle Schools*. New York: Longman.

Hunt, D.E., & Hunt, Joyce, B. (1967). "Teacher Trainee Personality and Initial Teaching Style." *American Educational Research Journal 4*, 253–59.

Hunt, D.E., Greenwood, J., Brill, R., & Deineka, M. (1972). *From Psychological Theory to Educational Practice: Implementations of a Matching Model*. Symposium presented at the annual meeting of the American Educational Research Association, Chicago.

Hunt, D.E., Hunt, Joyce, B., Greenwood, J., Noy, J., Reid, R., & Weil, M. (1981). "Student Conceptual Level and Models of Teaching." In Joyce, Bruce, Peck, Lucy, Brown, & Clark, *Flexibility in Teaching*. White Plains, NY: Longman.

Kellough, R., & Kellough, N. (1999). *Secondary School Teaching: A Guide to Methods and Resources*. New York: Prentice Hall.

Kohl, H. (1994). *I Won't Learn from You*. New York: New Press.

Kozol, J. (1992). *Savage Inequalities: Children in America's Schools*. New York: Trumpet.

Maine Commission on Secondary Education. (1998). *Promising Futures: A Call to Improve Learning for Maine's Secondary Students.* G.E.R.I. Contract #196006401.

McLaren, P. (1994). *Life in Schools: An Introduction to Critical Pedagogy in the Foundations of Education.* New York: Longmans.

Mehlinger, H.D. (1995). *School Reform in the Information Age.* Bloomington, IN: Center for Excellence in Education.

Meir, D. (1995). *The Power of Their Ideas.* Boston: Beacon Press.

Michie, Gregory. (1999). *Holler If You Hear Me.* New York: Teachers College Press, Columbia University.

National Association of Secondary School Principals. (1996). *Breaking Ranks: Changing an American Institution.* Reston, VA: NASSP.

Noddings, N. (1992). *The Challenge to Care in Schools.* New York: Teachers College Press, Columbia University.

Perkins, D. (1992). *Smart Schools: Better Thinking and Learning for Every Child.* New York: Free Press.

Powell, A.G., Farrar, E., & Cohen, D. (1985). *The Shopping Mall High School.* Boston: Houghton Mifflin.

Sizer, T. (1984). *Horace's Compromise.* Boston: Houghton Mifflin.

Sizer, T. (1992). *Horace's School.* Boston: Houghton Mifflin.

Sizer, T. (1993). *Horace's Hope.* Boston: Houghton Mifflin.

Sizer, T., & Sizer, N. (1999). *The Students Are Watching.* Boston: Beacon Press.

Tomorrow's Teachers. (1986). East Lansing, MI: Homes Group.

Wheelock, A. (1992). *Crossing the Tracks: How Untracking Can Save America's Schools.* New York: New Press.

CHAPTER 10

Making Learning Personal

Educational Practices That Work

JOHN CLARKE and EDORAH FRAZER

(with Joseph DiMartino, Pamela Fisher, and Patti Smith)

During the year 2000, teams of field researchers from the Lab at Brown traveled to seven high schools in New England noted for their attempts to personalize learning for high school students. The research teams wanted to assemble a definition of "personalized learning" based on events occurring in a regular school day, aiming to assemble those events into categories that might explain how high schools can organize themselves to personalize learning for all students. Our strategy was to "shadow" a representative selection of students to see when and how these students became personally engaged in their daily work. Applying New England Association of Schools and Colleges guidelines for "shadowing" during school accreditation visits, we wanted to see how different students became personally involved in different program options during their high school experience. At the end of each day, the researcher teams regathered to share their notes, debrief with school teachers and administrators, then try to characterize "personalization" within the whole school, generating from all visits a list of strategies for personalizing learning.

By shadowing twenty-one students in seven different high schools, the teams aimed 1) to characterize developmental needs that students may meet through personal engagement; 2) to describe the many structures schools can organize to meet those needs; and then 3) to characterize the interactions between students and high schools that constitute personalized learning. After outlining one student day from our sample of twenty-two, we will explain how personalized learning may result from the interaction of young adults with aspects of school life arranged to encourage student interaction with a wide community, with illustrations of high school practices that increase personal engagement in learning.

BART'S DAY: FIELD NOTES FROM A HIGH SCHOOL VISIT

As the other researchers follow their assigned students out of Guidance into the teeming halls, I meet Bart in the main office, a bright and courteous junior, friendly and anxious to please. Off the teeming halls, I become a hulking, gray mass, lurching behind Bart's slight frame. I try for that easy banter I recall as "peer interaction" from my own schooling more than forty years ago.

Homeroom

We recite the Pledge of Allegiance, listlessly.

We take our assigned seats.

Announcements on the PA feature looming PSAT exams.

Our home room teacher hands out school pictures so kids can write their own blurbs.

Aesop's fable comes in over the intercom: Lion and Mouse = "cooperation."

It's weird hair and hat day, so the teacher counts weird hats to win a Home Room Prize for the competition. I see unique hair and hats in our homeroom, but probably not enough to bid seriously for the award. The bell rings. We're in the halls again.

Period 1: Communications

To support musical composition on computers, the class was planned to begin with playback of student work. Technological difficulties with the playback machine halt the planned critique. So, the teacher assigns students to listen and match scales and tones programmed on their MIDI machines, a process known as dictation. Bart tells me he has been identified as learning disabled, with clear limitations on his ability to decode symbolic forms. After twenty minutes of dictation, the hyperactive student at the next MIDI station has racked up twenty-six points; Bart, with his decoding disability, has none. Still, he hits the keys forcefully with the hope of identifying the notes that appear randomly on his computer screen.

Two kids teamed at another station surreptitiously tap into Bart's computer to work up some interesting "discord." Cacophony ensues, until Bart shoos them off, fearing that the teacher might spot them.

I decide to mediate frustration with some questions about Bart's interest in music. "I write and play classical music," says Bart. "A couple of recitals so far, mostly Beethoven and Christmas songs. I have taken nine years of music training . . . piano." Bart comments that media is where he gets "hooked in," but no one in school seems to know he plays Beethoven. As the exercise ends, Bart submits no points for his dictation.

The media teacher turns on a videotape showing how "producers" during the '80s used a mixing board to fuse a popular song from scraps of noise. The class watches until the bell rings and the lights go on. We're off to bio.

Period 2: Marine Biology

The teacher has organized a guided tour of a local marsh.

She is remarkably knowledgeable about flora and fauna and the history that shaped their present distribution. We walk down to the marsh in the bright sunshine. At several places in the tour, we listen as she describes the indicators of salt/fresh water incursion.

As we walk and listen, Bart describes his adult contacts and personal involvement in the high school:

Media: "I got hooked in freshman year," he says, "We made advertisements and short programs."

Science club: an afternoon activity.

Costa Rica trip: collected samples from the rainforest.

Sailing club: summer only.

Eagle Scout: after 6–7 years of concentrated work, he earned the highest rank in that organization.

No one but his bulging "shadow" talks with Bart as we tour the marsh, but other kids find amusing things to do along the road, most of which attract a stern warning. We return to the school as the bell sounds.

Period 3: Learning Center/Resource Room
(Special Education)

Bart starts some worksheets for his marine bio class. I look at the kid next to me, who is slouched down in his seat, staring at a pile of grammar review sheets. He is angry. "This is bullshit," he tells me. I ask to take a look at the worksheets piled on the desk. "Bullshit," he says, loud enough for all to hear.

By necessity the special educator and I focus on him, a 17-year-old sophomore with a history of resistance. "Why are we doing this?" he repeatedly asks the teacher. She tries to explain the importance of skills development for his regular classes, but he folds his arms defiantly. The struggle continues for fifteen minutes. A serious educator, his teacher sends a note out to parents each biweek—and Dana's next note has now been defined by this interaction.

"Dana is talented with computers, but he doesn't seem to use his talents around here," she tells me. Bart has abandoned his bio worksheets to listen in as the bell rings.

Period 4: School-to-Work Class: "Journey of Introspection"

The blackboard contains indications that the group is using the Meyers-Briggs Type indicator to compare learning and thinking styles within the class and to speculate on the fit between individuals and the demands of work.

At the teacher's request, two kids explain without energy their Meyers-Briggs profiles, as if fearful of responses from others. There is no response from teacher or class, though one scores "introverted" and the other "extroverted."

The teacher reads a new article on current job pressures and trends.

Student heads hit the desks. "The traditional workplace was designed by Ford for mass production, not for people who think on their own—like today's workplace." No students respond.

The teacher turns on a video about Japanese/American conflict in the workplace. Individual kids have conferences with the teacher on their midterm "Progress Notes." The class watches TV until the bell rings.

Lunch

Bart waits in line, then goes to a table and talks to a few other kids, without passion. I let him have some peace until the bell rings. Besides, I have a headache.

Period 5: English

Class starts with ORBs (Outside Reading Books). Kids read independently for thirty minutes. The teacher hands out the day's newspaper: Kids read, looking for articles in categories: sports, politics, world. . . . No interaction occurs about the articles. Kids write in their journals on the articles they have read.

As the period draws to a close the teacher reads aloud an article on working.

"Work sucks," says Melissa, next to me in the circle of desks.

"I hate working," says her friend.

"It's like bees," says Cathy, who works afternoons at the local Shop & Save, "Buzz, buzz buzz . . . die."

"The better you do in school, the more you earn in a lifetime," explains the teacher, as the bell rings and kids rush to the gathering buses. Bart runs, too, and I wave, admiring from a distance his forthright courage and determination. He is aiming for a communications major in college.

Researcher's Impression

Students run by the bells.

The bells run the day.

The schedule runs the bells.

The curriculum runs the schedule.

The curriculum is designed to convey a core of knowledge to all kids, divided into career clusters that help them choose electives and aim roughly for their future. Bart has not had a meaningful interaction with any adult all day, or with any student, from what I have seen.

Debriefing and Team Conclusions

We believe we have discovered that personalization is not the same as individualization. Personalized learning requires the active direction of the student; individualization lets the school tailor the curriculum to scaled assessments of interest and abilities. The difference between individualization and personalization lies in control. "How much does the student direct the process of his own learning? The answer to that question plays out in student commitment. We have seen few students committed to their learning in this school, except as an expression of their hope to attend college. Despite Bart's interest in music, media, and nature, events of the school day are organized to fit generalized career tracks, rather than his individual hopes and dreams. The structure and process of the day are controlled by others. If students want to go to college, they comply. If not, they resist, probably without effect. Even Senior Seminar, a required inquiry project, inspires student dread; it is a set of written requirements jammed into a nine-week quarter. The block schedule, designed to promote engagement, has the detrimental effect of forcing kids to change their classes, teachers, and acquaintances twice a year, filling their days with strangers who become familiar only when the semester is about to end. We did not see a great deal of personalized learning today.

IMAGES OF PERSONALIZATION

In fact, the shadowing visits as a group revealed a great deal more about depersonalization than personalization. Still, by gathering descriptions of engaging events during a high school day, we began to recognize essential elements of personalized learning across our sample schools that could characterize the ideal of a personalized high school experience. From all the shadowing visits, the research team assembled long lists of specific events that engaged high school students personally. From each of those lists, several hundred items in length, Edorah Frazer began to group similar events into categories representing:

1. The developmental needs that students appeared to express through the event;
2. The school practices that allowed students to meet those needs;
3. Descriptors for interactions between students and school professionals that may characterize personalized learning.

We identified six categories of supportive interactions across all schools, each reflecting a developmental need of high school students that could be associated with a set of school practices organized to meet that need. The following summary illustrates each of the six interactions, with selections from field notes for both developmental needs and school practices. Figure 10.1 represents the six developmental needs, six areas of practice that respond to those needs, and six principles that describe the effect of interactions between the developmental needs of young adults and supportive school practices.

1. Recognition

A large number of events in our field notes represented the young adult's need to test her voice among peers and adults. School practices that allowed students to test their "voices" required a platform of equity; democratic processes established within the community, school, and classroom. In such settings each student could receive recognition for a unique perspective, contributing to the larger group process. Recognizing the individual's unique contribution to school life was clearly apparent in a large number of events from our shadowing visits. Although many schools arranged formal award ceremonies to showcase student achievement, personal recognition with the power to keep students engaged appeared moment-by-moment in the daily interactions among students, teachers, and administrators in all aspects of school life. The most powerful moments of "recognition" occurred during fleeting interactions in the halls, classrooms, and central areas, usually as students and teachers greeted each other with deep familiarity. When students, educators, and adults in community-based projects

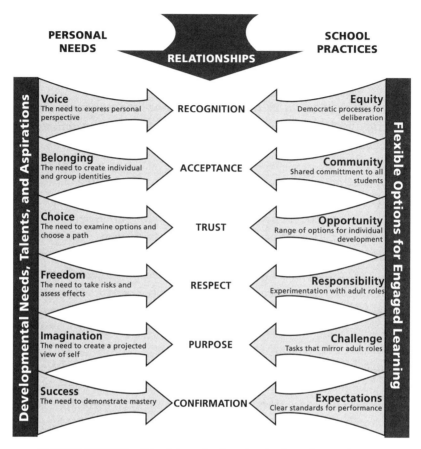

PERSONAL LEARNING: Using information from the school experience to direct
one's own life and to improve the life of the community

Figure 10.1.   Personalization rubric.

responded to each other with shared concern, as in a continuing but fragmented conversation, mutual engagement was likely to occur.

In personalized settings, students and teachers knew each other, often using first names in greeting. By far, recognition exerted the most powerful force in the interactions between students and their teachers. As one field note says directly, "I ask K——— why this is her favorite class. 'Because my teacher loves me!' she beams. Teacher smiled. (It's clearly true.)" Momentary and evanescent, such moments accumulate during a school day, lending the whole school a friendly atmosphere. When students wanted to show us their work, we came to believe that they were being recognized for a unique expression of personal perspective. When the school arranged schedules, classes, advisories, schools meetings, and student travel equitably to promote individual success, the chance to be recognized pervaded the whole school day, reducing the need for control by adults. The team proposed (see table 10.1) that the need for "voice" and the practice of creating democratic processes created a changing array of opportunities for gaining recognition.

2. Trust

Students in all our schools expressed their need for real choices, not in course selection, but in the daily work of school learning. Personalized schools responded with challenges that mirrored the challenges of adult life in the community. When students made choices to meet those challenges, they earned trust from the whole community. When mutual trust marked student/faculty interactions, shared purpose took the place of force, suspicion, and resistance. Instances of mutual trust between adults and students reinforced a sense that both were committed to school learning, but that students would have to take the lead. Teachers and administrators developed structures in which students would have to take on a challenge, then seek support from within the whole community, school, businesses, and local agencies. The mark of effective teaching was not command of academic material, but commitment to student control over information. "Mr. M_____? He's a genius, that man. He has so many ideas about how I could improve. . . ." Our research team talked about how much schooltime was wasted on command and control efforts in schools where personalization was not prominent—and how much learning time appeared when students were pursuing their own questions and finding their own answers with wide access to adults in the community (see table 10.2).

In relation to personalized learning, trust at the secondary level seems to require an appreciation of the age or developmental stage of the young people being taught. Young adult learners need to experience

Table 10.1. Comparison of voice and equity.

Developmental Needs	School Practices
VOICE: the need to express a personal perspective	**EQUITY:** Democratic processes that encourage all to take a personal stand
◊ He was greeted with a handshake and they began their time with Paul saying, "Show me what you got." J. maneuvered his way through the HTML language with Paul and maintained focus for the entire hour. ◊ Student presenter continued to lead class and rest of class listening -- engaged, and taking notes as she presented. ◊ Halls and classrooms are filled with student murals; all the murals were beautiful and unblemished ◊ M_____ tells me she has lunch with her English teachers sometimes; they know her best of any adults in the school. ◊ One student is doing a short movie on Thoreau, can you imagine; it came from him and so he is thrilled. ◊ Two kids in wheelchairs are frequently greeted by other kids ◊ He glows with pride as he shows me a "light-saber" fight scene from his movie that looks nothing short of Spielberg. ◊ She showed me her photography portfolio and her working notebook.	◊ Then after a moment of thought the advisor suggested that he might want to modify his goals to include his work on the family house. ◊ Individual kids have conferences with the teacher on their grades and Progress Notes. ◊ Student work used as a basis for discussion in class and among teachers. ◊ Advisories flex to allow students to pursue their own interests ◊ Many of these students have been together with each other and the teacher for two years ◊ School structure based on smaller, two-year "divisions" ◊ The high school funded all three to attend the Women's LEADS conference at Dartmouth last weekend. ◊ Senior projects, junior research papers, portfolio presentations celebrate unique passions and gifts ◊ The principal commended everyone involved naming the kids who had been fighting and spoke of them as if they would be familiar to everyone.

some of the autonomy that marks adulthood and adult decision-making. They need to experience "knowing things" as an essential prop to their own autonomy. This autonomy does not mean teachers make no claims to authority, but it does mean that teachers must consciously create scenarios in which students are called upon to exercise judgment and to take ownership for a task.

Our schools had devised many ways to endow their students with trust. For example, schools can give students control over the funds they need to pursue their own learning: one school gave $50 to a student interested in photography to help that student set up a darkroom at the school; another responded to three students' requests by paying

Table 10.2. Comparison of choice and challenge.

Developmental Needs	School Practices
CHOICE: The need to choose a path and test choices against results	**CHALLENGE:** Tasks that ask students to take the lead & help each other
◊ "I feel like I have a lot of control now, especially in this school. You aren't limited and that really helps." ◊ "Students have tremendous freedom of expression and movement in this class," M. says. "I can do what I want when I want and I am not sitting at a desk listening to a teacher talk." ◊ choice in demonstrating learning: choice of final project, presentations, ◊ student involvement in designing rubrics to assess work ◊ no bells or halls passes or other indicators of external controls ◊ teen culture allowed to stretch and breathe in hallways (music, chatter, light jostling about and horse-play) ◊ The girls work on the floor of the PLP coordinator's office. Two other students enter individually during the period, one to use the counselor's computer, the other to talk with these girls. The counselor never appears. ◊ J. and friend D. look over database list of possible placement sites in business and discuss who they want to call and what they will say. D. calls and makes them an appointment for an interview.	◊ "Yeah, that's what I like about my Community Service placement. I'm not good with a schedule. Freedom is good. I like freedom." ◊ Lots of computers, kids working independently on them and helping each other (kids have passwords) ◊ I like Mrs. _____ 's World History class. She tells us what we need to do and sends us off to do it. I do not like things that are structured . . . the same-old, same-old. ◊ Teacher hands out evaluation rubrics that students will use to evaluate each other ◊ Teacher says of the class, "It always amazes me how interested they are if they pick what they want to do." ◊ Teachers enter and leave classrooms without concern for student behavior. ◊ S. had "Independent Study." She told me she uses this time to get extra help in music ◊ In every way students are encouraged to do independent projects, either as a group or as an individual activity ◊ The program office helps people become more independent in their learning.

for them to present at a "Women LEADS" conference at Dartmouth College. Financially, these are minor expenditures, but it is striking to think of how atypical it is for students to have any input into even the tiniest portions of a school budget.

3. Respect

High school students also expressed their need to take control of the situations they faced during a school day, assuming responsibility for their own direction. Personalized schools responded by offering a wide variety of opportunities for students to take responsibility, in small projects, in leadership roles, and in defining problems for solution within the community. During moments of student engagement, mutual respect removed the tension and strain that characterizes interactions between young adults and their older teachers in many high schools. Feeling control over their own destiny, students turned to the faculty for guidance and support, but not for admonition or direction. Students come to see that there are many ways to earn respect. As one commented, "In my ninth grade year I did a community project with some other kids by teaching an elementary school class about racism. I was proud to see how the kids felt about themselves afterwards and how much they learned about racism. This was the first big project I had ever done in my life." Students need to take control of their learning. Self-respect, like mutual respect, needs time and a wide assortment of opportunities to develop. The research team proposed that students who wanted to take responsibility needed the opportunity to experiment with adult roles within the adult community (table 10.3).

4. Acceptance

The adolescent need for belonging has been featured in most descriptions of young adult development. As the persistence of high school cliques may attest, students crave a sense of belonging, even if they belong to a small group that is angry, rebellious, sullen, or violent. In response to the need for belonging, personalized schools in this study deliberately fashioned community roles and processes that allow all students to become personally engaged (table 10.4). Through engagement in many aspects of school life, each student could gain acceptance as an identifiable member of the school community. High schools that successfully personalize learning provide all students with a means of gaining acceptance from the school community, not for conformity but for achievements that are unique, self-organized, and carried out independently, often with other students working as a team. To support acceptance, schools can announce a shared commitment to all students, offering an audience prepared to recognize and applaud contributions of any kind to the life of the school. When students complete a task with others that reflects the community's shared hopes, the

Table 10.3. Comparison of responsibility and opportunity.

Developmental Needs	School Practices
RESPONSIBILITY: The need to take control of the personal situation	**OPPORTUNITY**: Access to tasks relevant to adult roles
◊ "I've been to a lot of schools, and this is the school that I feel caters most to the individual, because if they see that you have motivation they'll support you and let you run with it." ◊ S_____ good-heartedly gets out of her seat, walks up to the map in front of the room and says, "I'll show you." She goes up and shows him kinesthetically on the map to get her point across. Teacher says, "Oh, okay, I can explain this." ◊ Rubric on board that was <u>developed in class with students</u> ◊ For her photography independent study, a teacher found H_____ a very small room that she could use as her own darkroom. The school provided her $50 for supplies. ◊ The <u>advisor</u> opened the class with an apology. "Its one thing to be under stress, its another thing when you allow yourself to be disrespectful because of your own circumstances. <u>I'm sorry</u>."	◊ Food consumption is seen as a normal human activity ◊ Permission to move about as if school were home ◊ Teacher tells students to use assessment rubric to evaluate him. S. focuses on the sheet and completes it. Students give their comments. Class discusses his weaknesses/strengths. ◊ Teachers not "on duty" watching students ◊ allow students to individualize all or part of their program ◊ Adjusting deadlines to meet student needs ◊ No bells or hall passes or other indicators of external control ◊ <u>State of the Community Day</u>: Group comments and open mike in gym at end of day. Last year resulted in students presenting a new smoking policy to the school board ◊ Natural Helpers program, <u>a one-on-one support for kids</u> (20 kids have been trained so far)

"vision" that organizes school life grows more robust, more flexible, and more personal for all.

5. Confirmation

Despite wide differences in purpose and style, all our shadowed students seemed to need successful moments during the school day during which they could recognize and test their growing individual competence in areas of the sharpening interest. Successful school practices appeared to spring from widely held and very high expectations for performance, not emanating from written standards and guidelines alone, but from a shared sense of how good things happen within the school, a subject of general conversation. When students were experi-

Table 10.4. Comparison of belonging and community.

Developmental Needs	School Practices
BELONGING: the need for identity within a whole school.	**COMMUNITY**: Public support available to all students
◊ As she moves through the school, T_____ greets many people in a very warm way, often touching them and asking how they are. She seems to know everyone and be well loved, authentically or not, in a social butterfly kind of way. ◊ Kids were cheerleading each other all over school ◊ "Everyone's voice should be heard. I'll start with Chris," says Mrs. M___. "Travis, what did you pick?" "Marybeth, how do you see it?" ◊ Students are set on task of performing a fellow student's "one act" play or at least as much as he had written so far. Then they are to dress up in costume and improve so that he could get ideas for more characters and further plot. ◊ Lots of banter as kids try to use the calculators in a new way; people calling out questions and helping each other. ◊ Kids encourage one of the boys to practice a lift with the smaller girls. They hoot and clap, and he grins for a long time afterward ◊ Kids easily get in pairs for swing dancing. Teacher circulates and helps couples, taking the place of one partner in each couple and demonstrating the rhythm. When she dances with kids, she makes them all look great.	◊ At some point in the class, uses every student's name and walks over to each student, engaging with each about her work. ◊ teacher reinforcement of student behavior ("I was proud of you when . . .). A Socratic Seminar brings many minds together in the search for depth. ◊ House system designed to help people know each other better ◊ Two student reps are elected to the school board ◊ Academic events to celebrate unique passions and gifts of students ◊ Postcard program: postcards are given to each parent to write to school about what they'd like the school to know about their child. ◊ When I first started going to school and really getting to know Amy (my advisor) for the next fours years, she was the greatest. Our classes were very diverse. But it didn't take long before we were called "Amy's Clique." ◊ The school feels small to her (800-900 kids), because she at least recognizes everyone, and knows most ◊ Small group work, with students choosing roles within groups

encing success in class, hallways, community settings, or common areas, they were able to confirm the trajectory of their own hopes and beliefs for the future (table 10.5). Moments of confirmation underscored the unique talents an individual could bring to the situation, celebrating the discrete individuality of each student. Summer programs, community-based learning, senior projects, and community service all represented opportunities for students to confirm for themselves and others the direction of their own aspirations.

D——— got up to talk about a summer program he participated in which had taken him to Alaska. He did community service work there.

"I'm from the ghetto and ain't nobody in my neighborhood that can say they went to Alaska for free and had a good time. . . . Try Summer Search. It's about whatever you're about, whatever you like, whatever you do."

A student asked him, "What did you learn about yourself as a person?" His reply: "Whatever I've got here I'm really glad to have, even though I don't have that much."

Advocates of yearlong schooling should look carefully at options for learning and work in a wide variety of settings beyond the high school walls and throughout the school year.

6. Relevance

Unlike the idea of "relevance" in earlier decades, relevance in a personalized school allowed each student to imagine herself engaged in an adult role, wrestling with the real and complex problems that shape human experience. In such experiences, students could imagine themselves working in an adult context, using skills and information to propose workable solutions. Academic classes that personalized learning often aimed to clarify issues of concern to the community: insect trapping to "map" the ecology of the school setting, for example, or estimating road curves and angles to reduce traffic accidents, then modeling and testing alternative designs in a design competition. Schools with active independent study, community service, and school-to-work options were most powerfully "personal" when students used their adult work to stretch their academic skills, and to represent their accomplishments in portfolios or roundtable presentations. Schoolwide requirements for active engagement in adult roles made each student an "expert" in a distinctive context related to his or her hopes, empowering students to relate their learning to others who could learn from their experience (table 10.6). Students described community-based learning as an opportunity to be treated as "equal," though free to ask probing questions and try new approaches. Relevance, in short, was a chance to practice voice, choice, and responsibility to

Table 10.5.   Comparison of success and expectations.

Developmental Needs	School Practices
SUCCESS: The need to extend competence	**EXPECTATIONS:** High standards pervading school life
He showed me the <u>flyer</u> he had designed and that had been approved <u>for distribution</u> by the director of the center who also serves as his official mentor. proudly shows me <u>her book</u>, which includes a front cover made by her and a back cover made by her friend just before she moved away. decides on a topic <u>and shoots a scene</u> with a friend. They are laughing and enjoying this work tremendously. They do not go off task the entire time. R_____ brings me in the Horizons office; she wants to physically <u>show me her PLP</u> The entire period is used <u>to play music</u>; very little is spent in conversation, and the band sounds very good. When he got back from Alaska, he realized that everyone in his neighborhood was doing the same things as when he left. <u>They hadn't grown, and he had.</u> He then goes into <u>detail showing me the pain-staking process of creating the special effects</u>. It is clear he enjoys this work. He described how his LTIs at <u>several Providence restaurants</u> had shaped his selection of a college program and, relatedly, his selection of a career trajectory.	School vision explains <u>six common expectations</u>, featuring mutual respect Independent studies involve <u>a contract of study</u> linked to several Standards, a reflective journal, a daily log of activities, and a final presentation <u>rubric for grading</u> that fairly clearly identified the level of expectation for the work. The girls <u>reference independent studies in bioethics</u> says "favorite class is English, a student <u>seminar that runs itself</u>. The teacher only interrupts us if the conversation stops." <u>Rubrics for each course</u> are distributed at the start of the school year. Senior projects become part of the <u>portfolio</u>, a course-based collection of best work linked to the "Maine State Learning Results" by reflective papers All students take <u>Seminar</u>, which is used for portfolio and junior exhibition/senior project preparation <u>A checklist</u> on the classroom wall outlines the due dates and Senior Seminar requirements, including 20 hours of community service, which A_____ completed with no trouble.

achieve and document a success where it counts—among adults in the community.

PERSONALIZED LEARNING FOR HIGH SCHOOL STUDENTS

Even if depersonalization is more acutely a problem in some schools than others, we believe that it is a problem in nearly all high schools (those in our study and nationwide). As a consequence, student learning falls short of what it could be and in nearly all cases means some students fail to achieve high standards. (Although school failure is dis-

Table 10.6.   Comparison of imagination and complex tasks.

Developmental Needs	School Practices
IMAGINATION: Projected view of the self succeeding in the future	**COMPLEX TASKS**: Adult roles in problem solving & communication
J. initially sat furthest away from the table but then jumped into the mix to assist the teacher in an experiment.	physics class was doing a noisy experiment off the front balcony with pulleys, toy cars, inventions of various kinds;
Each day of the week M. comes down to the A.R.T. program (Votec) for the morning school hours. Here he works on his independent study 'Star Wars' type movie, which he wrote and directs.	They begin to ask questions and realize that they can do anything they want to with all these cool machines
	advisories flex to allow students to pursue their own interests
we do have internships and we go out and help the Middlebury College Sports Info Office doing public relations. I really like it because now I know how good it is for you.	team time set aside for individuals to work on completing projects
	Students come in and out, making phone calls related to LTIs:
In his words, "I have to teach middle school teachers about materials that they have to use. So I have to know how to use everything first so I can help them learn by doing."	Setting: 4th floor of a building housing a college and other businesses. Individual kids coming and going on elevators.
Visiting student says he serves on a technology board for the R.I. governor, and that he has written and received grants for his technology work.	loves the internship and plans to major in political science at Colby or George Washington U. and become an attorney.
	Challenge Diploma - You need to do readings or writings each quarter and you set your own deadline but you still need to follow the dates for the evaluation committee
You can do internships like the one I'm doing now by helping teach 3rd graders Phys Ed. At the beginning of the class you talk a lot about yourself and you do a lot of community service. It gives you a head start and good background information.	If he was learning about plumbing and carpentry he could incorporate the learning into his program as long as he kept a daily account of his progress and his learning.
	They will have a public booth on December 14th on sexual violence and hope to get a professional in the field to be at the booth.

proportionately consequential for the student, the student is only one contributor to failure, with teachers, peers, schools, and/or larger society at least sharing culpability.) We have found that the personalization of learning requires substantial engagement by teachers and students, parents, and administrators, who must share a different vision of their work in order to develop their schools toward higher performance. Personalized learning, as illustrated in the six areas mentioned here, promises to improve student learning within a given student's interests and sociocultural context, even if that learning is not specifically included in whatever standards are formally measured in standards-based testing.

Personalization appears to increase performance, rather than detract from it. In personalized high schools, high expectations for all students and staff form basic assumptions, diversity is viewed as an asset to learning, and multiple talents are brought to bear on real challenges. At such schools, we saw administrators being academic leaders and lead promoters of a collaborative culture of school management, involving both faculty and students. They expected intellectual curiosity and application on the part of students, teachers, and themselves. Upon entering personalized high schools, we saw students coming and going from internships in the community, or community-based mentors and parents arriving for specific meetings with students and staff; community-centered learning creates access to multiple partners for inquiry and learning. We noticed students and teachers actively engaged in informal discussions in hallways and classrooms. These conversations were friendly and personable but also learning-centered, probing issues and discovering options for students to explore. "Mentor and mentee" ("Manatee" in the student parlance of one of our schools) or "advisor and advisee" better describe relationships in personalized high schools than "teacher and pupil." Sizer's (1996, p. 96) expression "caring rigor and rigorous caring" describes the interactions that support the development of skills, knowledge, and habits high school students need as they clarify their hopes for their future lives.

Our six categories of personalized learning did not appear as separable elements of the high school experience.

- recognition
- trust
- respect
- acceptance
- confirmation
- relevance

Instead, they formed a general framework for understanding a wide array of interconnected practices and beliefs. Each of the six descriptors of personalized learning emerges from personal relationships built through daily interaction among students and adults in their community, primarily between instructor and student, bounded by curriculum and current systems. However, the relationship between the student and the sociocultural context in which she or he is growing also influences personal commitment (Ogbu, 1987); some students have many reasons to be skeptical of school and schooling. Expecting students to defer gratification until college acceptance, college success, and distant economic rewards is inadequate, particularly for the many students who hold no hope for further education. Learning requires consent. Consent requires trust, but trust is not singularly coconstructed by teacher and student. Students look to peers, to parents, and to other role models (local or pop culture, real or fictitious [Fisherkeller, 1997]) as they try to determine what and who is trustworthy. Recognition and acceptance depend on relationships with the whole community (at school and outside it) that high school students are hoping to join.

The idea of personalized learning, as outlined previously in figure 1, suggests a wide assortment of solutions to a nearly ubiquitous high school problem. A high proportion of students in low-achieving high schools, and even in high-performing schools, feel disenfranchised, disconnected, and disengaged from schooling, and they perform accordingly. They comply, they resist, or they rebel. Withdrawal of personal commitment is more often characteristic of students who are placed at risk due to poverty, cultural differences, and/or the challenge of learning a new language, but it is hardly unique to them. The size, structures, traditional orientations, and practices of the high schools these students attend contribute to students' alienation and academic failure. Large and impersonal school settings, low expectations for student performance, and a continued overemphasis on teacher-directed instruction may all act as barriers to reform and as inhibitors of many students' academic success. Curricula guided by external mandates that emphasize coverage or manic test preparation rather than comprehension, or curricula determined by academic departments that do not ensure interdisciplinary coherence, also depersonalize schooling, leaving students suspicious, confused, and/or detached. Finally, philosophically inconsistent school policies (generated internally or externally) and public and administrative impatience with new reforms (in lieu of those reforms' steady incubation) can further interfere with personalized teaching and learning.

Personalized learning requires allotting time and means for students to reflect; such reflection is practically a prerequisite for tasks like autobiographical writing and also in the coproduction of a personalized learning plan with a teacher (and often a parent). However, creating powerful contexts for reflection can be realized through other less orthodox ways.

As an example, one shadowed student described his school's active encouragement for his participation in a "Summer Search" program in Alaska. That experience was potent for the involved student. In his words, through the experience of traveling "from the ghetto" to Alaska and then returning, he could see how much he had grown and changed in relation to his neighborhood peers who had passed the summer in the neighborhood. He had gained the perspective of one who has seen how things work a different way. He was also fortunate to be at a school that had faith in the positive prospects of away-from-school learning (so much so that it was willing to coordinate that learning with what happened within its walls).

From our study and our experience, we also believe that new institutional rearrangements are needed to support collaborative teaching and learning, decreasing student anonymity and increasing students' deliberation and control over how standards were to be mastered. Our lists of school practices that support personalized learning suggest that such arrangements have been developed widely but have rarely been organized so all students perform to high expectations. One urban, multiethnic high school included in our study embodies our belief in the feasibility of high school personalization: last year all of its graduates were accepted at four-year colleges, raising more than ten thousand dollars per graduate in scholarship support. Assuming high schools are committed to serving all their students, other very differently situated high schools could also gain substantially by exploring and developing personalized learning.

The collision of young adults (who vary along many dimensions) with school processes (which are products of different social structures, regional and community contexts, and different patterns of resource allocation) generates dynamic tension. Personalized learning occurs as students with different needs and perspectives respond to this dynamic tension by using multiple and varied talents to assert their own aspirations and address their own shortcomings, while checking their progress with adult mentors (usually teachers) who help them understand both common standards and their own hopes. The ability to relieve tension between personal aspirations and the larger context—by gathering information and solving problems—may be the most important outcome of high school learning. Managing tension between aspiration and expectation in behalf of personalized learning may provide a key to high school renewal.

RESOURCES

Boyer, E. (1983). *High School*. New York: Harper & Row.

Cresswell, J.W. (1998). *Qualitative Inquiry and Research Design: Choosing among Five Traditions*. Thousand Oaks, CA: Sage Publications.

Eisenhart, M., & Howe, K. (1992). *Validity in Educational Research*.

Erickson, F. (1987). "Transformation and School Success: The Politics and Culture of Educational Achievement." *Anthropology & Education Quarterly 18* (4): 335–56.

Fisherkeller, J. (1997). "Everyday Learning about Identities among Young Adolescents in Television Culture." *Anthropology & Education Quarterly 28* (4): 550–73.

LeCompte, M., Millroy, W., & Preissle, J. (eds.) *The Handbook of Qualitative Research in Education*, 643–80. San Diego, CA: Academic Press, Inc.

McQuillan, P.J. (1998). *Educational Opportunity in an Urban American High School: A Cultural Analysis*. Albany: State University of New York Press.

Moll, L.C., & Diaz, S. (1987). "Change as the Goal of Educational Research." *Anthropology & Education Quarterly 18* (4): 300–311.

Sarason, S. (1990). *The Predictable Failure of Educational Reform*. San Francisco: Jossey-Bass.

Sizer, T.R. (1984; 1996). *Horace's Compromise: The Dilemma of the American High School*. Boston: Houghton Mifflin.

Sizer, T.R. (1997). *Horace's Hope: What Works for the American High School*. Boston: Houghton Mifflin.

Sizer, T.R., & Sizer, N. (1999). *The Students Are Watching*. Boston: Beacon Press.

Vygotsky, L. (1978). *Mind in Society: The Development of Higher Psycholog-ical Processes*. M. Cole, V. John-Steiner, S. Scribner, & E. Souberman (eds.), 84–91. Cambridge: Harvard University Press.

Wolcott, H. (1999). *Ethnography: A Way of Seeing*. Thousand Oaks, CA: Sage.

CHAPTER 11

Toward the Creation of a
Personalized High School

ROBERT MACKIN

Souhegan High School is a relatively new public high school with students in grades 9–12. The school is located in Amherst, New Hampshire and serves the towns of Amherst and Mont Vernon, New Hampshire. Designed for 600 students in 1991, Souhegan was the culmination of a longtime dream of many residents—the opportunity to build their own high school. A decade later, with more than 1,000 students, Souhegan is an integral part of the communities of Amherst and Mont Vernon and has emerged as a national model of a personalized high school.

After approving the construction of a new building in 1989, the newly elected school board in August 1991 hired their first principal and charged him with creating a "high school for the 21st century." Their collective image called for a state-of-the-art, high-tech school that would foster student thinking rather than rote memorization and that was committed to *all* students' learning. They wanted a school that would coax and honor collaboration and teamwork and that would inspire teacher self-reflection and teaming. Above all else they hoped to see a humane and caring environment that would respect their children and nurture them to new heights.

In the fall of 1991, a planning team of five educators was assembled to begin the design of the school program and to hire a new faculty of fifty-five for a September 1992 opening.

While the story of the emergence of SHS is a fascinating one, suffice it to say that by the fall of 1992, Souhegan had established a powerful groundwork that has since led to its recognition as one of the outstanding schools in New England. Moreover, it has become a significant national model for reform. What follows is a look at how one high school has very consciously created an environment built upon respect, trust, and personalized support.

WHY THE EMPHASIS ON PERSONALIZATION?

When the National Association of Secondary School Principals first released the *Breaking Ranks* report in 1996, many parents and high school leaders were surprised by the prominence placed on personalizing our high schools. The theme of Personalization—one of six themes embedded and woven through the more than eighty recommendations included in this report—was characterized as follows:

> If one theme could be extracted that is overarching and paramount, it is a message that the high school of the 21st century must be much more student-centered and above all much more personalized in programs, support services, and intellectual rigor. These seven recommendations are illustrative of what we envision: Every student will have a personal adult advocate; the Carnegie unit must be replaced or redefined; student anonymity must be banished; teachers should meet no more than 90 students per day; every student should have a Personal Plan of Progress; imaginative flexible scheduling must be the order of the day; every principal and teacher will have a Personal Learning Plan.

Ironically, for most secondary educators who have been thoughtful and reflective about their work, this theme, so central and so accepted in our view of elementary education, has played a no less important role in the lives of successful high school students. In fact, an increasing body of research points to improved student performance:

- When teachers more actively engage their students
- When large schools are broken into smaller, more personalized units
- When schedules are designed to allow for fewer students to be taught for longer and more intensive periods of time

- When teachers become personal advisors or mentors to their students

With that thinking in mind and buoyed by the successful efforts of many other student-centered schools, Souhegan sought to personalize both its design and its instructional practices at the very outset. As a consequence, the most striking generalization drawn by visitors to Souhegan High School relates to its overall tone and ambience, not simply to practices that foster improved teaching and learning.

WHAT DOES A PERSONALIZED SCHOOL LOOK LIKE?

Many educators have traveled great distances to visit Souhegan, to see a successful model of the Coalition of Essential Schools in action. They are impressed by heterogeneous groups that work, by teachers excited to be engaged on interdisciplinary teams, by students "using their minds well" and demonstrating their knowledge and thinking skills through regular academic exhibitions. But the most common refrain heard as visitors leave the school deals with its personalized atmosphere:

> It certainly appears to be an ideal school community. The students were mature and showed respect for each other. Staff are so friendly and involved in being a part of everything. Every member of the school community showed a pride in being here. (A teacher from Massachusetts)

> The level of student-to-student respect is obvious. The 'unabused' freedom of movement is great to see. I am envious of the work you have done . . . and the quiet academic atmosphere. Trust is everywhere apparent. (A principal from New York)

> I am so very impressed with the sense of community that exists here. The true concept of democracy and the arduous effort to maintain it are remarkable and energizing. The philosophy engenders enthusiasm. (A professor from Indiana)

The intense blend of a highly task-focused school, pushing students continually to expand their comfortable limits, and an atmosphere that is almost compulsively humane and deeply personalized is ultimately what sets Souhegan apart from many other high schools.

When Souhegan first opened in 1992, the focus on personalization was not entirely popular. Amidst the publicity and political hoopla surrounding the Goals 2000 reform efforts started in the early '90s, the whole idea of personalization of high schools had taken on an almost negative connotation. Conservative groups in many communities around the country attempted to convince both parents and educators that concepts like self-esteem or human tolerance should not be the province of schools. The essence of their message seemed to be: "Forget about all this touchy-feely personalization stuff and stick to the basics! Humanization of schools? Bah, humbug! Stay focused on the consumption of knowledge. After all, how can our kids compete globally if they don't drown themselves in the ever-rising sea of information!"

In our view, such efforts to downplay the human side of schooling were missing the mark. In spite of the reticence, and in some cases the outright hostility, of certain parents and community members, we consciously strove to create a collaborative community. While the voices of our adversaries were loud ones, corporate and business leaders were also telling us that they wanted employees who were able to work in teams, to communicate effectively, to exhibit strong personal and interpersonal skills, to be adaptable to change and to know how to learn. These were viewed as the essential attributes for the new corporate culture and ultimately for competing globally in the 21st century.

Consequently, Souhegan, like many schools today, took on a more holistic mission than "Back to Basics" reformers advocated. It was a mission that called for basic proficiency in a broad range of personal and interpersonal skills in addition to the basic academic learning proficiencies that we all recognized were required. And it was a mission that could best be accomplished within a humane and personalized setting.

BUMPS ALONG THE WAY

After a year of planning, accompanied throughout by intensive criticism from a small but very vocal minority of the community, Souhegan opened in September of 1992. Our proposals around heterogeneous grouping, interdisciplinary curriculum, and an advisory system had drawn the greatest flak, but we were confident that we had weathered the attacks and that parents and students were supportive of our plans. What we had not bargained for were the attacks from the nonparent community. Their images of high school had been deeply ingrained from their own experiences long ago. Clearly they did not match with the design of much of Souhegan High School.

On a Saturday in the middle of September, two weeks into our first school year, one of our chief adversaries was encamped in front of the post office, the chief meeting place for Amherst residents. Atop his card table was a petition to place a "warrant article" (the equivalent of a referendum vote) on the March town meeting agenda that would solicit community opinion on the philosophy of Souhegan. Specifically, the petition, which needed only twenty-five signatures, called into question the concepts of heterogeneous grouping and of interdisciplinary instruction.

The signatures were easily gathered. Consequently, for the next six months we were placed in a position where we had to keep one eye on the careful growing of a school but simultaneously had to tend to public opinion. Out of necessity, we became as adept at good public relations as we did at nurturing good programs. Through regular community newsletters and meetings, through commentaries to the local newspaper, and through the mobilization of our students' voices, we waged a battle that portended to have major impact on our future as a model school for the 21st century.

When the March town meeting arrived, more than 500 citizens jammed into the gymnasium. Dozens of speakers, including several passionate and articulate students, either lauded our efforts or proclaimed the prospective downfall of education in America with the very existence of a school like Souhegan. The meeting went late into the evening, until a ballot vote was called. Anxiously we awaited the results. Visions of a year's work and a generation's worth of experience and wisdom being voided were at the top of our minds. We had no way of predicting the outcome. About a half hour after the ballot closed, the tallies were counted. Remarkably, we won by an 8–1 margin. Our philosophy and program had been vindicated.

Thereafter, while our adversaries were not entirely quelled, our work moved forward with a sense of affirmation. In a perverse way, the parent and student community came to feel an even stronger confidence in our efforts. By the end of our second year of operation, we were selected as the outstanding high school in New Hampshire, and that, in turn, gave us further license to maintain and refine controversial programs like "advisory" and "honors challenges."

THE KEY INGREDIENTS OF PERSONALIZATION

It goes without saying that people make an institution. In a school particularly, the quality of relationships and the openness of adults to reach out to, stimulate, and connect with students is doubtless the ultimate factor in making it a human, dynamic, and exciting place as opposed to an impersonal and debilitating brick façade.

In the case of Souhegan High School, the faculty and staff without a doubt became the critical elements in its success. At the same time, the very conscious efforts made by the planning team in 1991–92 to institutionalize a framework for personalization has ensured the creation of a culture that promises to maintain itself for the long term.

Unlike many schools that have achieved great success under the leadership of a dynamic principal, only to see their efforts and energy dissipate when that leader departed, Souhegan was different. It was mission-driven. The overriding belief in students—in respecting them, in trusting them, and in recognizing that they all had the capability to achieve high standards—was as much a part of the curriculum as were graduation requirements. The mission has become such an embedded and essential part of the overall school culture that it allows Souhegan to transcend the idiosyncrasies of any given leader or teacher or superintendent. Until the mission changes, the school will move forward with them or without them. But how does a school establish such a powerful sense of mission with such widespread support? It begins with a basic attitude shift.

1. The Mindset

At the very root of Souhegan's reform efforts was a set of beliefs that it sought to embed in all of its practices. The first belief was that a humane, caring, and personalized school—a place where all students were welcomed, were known well, and were heard, and consequently, a place where all students felt a stake in the institution, not simply in their own success—was central to fostering essential academic goals.

Students learn to think best, to use their minds well, to try out ideas, to express their views, to interact in teams, and to absorb themselves in a dynamic learning process in an environment where they feel trusted, respected, and encouraged. Consequently, at Souhegan a mindset was engendered in the faculty that all students unequivocally and without question can and will learn and that teachers must actively engage all students in meaningful and nonthreatening ways.

2. The Mission Statement

The formal expression of Souhegan's beliefs and values was found in its mission statement emblazoned in gold letters in the front lobby:

Souhegan High School aspires to be a community of learners born of respect, trust and courage.

We consciously commit ourselves:
   To support and engage an individual's unique gifts, passions and
      intentions.
   To develop and empower the mind, body and heart.
   To challenge and expand the comfortable limits of thought, tolerance,
      and performance.
   To inspire and honor the active stewardship of family, nation and
      globe.

Historically, most institutions, including schools, have a statement of philosophy or mission—a public commitment to a set of beliefs or values that drive the institution. Unfortunately, in practical terms, these statements often have little significance. In the case of schools, they appear in glossy documents—the front of the program of studies or perhaps in the appendix to the annual report to the board of education. Every ten years they are pulled from shelves and dusted off for the regional accreditation visit. Rarely does a mission statement serve as a true basis for designing school programs or affecting teacher practice.

In Souhegan's case, a very different phenomenon occurred. The mission statement acted as a daily guide for action and was the basis for defining very human expectations. The mission statement played such a powerful force in the school culture that students at times felt annoyed by continually having it "in their face." On occasion you would even hear students comment that a particular action was "so Souhegan," which meant in their view that the school had become overly concerned with a particular breakdown in trust or respect. For example, the principal would publicly announce a major schoolwide infraction, such as a theft, over the PA system and would make it clear that this was anathema to building a trusting community. This, in turn, would lead to advisory group conversations about trust and community.

3. From Mission to Practice

Unlike an "alternative school" of 80–100 students, or even a small charter school of 200–300, where the emphasis upon personalization and individual stakeholding is relatively easy to achieve, in a school of 980 students and 100 adults, implementation of these values becomes more difficult. A conscious and consistent focus on mission was essential.

For SHS the mission statement became the curriculum for the first part of each school year. On the opening day of school, advisory groups of ten students and one adult met for the first hour or so and focused on the new school year—both the pragmatic and the philosophical. The mission statement became the centerpiece for these conversations, and advisory groups became the backbone of the school culture. Words like *respect* and *trust*—the values that were most embedded in the culture—were defined, redefined, and absorbed through tangible examples.

Advisory groups, which met almost daily over the course of the year, talked about issues such as responsibility and freedom within the context of civil and respectful interpersonal conversations. A handbook that was developed for all advisors helped to ensure that some consistency of focus occurred by grade level. Ultimately, the advisor became the adult who got to know his students as well as a surrogate parent.

While some seniors found the constant concern about mission to be a bit obsessive, the need for ongoing reinforcement of beliefs and values was essential to the maintenance of a healthy and lasting school culture. For the ninth graders, the focus was most intense. The team-taught freshman humanities curriculum had as its essential question, "What is an American?" As prelude to a study of the nation's founding documents (The Declaration of Independence and the Constitution), ninth graders examined and discussed at length the mission statement as the founding document of Souhegan High School. Consequently, words like *respect* and *trust* took on real meaning, and gradually the overall programs and structure of SHS, which seemed very different and even confusing, began to make more sense to them.

In turn, the concept of culture was addressed. American democratic culture was dissected by looking at the attributes that had led to our country's success in fostering democratic values over a 200-year period of time. Then Souhegan High School was defined as their own home base for democratic practice, a place where they had a voice and ongoing opportunities to engage in true democratic decision-making.

4. Creating an Environment of Respect, Trust, and Caring

If, in fact, we believe that students should be respected and trusted and that those values arc part of the mindset and mission of the school, then many of the normal trappings of high school become unnecessary. Since students know how to tell time and since they need to become responsible for their own whereabouts, are bells really needed? If we truly trust and respect students, are hall passes and teachers serving "duty" in hallways or the cafeteria necessary? If all students are expected to learn and to meet high standards, then does tracking or homogeneous grouping make sense? Not remarkably, a belief that students can learn and that they can be trusted and respected led to self-fulfilling behavior. Students behaved in responsible and respectful ways because they were expected to do so, and they quickly came to perceive themselves as a "community of learners born of respect, trust, and courage."

From an organizational standpoint, then, rather than designing discipline structures and regulations around the 5 percent of students who inevitably will misbehave or challenge the system (which is the basis upon which most high schools build their rulebooks), SHS designed them around the 95 percent who would take the concept of "community of learners" to heart. Bells, hall passes, and duty assignments were nowhere to be found. While the dean of students had his hands full at times in dealing with the 5 percent who would challenge the boundaries of any school, even that number shrank in an institution where a premium was placed on individual responsibility, not on authoritarian power.

5. Democratic Principles

Perhaps the greatest hypocrisy of American schools is the longstanding pretense that they prepare students to be practicing democratic citizens. Unfortunately, high schools, next to prisons, may be the least democratic institutions in this country. Students are told where to go, what to do, and how to do it, and they have little or no voice in schoolwide or classroom decisions. As a consequence, they have little opportunity to practice being thoughtful democratic decision-makers.

Typically, student councils become the vehicles for "democracy in action" and for making seemingly important decisions like where the prom will be held or whether a soda machine should be installed. In such a context, how can we expect students to become true stakeholders in schools when the only decisions they make are of a perfunctory nature? Unwittingly, we teach them to be passive, dependent, unresponsive, and irresponsible—all those attributes that run counter to the expectations of a democratic citizen.

At SHS a personalized school culture meant a democratic one, a school where students were encouraged to express their views, to speak out if they felt they were not respected or trusted or treated fairly, and to participate in a school governance structure that gave them formal power. A community council was formed which consisted of forty-five elected members, twenty-five of whom were students. This forum, a truly democratic body, allowed students to have a majority voice in key policy decisions. For example, the community council enacted *all* disciplinary policies, abolished the traditional ranking system, and adopted a new modified block schedule. Much like the efforts we see in corporate cultures to empower employees, schools too can empower students to feel a human stake in a democratic community.

Challenge in a Democratic High School

Early in the fall of our first year, six freshman boys came to visit me, taking advantage of my open door policy. They made it clear that they were not being academically challenged and that if they were enrolled in honors classes, they would be much happier. Their disappointment was magnified by the fact that their friends at the neighboring high school were enrolled in four or five honors classes. They also wanted me to understand that they took my words seriously about being a democratic school, and that if I was truly listening to the voices of students, I would acknowledge their request.

I responded by asserting the philosophy of heterogeneous grouping and the belief that the "honors challenges" being offered in all their classes would ultimately prove as inspiring to them as honors classes per se. I went on to say that I would speak to their team of teachers and encourage them to work harder at developing more rigorous honors challenges.

It became evident quickly, however, that this small group of young men was not going to be convinced easily. Bright, articulate, and academically driven, they clearly had aspirations at the age of fourteen not only to be successful at Souhegan but also to get into the best colleges and become leaders in life. They did not want to see the school putting their futures in jeopardy.

At the close of our conversation, I asked them to bear with the program and give it a fair chance of being successful. The concept of heterogeneous grouping and of honors challenges was new to most high schools and needed time to develop and evolve at Souhegan. Furthermore, I indicated that their leadership and courage in confronting this problem was commendable and that they would become my personal barometer for testing the success of the evolution of our academic program. They agreed to go along with my request, not enthusiastically, but with the responsible commitment of young pioneers in the development and growth of a new democratic community.

Thereafter, about every five or six weeks, I would call them to my office (or occasionally they would remind me that it was time to meet) to discuss how well they were being challenged academically. Each meeting led to meaningful conversations that gave me insight into the growth of Souhegan and gave them a sense of how real issues can be discussed and resolved responsibly and without rancor. On each occasion, the refrain was the same: we would be more satisfied with honors classes but admittedly things are getting better. By the end of the year, we had established a deep and lasting relationship. While it was not until they were juniors and seniors that they truly saw the value of heterogeneous grouping, these young men were instrumental in the development and fine-tuning of our honors challenge efforts. One of them went on to be the chairperson of our community council, the policy-making and governing body for the school.

Upon graduation, four of the six boys, including our valedictorian, matriculated at Dartmouth College, and one at Duke. Certainly, Souhegan had not put their college futures in jeopardy. Today, as college graduates, they would be our staunchest advocates of heterogeneous grouping.

6. Teachers and the Academic Culture

It is all well and good to have students who feel cared about and who relish having a stake in their school, but the essential question becomes, "are our students being challenged academically, and are they being groomed to confront and understand a complex, confusing, and ever-changing world?"

The Souhegan Mission Statement called for students "to challenge and expand their comfortable limits." In practical terms teachers were charged with the responsibility of stretching the limits of each student, of pushing them to achieve high standards. This became much more doable when teachers knew students well and recognized what each student's talents were. Then they could take it upon themselves to push and cajole and inspire students to achieve and perform at levels that outstripped both their previous academic accomplishments as well as their own preconceived notions of what they themselves thought they should be able to achieve. Personalization became a tool for getting students to believe in themselves, but more importantly, it created a different kind of accountability between student and teacher, a spirit of mutual responsibility for the quality and substance of the learning that took place.

Authentic relationships with teacher "mentors" and "coaches" also fostered authentic learning for students. Learning became more than a paper/pencil exercise; it became a human dynamic where teachers confidently called upon students to become "workers" and to demonstrate publicly, in front of both faculty and student peers. All students were expected to show that they truly knew something—that they could talk about a physics concept, or do a mathematical exercise, or understand the meaning of a particular poem. Acquiring the ease and skill to perform or exhibit in regular and routine ways was a direct result of feeling cared for and supported. As Allison Rowe, Souhegan's former dean of faculty, once put it, "New norms of achievement result from new norms of respect and trust."

7. The Role of Principal

Teachers at Souhegan often referred to the founding principal (known throughout the school and the community as Dr. Bob) as the "vision-keeper," the one who would be persistent, persevering, and uncompromising in holding to the mission. As we all know, and as all the effective schools' literature attests, the leadership of the principal is the key influence in affecting the school culture—in establishing the tone, ambience, and overall commitment to excellence. The principal should be the ultimate role model and, in Souhegan's case, the most visible force in nurturing a humane and caring democratic community. The essence of his "practices" should revolve around accessibility and visibility.

Traditionally, principals' offices are found within a bureaucratic maze of front office clerical and administrative support. The inner sanctum mentality often isolates the principal from the school as a whole. While the original school design of SHS called for such an office location, the founding principal insisted that the plan be changed in order to move the office so that it opened onto the main student corridor. In this way, he was able to have a true "open door" with direct access and visibility to students, teachers, parents, and other visitors.

This tradition has continued with the new principal. Anyone was, and continues to be, welcome to stop in, say hello, express a concern, share a thought, as long as the door was/is open (which is most of the time).

Practically speaking, the "open door" was as much symbolic as it was real. In a school of more than 1,000 persons, relatively few of them took advantage of an open door at any given time, but the recognition was always there that an open invitation existed to stop by or at least to wave when passing the office. In a sense, a school community is analogous to a family, and in Souhegan's case, the symbol of the head of the household being home seemed to lend a calming influence.

8. Souhegan as a Holistic School

While the establishment of a personalized school culture goes a long way in providing an openness to learning on the part of students and a predisposition to collaborating and coaching on the part of teachers, it merely provides the context. Unless the school in turn introduces more engaging curricula, more diverse instructional practices, and more student-centered and performance-based assessment approaches, it will simply devolve into the same old thing—school as we have always known it.

Souhegan High School has attempted to understand and recognize the holistic nature of schools as institutions, as entities where all the components must fit and make sense in order for the school as a whole to become truly effective. In practical terms, this means that the mission of the school must drive the design of curriculum, which in turn leads to decisions about instructional and assessment practices. Likewise, how students are grouped or how policy decisions are made are a part of this larger gestalt—of this "systemic" approach to rethinking high school.

Souhegan had the opportunity to start from scratch and consequently to take all the components that collectively make up a high school and combine them in a way that allowed the school to be in synch with itself. For example, the report card and grading system fit with the assessment processes used by all teachers. The membership of all teachers in Critical Friends Groups connected with efforts to support teacher collaboration and self-reflection. The implementation of interdisciplinary teams at grades nine and ten aligned with the larger view of knowledge being connected, not disparate. Moreover, the teams became those smaller units (80–100 students), which insured personalized support to all students. In sum, it was this commitment to creating a wholly new conception of high school that truly distinguished Souhegan from most high schools in this country.

CONCLUSION

All of us recognize that public high schools face enormous challenges as they enter the new millennium. The impulse to look for panaceas or the quick fix has haunted reform efforts over the past century. Today, with the growing impact of information and communications technologies knocking loudly on the schoolhouse door and forcing us to question not only how to use technology, but the very role of schools as we have known them, the importance of schools as human places becomes all the more significant. No quick and easy fix awaits us.

Teachers and principals instead need to work hard at building school cultures not in a piecemeal fashion, but in conscious and systemic ways such as those described above. These new and more personalized "cultures" must seek to give students the self-confidence as well as the skills to ask good questions, to become thoughtful decision-makers, and to become effective team players. Moreover, they need to provide stability and safety in a world that is ever more complicated and perplexing to young people. It is that human touch embedded in a personalized and caring academic framework that will ultimately promote the kind of thinking and learning essential to the success of our students in the 21st century.

CHAPTER 12

Putting Student Performance Data at the Center of School Reform

New Expectations for Student Achievement and School Accountability

MARY ANN LACHAT
(with Martha Williams)

Today's high school students need a very different approach to education as they face the realities and demands of a technological and global society characterized by rapid change and unprecedented diversity. The workplace already expects individuals to understand multidimensional problems, design solutions, plan their own tasks, evaluate results, and work cooperatively with others. These changes represent a new mission for education that requires high schools to not merely deliver instruction, but to be accountable for ensuring that educational opportunities result in *all* students learning at high levels. The teacher's job is no longer to "cover" a time-based curriculum, "but to enable diverse learners to construct their own knowledge and to develop their talents in effective and powerful ways."

Establishing high standards of learning for all students in America is a response to widespread recognition that the education system must change to reflect the realities of the 21st century. Today's world requires many skills that are not being taught in schools, and reform efforts are defining the education standards essential for all students. For the past 100 years, our schools met the workforce needs of an industrial society by organizing learning around a standardized curriculum delivered in standardized time periods called Carnegie units. Within this structure, curriculum was defined as a set of units, sequences, and facts. Credentials (Carnegie units) were based on "time served," and the failure of significant numbers of students was not only accepted, but also regarded as an expected result of norm-referenced testing. For the most part, this system of education prepared generations of high school students to find their place in American society. Where it did not, the economy had a place for people who were willing to work hard even if they lacked the skills of formal schooling. The opportunities and demands of today's society are different. Conditions of secondary education that allow high school students to leave school without developing essential competencies or ever being challenged to fulfill their potential are unacceptable. Educational failure and undeveloped talent are permanent drains on society, and the current reform movement has shifted the emphasis from access for all to high-quality learning for all. The call to improve America's high schools isn't new, but the emphasis on high standards for *all* students is. It is hoped that this emphasis on high standards for all will raise the ceiling for our most gifted students, and lift the floor for those who now experience the least success in school (Lachat, 1994).

A commitment to higher levels of learning and rigorous standards for all students is a commitment to student-centered accountability. This new view of educational accountability is central to the paradigm that is driving today's educational reform efforts. It makes student learning and continuous improvement the rationale and evaluative criteria for statewide and for district-, school-, and classroom-level efforts. This emerging concept of schooling is different in several fundamental ways from the paradigm that characterized our educational system for more than 100 years. Some of these differences are illustrated in table 12.1.

Given this new paradigm, the central questions that drive today's high school reform efforts are: What do we want students to know and be able to do? What kinds of learning experiences produce these results? What does it take to transform schools into places where these results are achieved—by all students? Putting the learner at the center of school accountability means that high schools are responsible for effectively engaging diverse learners and ensuring their academic success. This shifts the focus from accountability for providing programs, courses, and instruction that lead to success for some students, to

Table 12.1.   Comparison of traditional and new paradigms for schools.

TRADITIONAL SCHOOL PARADIGM	NEW PARADIGM FOR SCHOOLS
◊ The "inputs" and process of education are emphasized over results. Curriculum is "covered," and instruction is organized around limited time units prescribed by the school schedule. Schools accept the failure of a significant number of students.	◊ The school mission emphasizes high levels of learning for <u>all</u> students. Diverse abilities, developmental levels, readiness, and learning styles are addressed so that all can succeed. There is flexibility in the use of instructional time with an emphasis on learning, not how much content has to be "covered."
◊ Learning is organized around a standardized curriculum delivered in standardized time periods. Credentials are awarded based on "time-served," issued in "Carnegie Units."	◊ Learning is organized around what students should know and be able to do. Credentialing is based on student <u>demonstration</u> of proficiency in these knowledge and skill areas.
◊ The curriculum is derived from existing content, which is most often determined by textbooks. The curriculum is organized around a set of units, sequences, concepts, and facts.	◊ The curriculum is derived from standards that define what students should know and be able to do. Subject matter is "integrated" around "real-world" tasks that require reasoning, problem-solving, and communication.
◊ Assessment is done at the end of instruction and is narrowly focused on lower-level and fragmented (end-of-unit) skills that can be assessed through paper-pencil responses. Norm-referenced standardized test results are the basis of accountability.	◊ Assessment is integrated with instruction and focuses on what students understand and can do. Methods assess students' competencies through demonstrations, portfolios of work, and other measures. Standards-based assessments are the basis of accountability.
◊ School accountability is defined in terms of programs offered, attendance rates, and dropout rates; the number of students who are credentialed, and the results of norm-referenced tests. There is minimal systematic monitoring of student progress on an ongoing basis.	◊ The school is accountable for demonstrating that all students are developing proficiencies that represent high level standards for what students should know and be able to do. There is an emphasis on frequent monitoring of student progress.
◊ School improvement focuses on improving the existing organization, e.g., by adding new programs, improving school climate, and increasing staff participation in decision making.	◊ School reform efforts are challenging and seeking to change the assumptions and practices that characterize how schools are currently organized.
	Lachat and Williams, 1994

accountability for producing positive results for all students. It means that as educators, we are responsible for demonstrating the impact of high school policies, programs, course offerings, learning environments, and instructional practices on learner outcomes.

Student-centered accountability recognizes that what we *really* mean by success for all students is success for each student: the school is accountable for ensuring that each and every student is acquiring the knowledge and skills that represent standards for what students should know and be able to do. It also means that the school is responsible for evaluating the extent to which students with particular characteristics or who are exposed to specific programs and practices are succeeding. The ability to systematically monitor the progress of individual and specific groups of students, then, becomes essential to ensuring success.

DATA-DRIVEN SCHOOL REFORM

The more that educators accept responsibility and accountability for helping all students succeed, the more they recognize the need for data that can inform the creation of learning environments that result in student success. A commitment to student-centered accountability is a commitment to a data-driven process that allows for continuous evaluation and improvement. Teachers and administrators need to examine student performance data in more meaningful ways, and to evaluate the extent to which new approaches to curriculum, instruction, and assessment actually result in higher levels of student learning.

More than a decade ago, one of the conclusions of the Office of Educational Research and Improvement's (OERI) State Accountability Study Group (1988) was that the pursuit of accountability in schools requires better systems for using data to improve low-achieving schools and to encourage high-performing schools. This conclusion has been supported by an emerging body of literature which underscores that better use of data is essential for improving the quality of learning in our schools (Codding and Rothman, 1993). Bernhardt (1998) made an impassioned case for using data as a lever for creating more effective schools for our students and emphasized that "what separates successful schools from those that will not be successful in their school reform efforts is the use of one often neglected, essential element—data." Properly used, data can make a difference in meeting the needs of every high school student. As today's high schools struggle to transform traditional structures into more personalized and engaging learning environments, data can be a powerful ally in stimulating positive change and improvement.

Data provide the power to make good decisions, work intelligently, change things in better ways, know the impact of our hard work, help us prepare for the future, and know how to make our work benefit all children (Bernhardt, 1998).

School reform is fueled by inquiry, and the systematic use of data is at the heart of this inquiry process. The process of questioning, exploring, and searching for new understandings is essential to creating more effective learning environments for high school students. In her work with the Regional Alliance for Mathematics and Science Education at TERC, Nancy Love has written extensively on the essentialness of effective data use in the school reform process, and she has posed the question, "How can classrooms be alive with inquiry if schools are not?"

We believe that the same process of inquiry that invigorates classrooms also breathes life into school reform. In inquiry-based schools, teachers and administrators continually ask questions about how to improve student learning, experiment with new ideas, and rigorously use data to uncover problems and monitor results. It's not that these schools have solved all of their problems. It's that they know how to tackle problems and continuously improve. Researchers in both business and education agree that these qualities are hallmarks of successful organizations (Love, 2000).

Effective data use strategies involving school staff in collaborative inquiry and problem solving can help create conditions that allow equity issues to be addressed, and that allow for change and improvement to take hold. Ruth Johnson (1996) examined many uses of data to measure equity and made the case that "data offers unlimited potential to districts and schools working to build their capacity to equitably educate students." A data-driven inquiry process is one of the most effective tools for achieving change in schools often considered furthest from current standards of excellence.

DEVELOPING THE CAPACITY TO USE DATA

Becoming "data users" requires new capabilities for schools. It's not that schools don't have data. In fact, they have lots of data. High schools have far more data than they can use effectively. Historically, however, schools have provided data rather than used data, and the "data provider" role has meant that others defined the criteria of progress upon which the school and its students would be judged (Johnson, 1996). There is an enormous need to understand how to analyze and use available information wisely (Holcomb, 1999). For years, researchers and practitioners have emphasized the limitations of aggregated measures of student outcomes that do not support an understanding of whether specific groups of students are benefiting from their educational experiences (Levine and Lezotte, 1990). What we have learned from decades of school improvement efforts is that focusing more on the process of change without a concurrent focus on results does not lead to any significant impact on student achievement.

Unfortunately, site-based innovations mean nothing if a school cannot determine if the efforts have had an effect on students. Most schools move from innovation to innovation and define success as the implementation of the latest innovation. To be blunt, this is nonsense. What difference does any innovation make if a school cannot determine effects on kids (Glickman, Allen, & Lunsford, 1992)?

Student-centered accountability recognizes that learner outcomes will not improve unless they are directly addressed, and it means that the entire culture of a school drives toward increasing student success. It grows from a belief that school staff must look at and be guided by the results they produce in their students. Focusing on student results creates an inevitable need for educators to accommodate diversity and to establish learning environments and instructional time options that are responsive to different learning styles. This vision of accountability requires school-level capacity to link student results to instructional practices and to disaggregate data so that results can be examined in meaningful ways. It means being able to obtain information about the performance of students with particular characteristics, the programs and practices to which they are exposed, and the knowledge and skills they have acquired. Student results have to be examined in the context of educational practice and the quality of opportunities that high schools provide for students—the question of *why* student results appear as they do has to be addressed. In short, database capacity that supports the current vision of education reform has to incorporate the capability to link information about student performance to information about the effectiveness of policies, programs, and practices.

A DATABASE SYSTEM FOCUSED ON STUDENT PERFORMANCE

For more than twenty years, research and development activities conducted by the Center for Resource Management, Inc. (CRM) have addressed the issue of how to build database capacity in schools that matches the level of data use necessary to support systemic change and that puts student performance at the center of the inquiry process. Our research highlighted several factors that act as barriers to effective data use in most schools:

1. Focusing on student achievement and using data for decision-making and planning is a major culture change for most schools. Few schools have any type of systematic process for examining results, developing targeted improvement plans, and monitoring progress.

2. Teachers and administrators don't have easy access to the data they need to examine the performance of specific groups of students and the effects of programs and practices on student performance over time. When data are available, the way that information is presented makes the analysis and use of data difficult.

3. Even in districts and schools where extensive data are maintained, there is limited capability to integrate and manipulate multiple types of data in meaningful ways. Data exist in multiple electronic and print files that include the school's student information system as well as data files from state assessments and other testing programs.

4. The student information system software packages most commonly used by schools were not designed to function as accountability systems. They create schedules, generate report cards, produce school and grade-level attendance reports, and in some cases, show grade distributions for specific courses. They were not designed to disaggregate performance data or to correlate performance data with demographic data or data on students' educational experiences. Schools, therefore, can't link multiple types of student performance data to specific programs, practices, and policies.

These factors have made the ongoing analysis and use of comprehensive data on student performance difficult for most high schools. "When it comes to using data to address problems, target improvements, or monitor progress, schools are ill-equipped. They lack good data-management systems along with the will, skill, time, and organizational structures to use data effectively" (Love, 2000). Even with outside expertise, most schools have not systematically looked at the effects on student achievement that result from changes in program structures and instructional practices. Most high schools struggle to produce data to answer the most basic questions about the performance of specific groups of students. In short, linking student results to specific programs, classroom practices, and learning environments requires database capacity that very few high schools have.

Our research also identified the essential features that practitioners and stakeholders want in a database system that supports a focus on student performance and school improvement.

A data system should:

- Promote a school culture that values and uses information.
- Focus school planning and improvement activities on ensuring success for all students.
- Be comprehensive—account for the wide range of data that address accountability and equity questions about the performance of specific students.
- Provide technology capable of merging and easily disaggregating different types of data.
- Present data in formats that relate to the questions posed by teachers and administrators and that lend themselves to analysis and decision-making.
- Help schools evaluate specific programs and reduce dependence on outside evaluators.
- Be sufficiently flexible to address individual school characteristics, priorities, and diverse information needs.
- Enable schools to communicate results to pertinent constituencies.
- Be interactive with school information systems to avoid redundant data entry.

These database system requirements represent powerful capacities for high schools seeking to create more positive and personalized environments for their students. They also reflect key elements for bringing high schools into the information age and for empowering school staff with information that directly relates to their mission of ensuring higher levels of learning for all students. To help schools acquire these capacities, CRM developed a highly versatile database system that was designed to make the complex possible and that supports ongoing data-based planning, monitoring, accountability, and program improvement. Because of its emphasis on the use of data to support a student-centered inquiry process, the system is called SOCRATES.

SOCRATES is a fully relational database application that integrates data from any source and permits virtually unlimited disaggregation. The system enables school administrators and instructional staff to use student performance data in combination with other information to monitor student progress and improve school programs and instructional practices. Because it utilizes relational database technology, it does not displace schools' current computerized systems, but has the capability to import data already entered into these systems to eliminate duplicate data entry and to create an integrated database. It was designed to be as flexible as possible. Standard field names can be easily modified to allow for the use of user terminology that varies somewhat across schools for certain data elements. Based on input from hundreds of educators, data profiles (reports) were designed to display data in formats that facilitate ease of use by school staff. We will draw from our experience in developing and using the SOCRATES system to illustrate the essential dimensions of creating capacity in schools to use data effectively.

THE CAPACITY TO INTEGRATE AND DISAGGREGATE DATA

Leaders in school reform efforts are very clear about one key aspect of effective data use—Disaggregate! Disaggregate! Disaggregate! (Bernhardt, 1998; Johnson, 1996; Lezotte & Jacoby, 1992; Love, 2000). Disaggregation allows a school to determine how various subgroups are performing, and as Lezotte and Jacoby pointed out, "it is not a prob-

lem-solving process, but a problem-finding process." Given the fact
that the emphasis on accountability has also escalated a defensive tendency on the part of school staff to "blame the victim," disaggregated
data can be an important tool for understanding the patterns of success
or failure in a school population, and as expressed by Holcomb (1999),
for "separating the *whys* from the *whines*." Less has been written about
the fact that meaningful disaggregation requires the capability to integrate data—the ability to link multiple types of student performance
data, student demographic data, and data on students' educational
experiences. Student-centered accountability means being able to
relate educational results to specific policies, programs, and practices.
SOCRATES was specifically designed to address these database requirements.

SOCRATES has import and data merge capabilities that bring together
data from school records and administrative files, from state assessments, and from testing programs and other data systems. It creates an
integrated database that merges three types of data: 1) Student Characteristics; 2) Student Education Data; and 3) Performance Data. This
means that data within these categories and across the categories can
be correlated in order to: 1) determine the extent to which students with
specific characteristics are achieving success across multiple performance indicators over time; 2) examine factors that affect student performance; and 3) determine the extent to which specific programs and
practices result in student success.

This integrated database becomes an important vehicle for helping
school teams develop shared understandings (a common language)
about student performance trends. Designed to enable school staff to
answer a wide range of questions about student success and program
results, it allows extensive data analysis and supports an inquiry process focusing on a comprehensive and meaningful examination of the
performance of specific groups of students and the effectiveness of
their educational experiences. Figure 12.1 illustrates the wide array of
data that can be brought together in creating an integrated high school
database that supports student-centered inquiry. These data include:
the demographic characteristics of students; multiple performance indicators; students' prior educational experiences; and current educational
experiences including such variables as learning community, programs

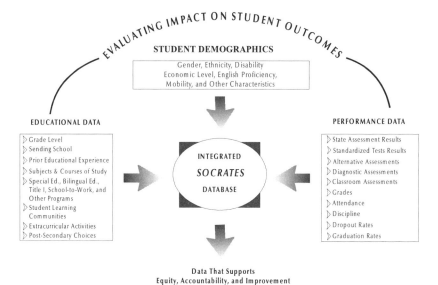

Figure 12.1.   An integrated database.

and course offerings, and instructional practices. The system's capability to incorporate and disaggregate multiple types of assessment data is noteworthy. Because assessment is a cornerstone of education reform, it has received extensive attention in recent years and has led to new ways of thinking about how student learning should be measured. However, while there is growing agreement that students should be able to demonstrate what they know and are able to do, there is less agreement about the measures that should be used to assess student capabilities. As highlighted by Visher and Hudis (1999), high schools participating in the *New American High Schools* initiative vary considerably in how they perceive and use assessment. "While some prefer standardized achievement tests, others are more committed to alternative assessment techniques or use a combination of methods." The authors also state: "Schools that use a range of assessment tools, each selected to meet certain objectives, are more likely to get the broad range of information they need to evaluate school and student progress and make program improvements." As schools use more varied assessment measures to make decisions about student progress, a data system must be able to accommodate these data.

DATA-BASED INQUIRY

Data-driven, student-centered high school reform is a process that engages school staff, students, parents, and other constituents in examining a wide range of evidence that can shed light on what is working well for students. An integrated database that has been specifically designed to focus on multiple dimensions of student performance provides a wealth of information that can be used to support this process and promote informed decision-making. Data can be disaggregated in hundreds of ways to answer questions about student results, program effectiveness, and the factors that affect success. These data become the essential pieces of evidence that allow staff to identify, understand, and solve problems. In our experience in using the SOCRATES data system with high school teams, data have been generated to address the types of questions shown in table 12.2.

Generating data to answer these questions is an important part of

Table 12.2. Guiding questions for data-driven improvement.

• How are specific groups of students performing on multiple assessments over time?
• How are students who are engaged in new and more promising learning opportunities performing on multiple measures and performance indicators?
• How are students in different school clusters or learning communities performing?
• To what extent are students enrolled in specific course offerings or program opportunities demonstrating proficiency on state assessments or other external measures?
• How do factors such as absence or mobility affect student performance?
• What are the proficiency levels of various student groups in specific content and skill areas?
• Are there knowledge and skill areas where there are notable gaps in student performance by gender, race/ethnicity, or language proficiency?
• What is the correlation between the grades or performance benchmarks given to students and their scores on state assessments and other standardized measures?
• To what extent are students enrolled in Special Education, Bilingual Education, ESL, or School-to Career programs achieving positive results on multiple measures over time?
• What is the participation rate of specific groups of students in higher level courses?
• Do grading patterns suggest inconsistencies in grading criteria across learning communities, subject areas, or course offerings?
• What students appear to be at risk of school failure due to excessive absence?
• What are the characteristics of students with high absence or discipline rates, or who drop out of school?
• What is the longitudinal performance of specific cohorts of students?

targeting areas of concern, identifying areas of instructional effectiveness, and developing plans for improvement. By itself, generating data doesn't drive high school reform. Data need to be looked at by people through a process of open discussion and inquiry. Inquiry is essentially collaborative, and it means that people need the opportunity to look at data as a group and have a constructive dialogue.

Data don't change schools, people do—people who are committed to working together and doing whatever it takes to improve learning. But they need to be armed with good data if they are going to uncover and understand problems, test the best solutions, and learn as they go. Data use and inquiry are inseparable companions on the road to reform and hallmarks of the most successful schools (Love, 2000).

Examining data through a process of collaborative inquiry allows all those who have a stake in student success to look deeply and broadly at the impact of policies, beliefs, conditions, and practices that influence success. School staff begin to recognize that monitoring student progress means being able to document success and also being able to pinpoint where the trouble spots are—determining which students are not succeeding and what factors seem to be associated with variations in achievement.

USING DATA TO SUPPORT STUDENT-CENTERED SCHOOL REFORM

As noted previously, data become the sources of evidence that grounds discussions and conclusions in actual results rather than assumptions and speculation (Lachat and Williams, 1996; Love, 2000). Using the SOCRATES system, we have worked with many high schools to build database capacity and to effectively use data to support the kind of substantive discussions that lead to better results for students. The following illustration is one example of how data were used to support student-centered school improvement.

A school team from a regional high school participating in a statewide school reform initiative wanted to explore the relationship between student success and factors such as students' long-term and short-term goals, attitudes toward school, perceptions about their high school educational experiences, and hours spent in work and other activities. The school wanted to directly involve students in examining factors that may be influencing their success or failure.

An advisor program was established to provide students with a relationship with an adult who could assist in developing long-terms goals and to set short-term grade average goals. Working with their advisors and parents, students selected long-term goals ranging from four-year college to the "world of work," and specified the grade average they would work to achieve. To engage students in looking at factors that impact success, the advisors administered a short survey that asked students how many hours per week they spent doing homework, watching television, and working. Students also were asked questions about their attitude toward school, their self-confidence related to success in school, and their educational experiences at the high school.

Because SOCRATES was designed with student data as its base, long- and short-term goals, hours spent per week on various activities, and responses to other survey items about students' experiences in the high school could be linked to performance indicators such as attendance, course grades, and performance on state assessments and other tests. The data profiles generated through the SOCRATES system illustrated these connections. A high school team comprised of school staff and the advisors involved students in examining the data profiles. They held discussions to help students gain a better understanding of how certain factors within their control (e.g., homework, working, and television time) may impact performance. Students also examined various performance outcomes achieved by students according to various short- and long-term goals, and the extent to which students felt positively connected to their high school experiences. The process engaged students in an examination of real data and gave them a voice in discussions about factors that affect student success.

The Northeast and Islands Regional Educational Laboratory at Brown University (LAB) is developing a data-driven model of systemic high school reform based on the framework of school change defined in *Breaking Ranks: Changing an American Institution.* Developed by the National Association of Secondary School Principals (NASSP) in partnership with the Carnegie Foundation for the Advancement of Teaching, *Breaking Ranks* provides a series of recommendations that capture the essential elements of a 21st-century high school that is both student-centered and intellectually rigorous. *Breaking Ranks* provides an overarching framework that helps high schools see the congruency and relationships across multiple aspects of school reform. CRM is a partner organization of the LAB in conducting this project, and the SOCRATES system is being used as a major database and research tool.

The emphasis on the systematic examination of data on student learning and achievement in conjunction with the collection of data on the quality of school change processes reflects a core *Breaking Ranks* vision that the "high school is, above all else, a learning community and each school must commit itself to expecting demonstrated academic achievement for every student in accord with standards that can stand up to national scrutiny" (NASSP, 1996). This vision requires not only the capacity for comprehensive school reform, but also the capacity to access and use data in ways that allow for the systematic evaluation of how a reform model impacts student outcomes. Many models of school reform have lacked the capacity to acquire comprehensive data on student learning and achievement as an integral component of validating the effectiveness and results of the models. The use of the SOCRATES system thus represents a unique component of this project. SOCRATES provides participating high schools with state-of-the-art information system capacity to address issues of equity and program effectiveness as they implement the *Breaking Ranks* framework, and also provides powerful research and program evaluation capability for determining the effects of the *Breaking Ranks Model* on student performance over time. The data-driven approach that is being implemented through the *Breaking Ranks* project is maintaining a consistent focus on student achievement and the quality of the learning opportunities provided to students. Table 12.3 presents the range of data capacities the *Breaking Ranks* high schools develop through the use of SOCRATES.

The following examples illustrate the types of issues that are being examined by the *Breaking Ranks* school teams.

An urban high school wanted to investigate an assumption that low test scores were resulting from high student absence. This investigation resulted from pressure on the school to improve test scores and a dis-

Table 12.3.   Data capacities of schools participating in the Breaking Ranks project of the Northeast and Islands Regional Educational Laboratory at Brown University.

Schools are able to:
• Track the performance of individual and specific groups of students on *multiple measures*
• Students in school clusters or learning communities
• Students participating in Title I, Special Education, Bilingual Education, School-to Work, and other programs
• Students in specific courses or classrooms
• Analyze student performance at multiple levels — school, grade level, subject area, program, course, classroom, and individual student
• Profile performance by gender, race/ethnicity, economic level, language proficiency, disability and other equity factors to identify achievement gaps
• Determine how students who took specific courses performed on state assessments and other standardized measures
• Correlate student grades to results on state assessments and other standardized measures
• Determine how factors such as absence and mobility affect assessment results
• Profile longitudinal performance trends on multiple measures
• Analyze trends in absence, suspension, and dropout rates for specific groups of students
• Track the longitudinal performance of specific student cohorts
• Make informed decisions about instructional improvement

trict mandate that the quality of instruction offered to students must improve. School staff had countered that the problem wasn't an instructional problem, but an attendance problem. Staff felt that students with high attendance were doing well, and students with high absence were not, on multiple measures that included a standards-based state assessment, another standardized measure, and course grades. Through the use of SOCRATES, performance results on multiple measures were disaggregated by frequency of student absence. The data showed that while students with high absence rates were certainly performing at failing levels, the same was true for the majority of students with the highest attendance rates. The data confirmed that the school had two problems—an attendance problem, and a problem with providing the quality of learning environment that prepared students who were in school most of the time to succeed. Reviewing the data and eliminating the assumption that the problem was only an attendance problem has allowed more productive discussions about the content and quality of instruction provided to students, teacher expectations for students, and the need to create smaller learning communities that would engage students more effectively.

Another area of interest to many of the *Breaking Ranks* high schools is the issue of course participation in higher-level courses. From an equity perspective, the capacity to track student enrollment in advanced course offerings over time by gender, race/ethnicity, and other factors is an important one. While many high school staff have a "general notion" of the types of students who are taking advanced courses, our experience has shown that when school staff are provided with actual data that shows long-standing and ongoing patterns of inequity in the types of students being offered higher-level instruction, they are far more likely to examine the conditions, policies, and practices that lead to these patterns. These factors may include low expectations for students, guidance practices that steer students into lower-level courses, and students not being adequately prepared to succeed in advanced courses.

An area of inquiry that has been raised frequently by the *Breaking Ranks* schools is the relationship between students' grades and their performance on state assessments and other standardized measures. Administrators and parents in some of the schools are increasingly questioning the differences between the grades given to students and their scores on external measures. The basic question is whether students who are given high grades by teachers also achieve high test results. All of the high schools participating in the *Breaking Ranks* project were provided with SOCRATES data profiles that allowed them to examine how students who received various grades in specific high school courses performed on external measures of performance. Many important issues were raised when school staff reviewed these data. A fundamental question, and one that has arisen many times in the past, is what a grade of "A" or "B" really means. Are teacher grades based on "progress" or "proficiency"? Is there agreement among teachers in specific subject areas about the criteria used for giving specific grades? These questions are not easily answered, and without leadership to sustain a positive and collaborative dialogue among teachers, the questions can feel threatening. While many considerations may influence the grades given to students, what the schools we are working with are increasingly recognizing is that these questions are connected to the more complex concerns underlying education reform in general— whether the high school's curriculum, course offerings, and the grading criteria used to assess performance are aligned with the standards and performance benchmarks reflected in the external measures used to judge the school's performance in preparing all students to succeed.

There is very little doubt today that high school reform efforts must be driven by a focus on learning and achievement. A commitment to providing meaningful learning opportunities that support the individual success of each student must incorporate the willingness to continually examine the results of our efforts. The fundamental principle is that continuous improvement must be supported by the best data available. Our students deserve no less than this. Student-centered accountability and the effective use of data can support equity of opportunity and individual and collective responsibility for results. As such, they can support reform initiatives aimed at ensuring the success and personal hopes of *each* student.

The growing emphasis on educational standards, learning, equity, results, continuous improvement, and accountability that now drives high school reform is itself driven by a recognition of the enormous diversity that our students represent—in abilities, learning styles, language and culture, attitudes and habits related to learning, prior educational experience, and home situations. This recognition requires a commitment to basing the decisions that influence students' lives on sound information rather than assumptions and subjective perceptions. The capacity to access and effectively use data from multiple sources is critical to a vision of education that embraces the belief of high standards for all students.

RESOURCES

Bernhardt, V. (1998). *Data Analysis for Comprehensive School Wide Improvement*. Larchmont, NY: Eye on Education.

Codding, J.B., & Rothman, R. (1993). "Just Passing Through: The Life of an American High School." In Darling-Hammond, L., Snyder, J., Ancess, J., Einbender, L., Goodwin, A.L., & MacDonald, T.M. *Creating Learner-Cen-*

tered Accountability. New York: Teachers College, Columbia University, National Center for Restructuring Education, Schools, and Teaching.

Glickman, C.D., Allen, L., & Lunsford, B. (1992). *Facilitation of Internal Change.* Paper presented to the annual meeting of the American Educational Research Association, San Francisco.

Holcomb, E.L. (1999). *Getting Excited about Data: How to Combine People, Passion, and Proof.* Thousand Oaks, CA: Corwin Press.

Johnson, R.S. (1996). *Setting Our Sights: Measuring Equity in School Change.* Los Angeles, CA: The Achievement Council.

Lachat, M.A. (1994). *High Standards for All Students: Opportunities and Challenge*s. South Hampton, NH: Center for Resource Management.

Lachat, M.A., & Williams, M. (1996). *Learner-Based Accountability: Using Data to Support Continuous School Improvement.* South Hampton, NH: Center for Resource Management.

Levine, D., & Lezotte, L. (1990). *Unusually Effective Schools: A Review and Analysis of Research and Practice.* Madison, WI: Wisconsin Center for Education Research, National Center for Effective Schools Research and Development.

Lezotte, L.W., & Jacoby, B.C. (1992). *Sustainable School Reform: The District Context for School Improvement.* Okemos, MI: Effective Schools.

Love, N. (2000). *Using Data—Getting Results: Collaborative Inquiry for School-Based Mathematics and Science Reform.* Cambridge, MA: Regional Alliance at TERC.

Marsh, D.D., & Codding, J.B. (1999). *The New American High School*, 3–17. Thousand Oaks, CA: Corwin Press.

National Association of Secondary School Principals. (1996). *Breaking Ranks: Changing an American Institution.* Reston, VA: Author.

U.S. Department of Education, Office of Educational Research and Improvement. (1988). *State Accountability Study Group.* Author.

Visher, M.G., & Hudis, P.M. (1999). *Aiming High: Strategies to Promote High Standards in High Schools: Interim Report.* Washington, DC: U.S. Department of Education, Office of Vocational and Adult Education.

CHAPTER 13

Using Breaking Ranks *to Engage a School Community in Cooperative Reform*

HAL HAYDEN

WHAT IS THIS CHAPTER ABOUT?

Reforming and improving high schools? What an undertaking. American creativity, drive, combined intelligence, and clear focus has placed men on the moon; certainly we can improve our secondary schools. It seems obvious that we should be able to identify effective educational delivery models and devise ways to assist high schools to better serve their students. We know, both intuitively and empirically, that smaller class size, well-trained teachers, active parent involvement, alignment of curriculum and assessment, expanded time on task, and good leadership results in improved student learning. The overarching question becomes, why is it that, with all our knowledge about what works, we still have such difficulty helping secondary schools reform in ways that will increase their capacity to excel in what they do?

Perhaps the answers are imbedded within a general failure to systematically examine what is happening, what needs to happen, and in what order change needs to be made. Researchers, building-level personnel, and the general public need to be able to answer several basic questions. They need to know: What is it that does or does not work for individual schools? How do you identify what is important and what is practiced in each school? How do you select what changes and/or direction specific schools can take? What cooperative reform can be attempted within existing or possible resources? We put a man on the moon—reforming and making high schools more effective may seem to be more difficult, but we will never know until we commit to developing and using a systematic process for implementing that reform.

This chapter describes the processes used by a group of educators/ researchers from Northeast and Island Regional Educational Laboratory at Brown University (LAB) to respond to the above questions and assist high schools to improve the way they deliver services. The LAB is one of ten federally funded educational research laboratories. Our primary foci are to: (1) Ensure that educators and policy makers have access to the best knowledge from research and practice; (2) Engage in ongoing research with practitioners; (3) Help schools conduct inquiries into the issues that most affect their learning environment; and (4) Work with schools to develop effective classroom approaches to address the needs of culturally and linguistically diverse students. It was under the charge of areas (1) and (2) above that we directed the activities described in the rest of this chapter.

In 1996, the National Association of Secondary School Principals (NASSP) published eighty-two recommendations which, when implemented, would assist high schools to better meet the needs of all students. The recommendations were published in a document entitled *Breaking Ranks: Changing an American Institution.* The recommendations threaded through six main themes as follows:

- Personalization—personalizing instruction;
- Coherency—alignment between what is taught and what is tested;
- Time—flexible schedules including abandoning or revising the Carnegie unit;
- Technology—developing long-range plans for use of computers and other technological devices;
- Professional development—preparing staff for new roles and responsibilities; and
- Leadership—expanding the capacity to lead to teachers, parents, students, and others.

The *Breaking Ranks* document itself sorts the eighty-two recommendations into three major sections: Priorities for Renewal—forty-five recommendations; A Web of Support—thirty recommendations; and Leadership—seven recommendations. The Priorities for Renewal section contains recommendations relative to Curriculum, Instructional Strategies, the School Environment, Technology, Organization and

Time, and Assessment and Accountability. The Web of Support section makes recommendations relative to Professional Development, Diversity, Governance, Resources, Ties to Higher Education, and Relationships. The Leadership section contains recommendations relative to the attributes of leadership that need nourishing.

WHY A SYSTEM?

The eighty-two recommendations contain detailed wording suggesting process, activities, and measures that high schools should consider when examining what they were doing and what they want to do. Sorting and placing these recommendations in priority seemed to be an impossible task. Each teacher, administrator, parent, school board member, and student could, and often did, suggest what had to be done, when, and how. The beliefs of these groups were strong and genuine but difficult to measure. What should be done? Where? When? By whom? These questions drove the need to develop processes to systematically measure the perceptions of staff relative to both the *importance* of these recommendations and the degree to which these recommendations were presently being practiced in their schools.

As a member of the Secondary School Restructuring Team, I was asked to work with other team members to develop processes, instruments, and report formats that would provide schools with data relative to the relationships between the *Breaking Ranks* recommendations and the schools' present activities. It was our sense that this taking stock process was essential before we could attempt to move forward. We needed to know where each school was before we could help them accurately describe where they wanted to go.

HOW WAS THE SYSTEM DEVELOPED?

Initially, the research team needed to make a case for what we were doing. We needed to explain why the data needed to be gathered, how the data could assist the school, and how we could protect the individual participants from individual identification. Our experience indicated that teachers wanted to tell their stories. Teachers wanted to reflect on and react to what was going on in their schools, and most of all they wanted a safe venue from which they could react to the school's level of practice as they perceived it without threat to their livelihood or positions. What was missing was a common "mirror," a common set of standards and/or even equal understanding of that on which to reflect. All teachers/staff needed to react to a common stimulus. The eighty-two NASSP recommendations became those stimuli.

After an initial exchange of basic information by phone and letters, the Brown University team met with the principal and members of the school staff to explain the process and gain acceptance for what was to be done. After a review of the instrument and process and considerable dialogue, the school team developed a degree of trust for the process and the value of the information the process would yield. The degree of time and effort required to gain entrance to different schools varied with the degree of risk each school was willing to take. In some cases the team and process were readily accepted. In other cases we had to explain in detail what we had done in other schools, what we expected to "discover," how and to whom we would report, and generally what might be the added value to the students, school, and school community.

WHAT WERE THE INITIAL ASSUMPTIONS?

After gaining entrance, our first task was to agree upon some basic precepts. We acknowledged that teachers were busy, the recommendations were complex, and the data gathering processes needed to be both quick and thorough. We also understood the necessity to garner the cooperation of the "client" while ensuring that the research objectives were met. We needed to honor the wording of the recommendations precisely while recognizing that accurate reaction to the many multi-part recommendations was problematic.

As an example, one recommendation states: "Decisions regarding budget and staff allocations will be made at the site level." This recommendation has two equally important elements—decisions regarding budget and decisions regarding staff. We understood that response to this particular recommendation, and similar recommendations, would vary depending upon the stress placed upon it by different readers. When we eventually administered the instrument, we coached respondents to read each of the recommendations in their entirety and to go beyond the individual words to the basic concepts. In the recommendation cited above, the stress was on making school-based decisions, not on the particular elements of budget or staff. Thus respondents were advised to "go with your mostly" (e.g., do you mostly agree that the statement is important in general or do you not; is the recommendation mostly practiced as part of your school or is it not?).

Next, we had to agree upon a reporting mechanism that would be easy to understand yet convey the important discoveries. We decided that we must report results in several ways. We agreed to report mean scores along with the standard deviations in rank order by "Perceived Importance," "Perceived Level of Practice," and "Difference between Perceived Importance and Perceived Level of Practice." We believed that this reporting scheme would provide the kind of analysis that would generate the deep discussions necessary when examining school life as it is presently perceived.

Thirdly, we had to acknowledge that, although we wanted to measure the perceptions of parents, students, and others and to measure the differences between and among these groups, such an undertaking was precluded by funding and staffing considerations. We anticipate that we will be able to expand the project in the future and redesign the gathering of information to include these populations.

Next, we had to identify schools that would be willing to participate in this activity. The Secondary School Restructuring Team presented our project at a gathering of principals in Massachusetts in fall of 1998. Four principals approached the director of the program and asked to be involved. The four schools represented two rural, one suburban, and one urban school. Within a year we had expanded the process to include all the high schools in the city of Providence, Rhode Island, and in several additional schools in New York City.

Finally, when the teachers and administration were comfortable with what we proposed, we scheduled a day in which we could meet with the staff for approximately two hours. At that meeting we described the process and administered the instrument, or we left the instrument with the in-house team for distribution over a brief period of time. The instrument was either returned to the LAB via mail or was gathered at the site for our retrieval.

WHAT INSTRUMENTS WERE USED?

The instrument consisted of three elements: A demographic sheet, a set of directions, and the instrument itself. The demographic sheet asked for such information as subjects taught, years of experience, and years at the school. Because of the concern of some teachers that their responses would be "discovered," the team agreed that, although we would allow for individuals to identify themselves, delineation of names was optional. Otherwise we asked that the participants provide us with as much demographic information as possible. In 90 percent of the cases we did receive the demographic page, but there were few (less than 5 percent) that were filled out completely.

The sheet of directions explained how the instrument was set up, "going with your mostly" in responding to the multipart recommendations, and how and to whom the responses were to be delivered.

The instrument contained five columns. Columns one and two identified the chapter and number of the recommendation; column three, the individual recommendations; column four, a scale of 1–5 for "Perceived Importance"; and column five, a scale of 1–5 for "Perceived Level of Practice." The 1–5 scale was used to indicate level of agreement with the "Perceived Importance" and "Perceived Level of Practice," with 5 being the highest level of agreement.

Table 13.1 is a sample of one recommendation with the recommendation truncated. The complete instrument is appended.

One element of concern permeated the entire process. The issue was acknowledging and defending the gathering of perceptions rather than "real" data. In virtually every school, the initial conversations eventu-

Table 13.1.   Assessment and accountability.

Chp	#	Recommendation	Importance	Practice
06	05	Decisions regarding budget and staff allocations will be made at the site level…	1 2 3 4 5	1 2 3 4 5

ally generated the query: "Will reporting perceptions of staff give us a picture of what is really happening at our school?" As a research team we first acknowledged that there is a difference and that the only real way to ascertain reality was to engage in systematic observation over long periods of time. The research protocol, the time available, and the willingness of the participants precluded this approach. After initial discussion the research teams and the school teams agreed that, although individual perceptions vary, the aggregate scores would give strong indications as to what was believed and that that set of beliefs frequently reflected reality and strongly influenced what was being done at the school. The teams agreed that this pairing of reality and perception, although not perfect, would provide important data from which further activities could proceed. As an example, we agreed that if the staff perceived "Decisions regarding budget and staff allocations will be made at the site level" as very "Important" while there was a very low level of "Perceived Practice," there was significant reason to examine this phenomenon more closely.

Essentially we all agreed that reporting mean scores along with the standard deviations from each of the recommendations would produce accurate, powerful, and useful information about how the schools' programs and staff relate to the recommendations.

While the introduction to the process was going on, many schools wanted to know what was a "good" score and what was a "bad" score. Additionally, they wanted to know how their scores compared to other schools. Although we were capable of making those comparisons, we determined that the most important information was examination of the scores within the school. The schools needed to know the beliefs of the staff relative to the recommendations; how those beliefs differed between their school and another school would be of interest at some later date but, for now, we reported only the schools' overall data, not comparison data.

HOW WERE THE SCORES REPORTED NUMERICALLY?

As indicated previously, the team decided to limit the reporting to rank order of "Perceived Importance," "Perceived Level of Practice," and

"Difference between Perceived Importance and Perceived Level of Practice." The report needed to be easy to read, have several "angles of analysis," and have the capacity to easily identify important recommendations. By ranking the recommendations by Importance, Practice, and Difference and giving the standard deviations for the means, we were able to capture all the salient information in one document. We retained all the raw data for future analysis.

Table 13.2 and figure 13.1 and table 13.3 and figure 13.2 are sample reports.

Note that these scores are reported in order of appearance in the *Breaking Ranks* document. Also note: Recommendations are truncated.

WHEN IS THERE TOOOOOOO MUCH DATA?

Breaking Ranks provided eighty-two recommendations grouped into thirteen chapters. We soon learned that, although all the recommendations were important, some had more impact on school reform than did others. After analysis of the data from more than thirteen schools, the Brown team selected thirty-one of the eighty-two recommendations and referred to them as "Core Elements." These thirty-one elements were grouped into one of three major categories: (1) Elements concerned with Curriculum, Instruction, and/or Assessment; (2) Elements concerned with Personalizing of the Learning Process; and (3) Elements concerned with Leadership and Professional Development.

Since graphic representation seemed to tell us more, we were anxious to develop a graphic presentation that would give us information

Table 13.2.   Local high school Breaking Rank scores by chapter and item.

Chap	No.	Recommendation for Curriculum	Imp	S.D. Imp.	Prac	S.D. Prac	Diff
01	01	Each high school will Identify a set of essential learnings.	4.34	0.80	3.89	0.91	0.45
01	02	The high school will integrate its curriculum to the extent possible and emphasize depth over breadth of coverage.	4.01	0.90	3.45	1.01	0.56
01	03	Teachers will design work for students that is of high enough quality to engage them, cause them to persist.	4.51	0.65	3.79	0.86	0.72
01	04	The content of the curriculum, where practical, should connect to real-life applications of knowledge and skills.	4.41	0.75	3.64	0.96	0.78
01	05	Assessment of student learning will align with the curriculum.	4.37	0.68	3.83	0.92	0.53

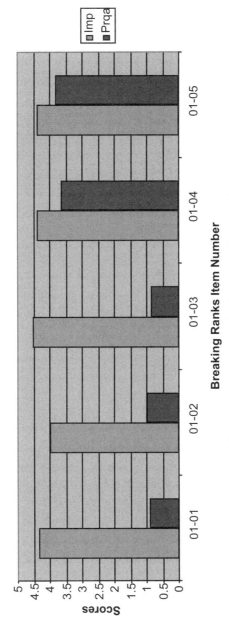

Figure 13.1.   BR scores by chapter and item number.

Table 13.3.   Local high school Breaking Rank scores by perceived importance.

Chap	#	Recommendation Ranked by Perceived Importance	Imp	S.D. Imp.	Prac	S.D. Prac	Diff
03	05	Each high school will ensure that any student who brings a weapon into a high school, or behaves violently will immediately forfeit the right to attend that particular school.	4.82	0.50	4.17	1.11	0.65
02	01	Each high school teacher will have a broad base of academic knowledge with depth in at least one subject area.	4.67	0.55	4.33	0.78	0.34
02	04	Teachers will teach in ways that help students to develop into competent problem solvers and critical thinkers.	4.61	0.58	3.93	0.81	0.68
13	04	The principal will foster an atmosphere that encourages teachers to take risks to meet the needs of students.	4.53	0.79	3.54	1.37	0.99
08	02	The curriculum will expose students to a rich array of viewpoints, perspectives, and experiences.	4.53	0.62	3.74	1.01	0.78

for scores over time. When it became possible and practical to use graphs over time, we chose to depict only the thirty-one "essential" recommendations. When we completed the graphs and the analysis of the data contained within, our estimation of the importance of these particular thirty-two recommendations proved to be correct.

WHO/WHAT DO WE BLAME?

At this point, it is wise to remind the reader that the most important considerations when using data to make decisions are the considerations relative to attribution. Although the graphs and data tables we constructed showed means and changes over time, there is no way to specifically attribute these changes to the particular actions being taken at the school. In the case of the graphic data, what we have at this point are *indications* that there is some movement in the areas of Practice and that the movement is in a positive direction. This information alone is significant, although not statistically significant, and gives the researchers and school personnel more information they can use to direct their activities.

In figure 13.3, twelve recommendations that are concerned with Curriculum, Instruction, and Assessment are reported by scores across time and the variables of Importance and Practice. In each column set, the first column reports the score for the school for that item for the

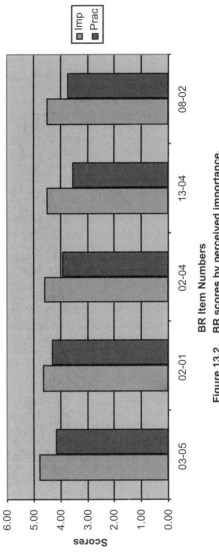

Figure 13.2. BR scores by perceived importance.

1999 school year in the area of Importance, and the second column reports the score for Importance for the year 2000. Columns 3 and 4 of each grouping reflect the 1999 and 2000 scores for "Perceived Practice" for each of the recommendations presented.

It is obvious from inspection that the scores for "importance" differed little from year to year, and that is to be expected unless there were some major changes in staff within the school. On the other hand, there are clear indications that the "Practice" scores for each of the recommendations reported are moving in a positive direction.

This kind of analysis has important implications for school change. It is only when there is some systematic examination of data that professionals can hope to make some sensible decisions about what is happening and what needs to be done to influence what is happening. Table 13.4 and figure 13.3 represent the twelve recommendations.

DISCOVERIES

In a comparison of the schools relative to perceived importance, the schools are more the same than they are different. Virtually all schools identified one recommendation as being the most important. That rec-

Table 13.4.   Twelve recommendations.

Cp	#	Comparison 1999/2000 Breaking Ranks Scores for Curriculum, Instruction, and Assessment	IMP. 1999	IMP. 2000	Chng	PRAC. 1999	PRAC. 2000	Chng
01	01	Each high school will Identify a set of essential learnings.	4.33	4.34	0.01	3.66	3.89	0.23
01	02	The high school will integrate its curriculum and emphasize depth over breadth of coverage.	3.93	4.01	0.08	3.2	3.45	0.25
01	03	Teachers will design work for students that is of high enough quality to engage them.	4.42	4.51	0.09	3.5	3.79	0.29
01	04	The content of the curriculum should connect to real-life applications.	4.49	4.41	0.08	3.43	3.64	0.21
01	05	Assessment of student learning will align itself with the curriculum.	4.23	4.37	0.14	3.48	3.83	0.35
02	02	Teachers will know and be able to use a variety of strategies and settings.	4.27	4.35	0.08	3.51	3.85	0.34
02	04	Teachers will teach in ways that help students to develop into competent problem solvers.	4.6	4.61	0.01	3.7	3.93	0.23
02	06	Teachers will utilize technology in their instruction.	4.07	4.10	0.03	3.3	3.32	0.02
02	07	Teachers will integrate assessment into instruction.	4.16	4.18	0.02	3.4	3.51	0.11
04	02	Schools will make technology integral to curriculum, instruction, and assessment.	3.91	3.99	0.08	3	2.99	-0.01
05	06	Each high school will present alternatives to tracking.	3.55	3.78	0.23	3.02	3.37	0.35
08	02	The curriculum will expose students to a rich array of viewpoints.	4.51	4.53	0.02	3.53	3.74	0.21

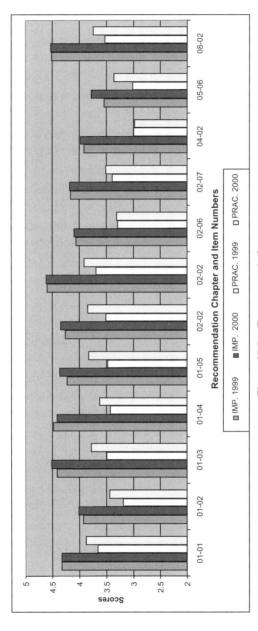

Figure 13.3. Recommendations.

ommendation was: "each high school will ensure that any student who brings a weapon into a high school, or behaves violently in the school will immediately forfeit the right to attend that particular school." In light of the recent activities associated with school violence, we felt that this was not an unexpected discovery. Pleasantly surprising were the next five recommendations that were perceived to be most important by the seventeen schools in which we worked over the last two years. Table 13.5 below illustrates the composite mean scores of the top five recommendations as selected by the schools.

The composite of those recommendations that were perceived as least important was equally interesting. As illustrated in table 13.5, the teachers reported as least important those recommendations concerned with the length of the school year, Personal Adult Advocates, and Personal Plans for Progress (for the students). This is especially interesting given that virtually all research confirms that a longer school year along with more personalized instruction and close academic contact between teachers and students would all contribute significantly and positively to student learning.

In addition, we recognized that the scores provide a great deal of "what data." What is missing is the "why data." As an example, when we inquired into why the teachers responded as they did to twelve-month schooling, the respondents indicated their concern with the fact that there were no indications within the recommendation for additional compensation, additional training, and even air-conditioning for those buildings here in the Northeast.

As was expected, we encountered large differences between schools

Table 13.5.   Recommendations ranked by perceived importance.

Chp	#	Recommendation	Imp	S.D. Imp.	Prac	S.D. Prac	Diff
03	06	Agreements that school systems negotiate with teachers, principals, and others will be accompanied by a student impact statement	3.28	1.38	2.84	1.36	0.44
06	06	Students will evaluate teachers and instruction on an ongoing basis in a variety of ways.	3.19	1.30	2.34	1.27	0.85
01	06	Each student will have a Personal Plan for Progress	2.99	1.15	2.44	1.11	0.55
03	03	Every high school student will have a Personal Adult Advocate to help personalize the educational experience.	2.70	1.17	2.12	1.11	0.58
05	08	Schools will operate on a 12-month basis to provide more time for professional staff development	2.35	1.37	1.73	1.05	0.62

when examining Perceived Level of Practice. Each school has its own history and environment. This variability was reflected in what was perceived as being practiced in each particular school; thus, there is no sense in reporting competitive scores within this document. Table 13.6 is a sample report generated for one of the schools.

SO WHAT?

Although all the above reports gave significant information, it was clear from the outset that no school could hope to address even the top five recommendations as measured by "Perceived Importance" and/or "Perceived Practice." What was needed was a way to further filter the information. The report that identified the difference between "Perceived Importance" and "Perceived Practice" proved to be the information source from which the best decisions could be made.

As an example, in the report shown in table 13.7, it is readily apparent that there is great disparity between what is perceived as important and what is perceived as practice in the areas of class size and technology. There is also disparity in the other three areas (funding mechanism, adequate budgets, and mandated programs), *but,* these three areas are usually out of the reach of a school undergoing initial reform. The two areas of class size and technology, although impacted by available funding, are areas where the reassignment of priorities and/or rethinking of how the school is organized may be addressed. It is by using this process of analysis that schools undergoing reform can make data-driven decisions that can and should be measured over time.

Table 13.6.   Recommendations ranked by perceived practice.

Chp	#	Recommendation	Imp	S.D. Imp.	Prac	S.D. Prac	Diff
06	06	Students will evaluate teachers and instruction on an ongoing basis	3.19	1.30	2.34	1.27	0.85
06	09	High school staff will assess the principal and the administrative team's performance periodically	3.90	1.26	2.26	1.25	1.64
12	07	The high school will require each student to participate in a service program in the community or in the school itself	3.66	1.28	2.22	1.11	1.44
03	03	Every high school student will have a Personal Adult Advocate	2.70	1.17	2.12	1.11	0.58
05	08	Schools will operate on a 12-month basis	2.35	1.37	1.73	1.05	0.62

Table 13.7.   Local high school overall summary report by difference between perceived importance and perceived level of practice.

Chp	#	Recommendation Ranked by Difference	Imp	S.D. Imp.	Prac	S.D. Prac	Diff
5	02	Each full time high school teacher will be responsible for contact time with no more than 90 students	4.34	0.98	2.38	1.13	1.97
10	01	Sufficiency of funding for education will be the top priority of state fiscal policy.	4.40	1.10	2.48	1.11	1.91
04	03	High schools will equip individual classrooms with the technology necessary to prepare students for life	4.22	0.99	2.35	1.09	1.87
04	04	Budget allocations will be adequate to maintain current technology and to provide for ever-changing technology needs	4.27	0.91	2.51	1.06	1.77
10	02	New programs mandated for high schools will be restricted to those that support learning objectives identified goals	4.17	1.05	2.47	1.07	1.70

SUMMARY—ENDING

Cooperative reform, particularly in social settings, is extremely difficult, but the process necessary to gather data to start that reform is not. The eighty-two recommendations of the National Association of Secondary School Principals are well grounded in research. They have the added value of having face validity. It just makes sense to have smaller classes, to have well-trained teachers, to have personal plans for progress for all students. The recommendations pass the "Reasonable Person Test." We can continue to argue, to add to the list, to wordsmith the *Breaking Ranks* document to tatters, or to otherwise ignore the obvious.

Our high schools need to be reformed, and we need to do that systematically and cooperatively. The process described above is relatively easy and provides important data to generate reform direction and scope. We need to measure what we treasure and set priorities that are based upon data. What is presented above is just one system for gathering one data set. There are many others that must be examined. When the examination of all data is done in a systematic process, reform becomes an ongoing, measurable process. Well thought-out, measured, and implemented reform will improve student learning and enhance our profession. What is left to do is to make a public commitment to examine data and base reform on what we know, not what we fear. We did, after all, put men on the moon.

CHAPTER 14

High School Capacities for Systemic Change

ANDREW SEAGER
RMC Research
CYNTHIA L. JORGENSEN
Education Alliance at Brown University

What happens when a high school makes structural changes in its program with the intention of bringing about long-term academic reform? This chapter reports on a retrospective study of long-term change in three American high schools. The chapter describes how we conducted our investigation and what we learned, and it poses some of the questions we are left with as a result of the study.

THE HISTORY OF REFORM AT BRANFORD HIGH SCHOOL—A CASE STUDY

When Dr. Ed Higgins became principal of Branford High School in Branford, Connecticut, in 1989, the school was experiencing problems with discipline, attendance, violence, and low community expectations. With a highly experienced but demoralized faculty, he began working to create a school that fulfilled the school's newly adopted motto, "Improved Learning for Everyone." A team of administrators, teachers, parents, and community members took the first step in the school's transformation. They revamped the school's learning program for students who needed an alternative to regular high school classes. This collaborative approach set the pattern for other reforms. In 1990, when the board of education supported the faculty's proposal to reduce the negative effects of ability groups (or tracking) on students, the school community began developing performance graduation expectations. With board support, the high school faculty's long-term planning committee coordinated a study involving all the teachers and large numbers of students and parents. Using research data, professional expertise, and personal experiences, they assessed the existing educational program and recommended changes designed to reduce tracking and adjust policies to improve learning for all students.

Among the first outcomes of the study were decisions to eliminate the lowest of three academic tracks within the school and to open honors courses to all students. In addition, faculty and administrators developed policies on grading and class size to improve consistency of standards, and they began to engage in curriculum revision to support the structural reforms. The resulting plan, *New Directions for Learning*, was presented to the board of education in 1991. The faculty reported to the board that they had learned that ability grouping did not result in increased achievement for any students, but that simply eliminating ability grouping would not increase student achievement either. Instead, the school needed to alter existing practices by fundamentally rethinking what was taught, how it was taught, and how student learning was evaluated at the school. *New Directions for Learning* was the beginning of a series of studies that led to the development of the first draft of the school's performance expectations for graduation.

Involving administrators, faculty, parents, students, and community members in developing the *Performance Graduation Expectations* document increased understanding of what high school graduates should know and be able to do and how specific courses and assignments fit into the achievement of those goals. It drew from Connecticut's Common Core of Learning to identify the knowledge, skills, attributes, and attitudes all graduates are expected to know and demonstrate. The school's goal was to have students demonstrate the skills and content-related expectations for a high school graduate rather than have graduation depend upon the accumulation of credits. Students are assessed on these outcomes in a variety of ways in their courses over the four years they are in high school.

Teachers now say higher quality work is expected of all students, and there is increased consistency in how student work is assessed across teachers, courses, and departments. On many measures, from state and SAT test scores to college attendance rates, Branford students are experiencing greater success. This has helped build the kind of faculty confidence and community support needed for continuing reform. The school has also developed a culture of constantly reflecting on its progress. The graduation requirements themselves, teaching strategies, and assessments are periodically reviewed and modified to make them manageable and appropriate in light of the school's goals.

Continuous learning and professional development are expected of all staff. Faculty engage in discussing research findings and their own beliefs, then examining the practices that emerge from beliefs. Discussion groups, committee work, peer observation, self-assessment, portfolios, and external professional development opportunities are some of the means for building faculty capacity. For newly hired staff there is an extensive induction process, and new teachers receive ongoing support throughout their first years of teaching from veteran teachers, administrators, and the committee members who recommended their hiring.

The faculty and administrators have also given ongoing attention to developing a culture in which all students are valued and differences are respected. Students are active decision-makers about their educational experiences. Many clubs and committees have been formed at the school that reflect the broad educational, athletic, and social interests of the students. Students are regularly involved in leadership activities such as interviewing prospective teachers. Each student is also a member of a student advisory committee involving teachers and administrators. These meet at least every two weeks to help students meet the school's academic, social, and behavior expectations.

Collaborative leadership and decision-making through teams of administrators, teachers, staff, parents, students, and community members are central to Branford High School's reform processes. Ed is perceived as an intellectual leader at the school and continues to be a significant catalyst for refining the long-term vision for the school. At the same time, he encourages and supports leaders from across the school. He has also been highly skilled in negotiating with the district office and the board of education in times of limited fiscal resources and in times of conflicting expectations between the school and the board.

After more than a decade of reform activity, the Branford High School community continues to:

- Pursue a powerful, evolving vision and improvement strategies that are clearly focused on students and their learning, a focus that has engaged the passions and long-term commitment of school reformers;
- Develop and support leadership from all segments of the school community to build capacity, maintain momentum, and sustain reforms;
- Promote and support ongoing experimentation, reflection on practice, and professional development to improve teaching and learning; and
- Build a collaborative school culture with connections to the broader community to ensure support for long-term improvement.

In contrast to high schools where old beliefs, structures, and processes have dominated for many decades or where attempts at reform have been sporadic, the ongoing process of change at Branford raises two major questions:

1. What capacities for reform do schools need to develop to improve student performance?
2. How can educators become aware of the complex dynamics of change that occur over time and manage them to sustain the improvement process?

These questions were at the heart of our study of high school improvement. Our team, from the LAB at Brown University and RMC Research Corporation, a LAB partner, focused on how high schools develop the capacities to support and manage deep change over time.

SEEKING INDICATORS OF CAPACITY

Reform is not as well documented or understood at the secondary school level as at the elementary school level. The structural characteristics of high schools (i.e., numbers of students and faculty, separate departments, and multiple staff roles) and the social forces arising from the context within which they function challenge the ability of practitioners and researchers to understand what it takes to change such large and complex environments. After discussions with secondary school advisors in the Northeast and islands region about elementary school indicators of capacity that we identified in previous research and the barriers posed by traditional high school structures, our research team decided to focus on schools that had a history of seeking substantial reform and of making changes affecting school structures (e.g., teaming, tracking, scheduling, faculty roles). We were interested in schools that had been able to sustain changes so that we could better understand both the antecedents and consequences of structural change.

Based on recommendations, we selected three high schools to participate in the study: Branford High School; Norwalk High School in Norwalk, Connecticut; and Yarmouth High School in Yarmouth, Maine. Each of the schools had begun making changes more than ten years ago and so provided an ideal opportunity to see long-term trends and to reflect with faculty, students, administrators, and parents about the progress of, and impediments to, reform. Because the LAB is interested in crafting opportunities for practitioners to learn by dialogue and reflection on their own and others' practices, the design of the study took the form of collaborative inquiry, reflection, and ongoing dialogue with members of the school community and among our research team.

Prior experience convinced us of the power of entering a school with a broad set of questions that enables us to document a school's history from the perspectives of those directly involved and to collect data in a nonlinear format. The latter increases the opportunity for making connections that have not already been identified or are not already part of the research design. We also sought a variety of perspectives in order to increase the range of information to which we had access, and so included administrators, teachers, students, and parents in the groups from each school. We asked them to collectively identify a structural reform the school had made in the past, the importance of which stood out for them. Then we asked the following questions:

1. What prompted the structural reform?
2. What preparation was there for the reform (e.g., training, research, staffing changes)?
3. What capacities were already in place that facilitated the reform?

4. What were the short-term (positive and negative) consequences?
5. What were the longer-term changes stimulated by the reform?

Using the format shown in figure 14.1, we recorded information as it was presented to us on a large sheet of butcher paper so that it was visible to all participants:

This strategy facilitated a wide-ranging discussion during which we were collectively able to make connections and raise questions about connections or discontinuities we observed in the data as it was recorded.

From the information we gathered at the schools, we then "mapped" the identifiable changes in structures and capacities that occurred during the reform process, using specific examples from the schools' histories as raw material for understanding more about secondary school reform. Like cartographers surveying the landscape and marking key points in the terrain, we developed for each school a visual "map" representing the path of its change. These displays provided opportunities to observe connections between elements of school reform that are otherwise not easily seen, to discern patterns of activity and consolidation that are part of the natural cycle of school change, and to generally

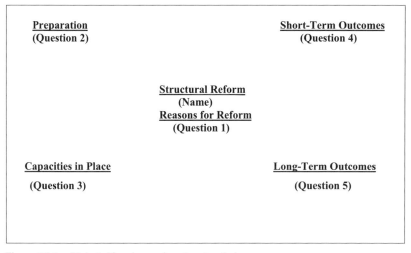

Figure 14.1.   Note-taking frame for structural change.

"make sense" of the experiences of representatives of each school's community.

We have learned that the mapping process can also help members of a school community to step back from their involvement in the everyday. When they do so they are better able to see patterns in their evolution that give them insights about their organization and help them gain new perspectives that can inform and invigorate their ongoing reform plans and strategies. The maps resulting from our study communicate that the particulars of each school's journey toward reform have been very different. Each of the maps, along with descriptions of the contexts for change in the other two schools, is included below to illustrate this point.

Mapping Change at Branford

Figure 14.2 shows the map of change at Branford High School, including key "markers" identified by school partners such as major activities, events, phases, and/or catalysts for reform. At the outset of the chapter we provided the history and context for changes at the school.

Focusing Change at Norwalk

Norwalk's map is shown in figure 14.3. "No student is allowed to fail" is a philosophy adopted by a group of Norwalk High School teachers a decade ago. Coined by a science teacher, it became the mantra for a group of teachers and administrators who acted on their concerns about the number of ninth-grade students dropping out of school because they lacked the requisite skills to succeed. Creation of ninth-grade teams of teachers and students was the result, a significant initial innovation at Norwalk High School. Thus began a decade-long effort to make changes in structure, content, and culture that would enable educators to pursue their vision of providing each student with the tools needed to be successful in high school—to allow no student to fail.

Norwalk High School, which has over 1,500 students, is located in Norwalk, Connecticut. While this city of nearly 78,000 is located in Fairfield County, one of the wealthiest counties in the country, Norwalk

Figure 14.2. Map for Branford High School in Connecticut, revised March 2000.

PHASES	Malaise/Ennui Potential Energy		Action	Consolidation of Beliefs About Expectations and Focusing Energy	Refinement of Teach/Learning	Seeking Validation
CATALYSTS		New Principal/ Beliefs Learning	De-Tracking/ CT Common Core	Initial Results	Positive Results →	
EVENTS	Group of teachers with common memories/ experiences of success Turnover of principals Lack of leadership		Alternative School/Horizons Project begun with 9th grade heterogeneous group Elimination of third track Everyone engaged in improvement committees Teacher study groups Research and piloting of new skills/processes Option of honors for all Teaming workshops Peer observations 8 release days Students and parents on improvement committees Faculty committee daily meetings Policy recommends: professional development, grading, curriculum revision and class size	Draft of performance based learner outcomes Ongoing discussions about teaching and learning based on common core Discussions of student work Encouraging the interests of students through multiple clubs and issue oriented teams Advisor/advisee concept	Outcomes guide most classes Increase CAPT scores Students know expectations of graduation exhibition Community service 70% take honors Social Studies	Graduation requirements are performance based Ongoing monitoring of progress
RELATIONSHIP TO EXTERNAL ENVIRONMENT	Little community support Divisive community Fiscal tightness Population growth Parents concerned about tracking		Used lack of $ resources as leverage to eliminate small classes/tracking Principal's style matched community	NEASC report cites strengths and needs $24 m. addition to school K-12 discussion on performance	Networking with other schools Recognition by CT Dept of Ed and external entities Board doesn't link changes in tracking to improved performance Board most interested in "discipline" issues	External validation continues Visits and requests from external groups energize reform efforts Change in Board membership may prove supportive

PHASES	Piloting/Review (1990-91)	Expansion (1992-94)	Diffusion (1995 +)
CATALYSTS	Principal's support/encouragement of staff plan Teacher Union support for structural change Motivated, professional school staff School concern for at-risk students and transition from eighth to ninth grade	Review of data showing improvement in TEEM group versus "control" group of students Increased teacher empowerment and decision-making responsibility resulting from team structure Creation of teams of teachers provided forum for reflection and energy, which enhanced teacher leadership	Professional development requests by staff in upper grades on TEEM and development of study skills materials Culture of school that supports risk-taking, research-based teaching, and expanded leadership roles for staff and students
KEY EVENTS/ CHARACTERISTICS	Essential Schools symposium "Students are not allowed to fail" slogan professional development of staff in multiple content areas The Essential Enrichment Method (TEEM) developed and piloted by team of 4 staff Structural change supported by curriculum changes in mathematics, science, study skills, etc. Creation of new scheduling system within existing house structure Initial teacher response to TEEM was one of being overwhelmed TEEM structure addressed need of individual students and recognized them as individuals	Identified and kept data of pilot group (25) And control group of at-risk students Continued expansion of TEEM concept to 50% of ninth grade students (1992) and to all ninth graders (1993) Included diverse group of staff in "teacher teams" including Special Education and Counseling	
EXTERNAL ENVIRONMENT/ INFLUENCES	Support from district for school-level decisions District mandate to develop plan for at-risk students followed first year of pilot	Positive parent and student reactions to team concept	Teachers and parents of upper grade students would like program expanded

Figure 14.3. Map for Norwalk High School in Connecticut, derived from data collected April 1999 and revised March 2000.

is a working-class community with a per capita income in 1998 of under $33,000. Its school population is racially, ethnically, and economically diverse.

When Dr. John Ramos became the principal in 1989, faculty professional development and teacher leadership became central to the life of the school. He and a team of faculty attended an Essential Schools Symposium that year, and the experience resonated with their desire to reach all students and address their concerns about ninth graders at risk. Following this event, the teachers and other key staff, with Ramos' support, designed a pilot project for at-risk ninth graders called The Essential Enrichment Method (TEEM). It was initiated in September 1990.

The teacher-led Essential Enrichment Method pilot project involved teaming four teachers with a group of 25 at-risk ninth graders as a means of assisting students to make the transition from middle to high school. The pilot was not an instant success. In fact, by midyear, teachers feared it was not working. However, they had had the foresight to establish a control group of similar at-risk students not on a team. When they compared the two groups, they discovered that teamed students were doing much better than those in the control group. The net result is that by the 1993–94 school year, all ninth graders in the school were teamed, all of their teachers were involved, and team membership had increased to include guidance counselors, special education teachers, a reading consultant and interns from higher education. This structure continues today in the ninth grade, and on a host of student performance measures, Norwalk High School has made steady progress in recent years.

TEEM was designed to "engage students with an interdisciplinary, learner-centered curriculum, motivate the uninspired, challenge the academically talented, and shore up the self-esteem of those in need," but faculty also reach out to parents to develop shared methods for promoting student success in school. Common planning time allows all team teachers to meet jointly with parents and students, and students are responsible for heading meetings. Parents can speak with all of their child's teachers at one time.

In addition, TEEM faculty have been engaged in using a variety of scheduling variations, including block schedules. However, after extensive study and a pilot, in 1999 the faculty and students did not support adoption of a formal block schedule for the school. Other recent initiatives include, for example, efforts to increase student involvement, an after-school program to help students academically, expanded outreach to minority and other parents, recognition programs, a grade-ten collaborative linking U.S. history and English, and assistance for sophomores who do not reach state goals on the tenth-grade Connecticut Academic Performance Test.

Norwalk High School remains a work in progress in terms of striving to meet the needs of all its students. About one-third of the staff is leading the reform process with the support of the principal. Bringing along others, across all grade levels, has been discouraging for these leaders at times. They hope the structures are in place now to assist them in effecting whole-school reform. It is no longer fashionable for faculty to complain about changes, and the leadership group views the school as less traditional than in the past.

Integrating Prior Changes at Yarmouth

The map for Yarmouth High School, figure 14.4, tells another story. Teachers at Yarmouth have been engaged in many individual and small group reforms over the past fifteen years. Structural, curricular, and assessment changes have been piloted and implemented by departments and individuals. Recently it appears that common expectations about student outcomes based on jointly designed performance assessments may be bringing together the separate strands of reform for the whole school and engaging individuals and departments that had not been pioneering changes on their own.

Yarmouth High School, located in the small, affluent community of Yarmouth, Maine, is racially and ethnically homogeneous. It is a school of about 500 students in which all the external doors remain open during school hours and few student lockers are locked. There is a strong spirit of community in the school, and teachers, who are generally highly experienced, are called by their first names if they wish. The school's parents, most of whom are very well educated, are committed to having their children participate in the kind of education in which they were themselves successful, and they question school policies and practices when they have concerns.

Change at Yarmouth often takes the format of:
New external influences and ideas——▶ lead to Piloting and programs——▶ that may create
Limited Spread to other staff——▶ sometimes followed by realization that reform may "not be
quite right for us"——▶ individuals and groups reconceptualize the reform——▶ and then refine
how it is implemented——▶ may lead to final adaptation by other staff or whole school with
recognition that not everyone will be happy with the changes.

An emergent interest in creating alternative curriculum offerings led to piloting of structural changes
                                    Core Principles
Structural Change ~ ~ ~ ~ /~ ~ ~ ~ ~ /~ ~ ~ ~ ~ /~ ~ ~ ~ ~
                        block schedules   A/B student grouping

An emergent need for content and process that support student learning led to exploration of Teaching/Learning Strategies
                        Critical thinking skills   Experiential learning
Teaching/Learning Strategies ~ ~ ~ ~ /~ ~ ~ ~ ~ /~ ~ ~ ~ ~ /~ ~ ~ ~ ~
                                        Writing samples

            Integrated 9th grade science   Standards   K-12 Coordination
Curriculum ~ ~ ~ ~ /~ ~ ~ ~ ~ /~ ~ ~ ~ ~ /~ ~ ~ ~ ~ /~ ~ ~ ~ ~ ~ / ~ ~ ~ ~ ~ ~ ~
                    Foxfire/AP English   Mathematics outcomes/integrated courses

Curriculum reform resulted in emergent learning that "we should not do process at the exclusion of content and vice versa"

An emergent need for methods to assess content & process led to development of Assessment processes, tools, and reporting system
                Standards/rubrics   9th grade science assessment
Assessment ~ ~ ~ ~ /~ ~ ~ ~ ~ /~ ~ ~ ~ ~ /~ ~ ~ ~ ~ /~ ~ ~ ~ ~
                Authentic assessment   Senior demonstrations

An emergent need to better understand students led to increasing opportunities for student input
            Input into decisions   Developers of courses/senior seminar
Student Input ~ ~ ~ ~ /~ ~ ~ ~ ~ /~ ~ ~ ~ ~ /~ ~ ~ ~ ~ /~ ~ ~ ~ ~
                    Source of information   members of teams
~ ~
            Loose Organizational Structure at School Level
            Is reflected in the variety of decision-making groups over time
        Strategic Plan ——▶——▶"Big Blue" Planning Document ——▶——▶ Guiding Principles

From curricular departments——▶ faculty council——▶ school improvement team——▶ learning area leaders——▶
    Learning teams ——▶ to balanced roles of self-actualized faculty and supportive principal
~ ~
                    Stable Environment
            Yarmouth Community and District Provides/Offers
    • Continuity   • Fiscal resources   • Strong academic focus   • Encouragement
            • Community expectations for "excellence"/high expectations

Figure 14.4.   Map for Yarmouth High School in Maine, derived from data collected May 1999 and revised March 2000.

The current history of reform and restructuring at the school began in the mid-1980s with a change of principal after a period of faculty and principal conflict. Both the teachers' union and district staff wanted a fresh and collaborative start. Teachers were invited to take significant responsibility in selecting the new principal, and then core faculty and the new principal began to engage in ongoing conversations about reform. They focused their discussion on curriculum and authentic assessment, and the school began to offer professional development on these topics. The Essential Schools movement influenced the thinking of school faculty as well. The approach and content of their discussions moved the school toward a collaborative culture and away from a congenial one in which debate and disagreement were avoided. Faculty and staff were increasingly able to explore and argue about significant issues of teaching and learning. As the Yarmouth map illustrates, from these initial changes individuals and small groups have pursued a range of reforms over the ensuing years. Some involved structural changes like block scheduling, which was initiated by the principal, but the change did not persist at a schoolwide level because it brought resistance both from some of the faculty and from the community. Other innovations focused on instructional strategies or curriculum, often confined to a given grade level or department. Over the years a variety of governance structures and decision-making groups have also been tried in an effort to support broader reform.

Throughout this period the district has supported ongoing reform through professional development and has provided more time for staff to plan and work collaboratively. One result was an integrated mathematics curriculum, but parents had not been involved in the development and reacted negatively to course offerings unfamiliar to them. The outcome was a new rule that no major change initiative can be submitted to the board of education unless it is research based and has involved community members in its development. Over the course of reform the school has fully supported individual faculty empowerment, but it has not on its own moved reform to the level of the school as a whole organization.

A more recent generation of whole school and system improvement seems to be taking hold in light of new expectations for students established at the state level in the Maine Learning Results document. Faculty and administrators have been working on issues of performance assessments. In most learning areas, staff have now developed an exhibition assessment for graduating seniors. Pressures against the adoption of a graduation-by-exhibition requirement, however, are strong from the community, and the elite colleges to which most students go do not generally support portfolios or assessments outside of traditional measures like the SAT. Still, it appears that shared expectations about student outcomes, along with performance assessments developed jointly by staff and supported by the principal, may be the catalyst for bringing together the separate strands of innovation for the whole school and increasing the level of engagement of school staff.

DILEMMAS TO MANAGE

Analysis of the three high school reform histories and maps led us to identify a set of interrelated dilemmas that each school has continued to face as staff and constituents have engaged in reform, and which each school has addressed differently. The differences appear to result from different conceptions of what was most effective and from unique internal and external contexts that have created particular landscapes in which they have operated. To illustrate the different strategies that each of the schools used in the face of these dilemmas, we have charted them on a series of continua.

REFORM ISSUES ARRAYED ON CONTINUA

We observed a set of fourteen issues with which each school had to deal that played out in each of them over the course of their reform processes. In the discussion below we will explore the dynamic inter-play schools must engage in around these key issues and the inherent dilemmas they pose for schools. Each can represent potential benefits as well as potential problems or barriers to reform, depending on how a school addresses the issues at important junctures.

Figure 14.5 depicts these as fourteen characteristics. It also includes notations showing where we perceived that each high school predomi-nantly fell on the continua at the time we conducted the research (com-pleted in the spring of 2000). For example, on the first continuum, "divergence from community expectations/close alignment with com-munity expectations," Branford High School seemed quite divergent from some vocal segments of the external community in having high expectations for all students, creating a culture of student responsibility and freedom, and pursuing comprehensive change over a considerable period of time.

Depicting these issues as continua is intended to convey several messages. The first is that these are matters that schools undergoing reform will have to address along the way and so they may wish to attend to them and adopt strategies to manage them that are aligned with their long-term goals. A second is that the position on the continua where a school may be placed will, and probably should, change over time, depending on student and staff needs, resources available to the school, and the context within which the school is operating. Third, the "correct" position for any school on each of these continua is related to its current context and the trade-offs that may be required for a school to continue to pursue its goals. Our observations suggest that it is not useful to prescribe the approach to these issues that any given high school should take, but the more the issues are identified, understood, and approached thoughtfully over time, the greater the choice and flexibility the school will have in its improvement effort.

Either end of each continuum offers potential benefits as well as potential negative effects. Moving entirely to one end of any of them may increase the associated negative effects of that end and eliminate the potential benefits from the other end. Consequently, the continua represent ongoing issues, dilemmas, and essential "unsolvable problems" that have to be continually managed within the complex environment of a school and its community.

Leadership, as an example, is one issue central to reform where these dilemmas can play themselves out along a "teacher-led reform/administrator-led reform" continuum. That is, an administrator may initially lead a reform initiative, but if it remains so it is likely to suffer from teacher resistance and a rapid demise with a change in building administrators. At the same time, an innovation initiated by teachers is likely to have limited impact and longevity if building administrators do not play a supportive leadership role. Similarly, the issue of whether to institutionalize changes in policy can pose a dilemma. Early on in the initiation and development of a reform, spending time institutionalizing it in policy may divert energy from the task at hand and "freeze" change before it is fully developed. On the other hand, it may be very important to concentrate on policy at certain points so that changes can

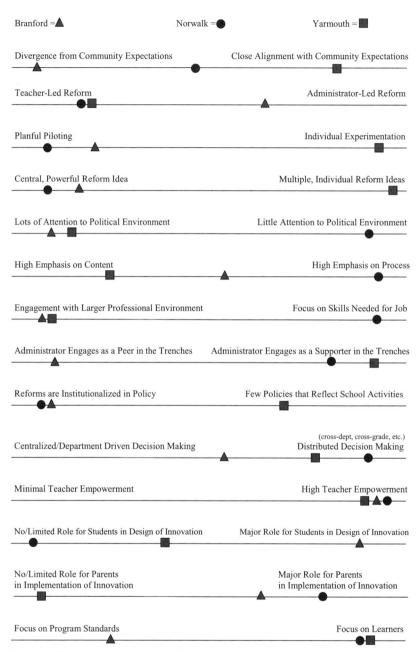

Figure 14.5.   Fourteen characteristics.

become part of the organizational structure and culture and attention and effort can be moved elsewhere.

Interestingly, the dilemmas that these continua represent may also be resolved by school staff as a consequence of their beliefs, the ways they think about issues, and their own actions. Branford is currently at this stage on the "high emphasis on content/high emphasis on process" continuum. School leaders believe that the two ends of the continuum can be fully reconciled, that process and content are mutually reinforcing and essential to their success. They have developed the skills and strategies to be simultaneously "high content" and "high process."

The experience and histories of the high schools that participated in this study have reinforced our understanding that the pace of reform and the cycles and patterns of change will differ for each school. Within the context of each school, initiating and sustaining reform requires attention to a collective guiding vision, the beliefs and roles of adults and students, and organizational structures, content, and processes. In addition, managing the dilemmas posed by the issues in the continua requires ongoing attention as schools navigate their environment in order to meet the needs of their students and community. As we observed over the course of our study how the schools were addressing these challenges, we identified six reform themes and related capacities that are important in supporting successful change over time at the secondary level.

HIGH SCHOOL CAPACITIES FOR REFORM

As a synthesis of our study, we produced summary statements of the capacities demonstrated during the schools' reform histories that seem integral to success. The maps and the combined continua for these schools reveal what we consider to be six major fields of action that support the long-term and complex process of whole-school reform.

Pursue an Evolving Vision and Expand Commitment

A school's vision can serve to generate direction and energy for reform, particularly when it focuses on meeting student needs and improving teaching and learning. A vision needs to be described as evolving, one that the school community can continuously approach but that it must revisit regularly, refine, and extend. A "picture" of the future that can be interpreted as readily attainable or that is limited to particular aspects of the organization can stall reform when it is perceived to be "done." Moreover, a vision that is not well defined or one to which a critical mass of staff is not committed may still generate actions, but they are less likely to be coherent or to lead to whole-school reform.

School staffs need to develop the beliefs and skills to "operationalize" their vision through concrete practices and to make a commitment to ongoing dialogue and collaborative action over the period of time it takes to accomplish significant change. Our study involved looking at a decade or more of activity and, in spite of substantial progress on many fronts, in none of the schools was the work "done." Moreover, based on the experiences of these schools, the success of reform also becomes increasingly likely as increasing numbers of staff take personal and professional responsibility for achieving the vision. At Branford High School most staff are involved in continually examining their actions in light of the school's vision. They are always filling in details of their "picture" of their school or modifying their practices based on experience and emerging research.

Expand Leadership across Roles

Schools can be leadership rich or leadership poor. In schools that are rich in leadership, all staff members have opportunities to develop and exercise leadership capacity. In these schools leadership is not the sole responsibility of those in formal leadership positions. The history of the schools we studied revealed that successful reforms at the high school level are designed, led, managed, supported, and evaluated through the leadership of administrators, teachers, community members, and students. Norwalk's ninth-grade intervention program was a teacher-led initiative supported by the principal, as were many of the improvement activities in Branford and Yarmouth. So a school's capacity for reform is highly dependent on the amount of leadership available across staff, students, parents, and community members. In each of these schools there were core groups of experienced individuals willing and able to take on leadership roles, and they were supported in doing so. Professional development over time has increased the numbers and skills of these people.

As leadership capacity expands, principals need to be prepared to adjust their roles. The principal may actively lead some of the reform efforts from the front, support others' reform efforts, or opportunistically take advantage of events to move reform ahead. Ed Higgins walks a tightrope between making decisions himself and giving responsibility to others. He sees himself as "a facilitator who also gives direction." Because principals often have the advantage of greater access to the broader educational environment than other staff, sharing information and leadership opportunities across roles is central to expanding leadership capacity. And principals need the capacity to develop and support other leaders across the school.

Moreover, principals themselves need the base of support that expanded leadership provides as they confront the challenges inherent in secondary reform. In Branford, it was the teachers who proposed comprehensive reform to the board of education, but students went before the board and supported the faculty in creating a culture of student responsibility. In Norwalk, it was teachers who designed and led the initiative to create ninth-grade teams. In Yarmouth, students have increasingly taken on substantive leadership roles as responsible participants in their own education, and parents and community members have also been partners in reform at each of the schools.

Support Ongoing Reflection and Professional Development

In each of the schools we studied, a necessary precursor and adjunct of reform has been time for reflection and professional development. Schools face many demands, and often the school day is structured in ways making it difficult to organize time for collaborative activity. In many schools time in the classroom is such a high priority, including for political reasons related to community pressures, that staff members have very limited opportunities for new learning. In the study schools, Branford and Yarmouth in particular, the school staff is regularly able to come together for significant conversations. Faculty and administrators bring new research, practices, and locally generated data into these conversations as they strive to better focus their work and improve their effectiveness. In Norwalk, the ninth-grade teacher teams work together and confer regularly about the students with whom they interact.

In the context of ongoing reflection and professional development, the opportunities available to staff must meet their needs and continue to stimulate them. Activities appropriate to new staff are unlikely to meet the needs of seasoned veterans. As faculty members' skills and knowledge mature and their opportunities to exercise leadership expand, their professional growth opportunities must expand and increase in sophistication. The Yarmouth staff has had access to nationally known figures to provide some of their professional development. Branford teachers travel the state and region to talk with others about their reform process. In general, staff with well-developed skills can often improve them further when they become presenters, first to peers within their school and then beyond its boundaries.

Link Robust Ideas to Significant Changes in Content and Structure

Small-scale change often addresses issues that are not significant to the whole school or will have minimal impact on most stakeholders, and thus are relatively "safe." To mobilize an entire high school community in pursuit of reform, the changes envisioned must be powerful and meaningful enough to engage members and substantive and comprehensive enough to persist as significant issues over time.

At the secondary school level, successful changes in process and structure are integrally linked to changes in content. Early in reform, leaders must identify changes in school structures, processes, and content that are aligned with the school's vision and robust enough to promote long-term, fundamental improvements in teaching and learning. Short-term wins are important to long-term success, but launching reforms that can be addressed relatively quickly can limit the continuing impetus for change, and momentum for change will dissipate. In addition, teachers, like their professional peers in other organizations, are suspicious of short-term change efforts of a year or two. They have the tendency to wait them out.

In the schools we studied, reform efforts that put students in the forefront, addressed core issues around teaching and learning, and involved implementing new structures to support changes in approaches (e.g., time for faculty collaboration, new faculty roles) have engaged staff in ways and over periods of time that less substantive reforms could not. At Yarmouth High School specifically, reform has centered on designing curriculum and instruction to address Maine's expectations for all students, developing assessment methods to measure them, and calibrating assessment scoring to provide consistent standards across teachers. All of this collaborative work has increased professional interactions and served as powerful professional development.

Engage in Planful Piloting

None of the three schools implemented a reform effort that involved importing a model developed elsewhere. Rather, a key strategy the schools used was piloting innovations and building their own knowledge to inform decision-making. While some of the literature on high school reform suggests that pilots may be an ineffective reform strategy, the features of piloting in these schools made them an effective choice. Importantly, the pilots were not just an administrative first step to a predetermined change. Instead, pilots were carefully linked to the overall goals of the school so that they would support broader reform processes already in place. In addition, they were structured to enable the school community to learn from them, decide their utility, and then determine the next steps to take in the reform process.

Norwalk High School had a very successful experience with the process of piloting when some teachers initially proposed and then piloted four-person teacher teams, each with a cluster of twenty-five at-risk students. As part of their plan, the teachers also established a comparison group of similar students who were not in a cluster supported by a teacher team. When the pilot teachers compared data on the two groups at midyear of the first year, they discovered that the students in the clusters were doing much better on both academic and discipline measures than those in the control group. The school then used the data and new knowledge for decision-making. Within three years, all ninth graders, not just those at special risk, had been included in the team and cluster model.

Recognize and Respond to Community Expectations

High schools often have high profiles in their communities and are therefore subject to many community expectations and social pressures. Identifying and understanding how the community defines "school success" is essential in navigating the political environment of the secondary school. In the words of Ed Higgins, high schools have to learn how to "deliver the coin of the realm" to ensure a base of support for ongoing reform. In the current era of school accountability, the "coin" is often high or at least improving scores on a state test, which is the case in Branford. On the other hand, Yarmouth High School serves a community in which a large percentage of the parents have graduated from high-status colleges. These parents expect the school to deliver to their children the kinds of instruction and courses that made them successful, as well as the kinds of data that elite colleges are most likely to appreciate on college applications. School leaders need to recognize the elements of education that different constituencies value and learn to craft messages in language that communicates clearly with various stakeholders. By doing so it is possible to mediate against the boundaries placed on a school by the community that can limit the options for reform and renewal.

If community expectations can be met, a school is more likely to be given leeway to pursue policies and strategies that may be less popular but that educators believe will improve learning. An example of this has been the extent to which Branford High School has been able to create and sustain a culture of student responsibility and leadership, despite board members' concerns that the school has provided too much freedom of choice for students. In this case the students even took leadership and publicly supported the school's policies at board meetings. It goes without saying that students are also community members, and Branford students served as important links to the community at large.

CONCLUSIONS

One factor that emerges from this exploration of just three high schools is the way short-term foci often constrain our capacity to implement change. All high schools have a history that influences efforts to bring about significant reform, yet those histories often do not reside in those who attempt to implement change. Our study looked back over more than ten years of institutional history, and that length of time was scarcely adequate to complete comprehensive restructuring. If that is generally true of high schools, then successful interventions need to tap into knowledge about longer-term history and have a long-term future focus. We have sought to communicate the latter lesson by emphasizing the need to generate robust ideas with which a school staff can engage for a significant period of time. Two to three years is not long in the life of a high school, yet this is the time frame for too many projects that are not an integrated part of a longer-term effort.

A second factor that we identified is the power of context. All high schools have different histories and capacities and function in different contexts. Schools are constrained by their own histories, by the communities within which they function, and, more broadly, by the colleges to which they send their graduates. Change initiatives are likely to be more successful if they begin with an assessment of the capacities that already exist within a particular school, and if the boundary between the high school and its environment is carefully attended to. While this may be a principal's role primarily, it can also be the responsibility of the whole school community.

Change strategies may, and we argue should, be informed and shaped by local context, but in each of the three study schools they were also informed by both the research literature and internal research and evaluation. These sources of information deepened discussion and enabled reformers to embark on change initiatives that capitalized on knowledge not available in the school staffs at the beginning of the initiatives. Consequently, although the schools had well-defined visions and operating principles, they were unable at the outset to plan the details of the change on which they were embarking. There are limits as well as benefits to formal planning processes.

Finally, this small study raises a number of questions in our minds.

For example, to what extent are the patterns of change that we discovered common across all high schools? What are the differences in pattern between urban and rural high schools and between those with student populations of relatively low or high socioeconomic status? How do the dilemmas we cited play out in other schools? Could they be better articulated, or are there other significant dilemmas that we did not identify? Is there more that could be said about the capacities and more and less successful strategies for resolving the dilemmas, or is seeking to deepen understanding about how to explore them in context of greater use than providing generalized advice on how to resolve them? We look forward to exploring these and other questions in the company of others who support or are engaged in high school reform.

RESOURCES

Dufour, M., & Eaker, R. (1998). *Professional Learning Communities at Work: Best Practices for Enhancing Student Achievement*. Reston, VA: ASCD. Michael Dufour turned around a high school that was in the pits and promotes a comprehensive learning community approach.

Fullan, M. (1999). *Change Forces: The Sequel*. Philadelphia, PA: Falmer Press. This book builds on his earlier *Change Forces*, addresses issues of equity and poverty, is written from the perspective of complexity theory, and seeks to suggest approaches from multiple levels of system.

Wheatley, M. (1999). *Leadership and the New Science: Discovering Order in a Chaotic World* (2nd ed.). San Francisco: Berrett-Koehler. If people get this, then a whole new way of thinking about change is possible.

Senge, P. (Ed.). (2000). *Schools That Learn*. New York: Doubleday. While this book focuses on schools as learning organizations, it builds on his earlier ones, including *The Fifth Discipline*, *The Fifth Discipline Fieldbook*, and *The Dance of Change*, all of which are about the art and practice of building learning organizations in various other types of organizations.

CHAPTER 15

Making Personalization a Statewide Priority

Maine's Promising Futures Movement

GORDON DONALDSON and GEORGE MARNIK
University of Maine

Some might consider it an oxymoron to claim that a state could help to personalize the learning of all of its adolescents. Indeed, at its heart, personalization is a very human process involving student and teacher, child and parent—but not the state. Maine, however, has over the past three years launched a campaign to personalize learning for all its secondary students. This chapter describes how this movement came to be and some of the reception and results it has met with to date.

We were recruited to serve on a statewide commission to examine the status of secondary education. Gordon served as cochair of the commission, while George (a high school principal at the time) was one of twenty-six members. The commission, appointed by state commissioner of education J. Duke Albanese, did not set out with a mission to "personalize" learning. Rather, its goal was to examine how current practices in the classrooms, corridors, and playing fields of Maine's high schools could be reinforced or reformed so that every one of Maine's high school graduates would meet the standards set by the Maine Learning Results, a compilation of "what every youth should know and be able to do" to succeed in the 21st century.

The Maine Department of Education and the Northeast and Islands Regional Educational Lab at Brown University supported the eighteen-month journey of the Maine Commission on Secondary Education. It took us to high schools, regional vocational centers, and academies throughout the state. A linchpin of our data collection process was the hosting of three regional "student and teacher forums" to which members of every Maine secondary school student body and faculty was invited. We gathered data on outcomes and on common practices. And we read widely and heard from a variety of people about the challenges faced in our secondary schools and about the various visions put forth nationally for high school reform.

From all this, we fashioned a description of "current realities" and, from that, the commission generated its own vision for a better future. Our report, entitled *Promising Futures: Improving the Learning of Maine's Secondary School Students*, was published in the fall of 1998 by the Maine Department of Education and distributed widely throughout the state and, since then, the nation.

Neither of us would have guessed at the outset that the commission's thinking and, later, its report, would develop the student-centered quality that they did.

But *Promising Futures* became a testimony both to the neglect of individual learning that has befallen many of our adolescents and to the need to rethink, restructure, and reculture our high schools so the personalized learning journey of each student lies at the center of the school experience. Indeed, the reform literature abounds with strategies for restructuring schools, for reinventing systems of accountability, for reorganizing the schedule, the curriculum, and the physical plants of high schools. Our commission could, too, have traveled into that maze of prescriptions and structural solutions. But something—we believe it was largely the presence of students and teachers on the commission— saved us from this fate. In its place, we created a vision for Maine high schools that seeks to ensure personal attention and a personalized learning experience for every Maine youth.

STATE REALITIES AND THE COMMISSION'S VISION

The commission's mapping of "the current realities" in Maine's secondary schools mirrored the findings of a 1997 national study by Public Agenda: "Most teenagers are not as hostile or indifferent to education as many adults fear. To the contrary, most echo beliefs about education that are widely held by adults. Most teenagers are not 'turned off and tuned out. . . .' [But] most teens view the academic side of school as little more than 'going through the motions'—a monotonous and meaningless series of exercises that teachers and parents expect them to complete" (p. 13).

Our major observations are described in *Promising Futures* and can be summarized as follows:

1. Maine secondary schools are currently graduating the highest proportion of eligible students in the state's history (80 percent of eighth grade cohorts graduate from public high schools four years later).
2. Secondary school students exhibit more varied and complex learning, social, and emotional needs than in the past.
3. Every Maine student does not have equal access to learning in comparison to other students in his or her school.
4. Academic achievement is, on average, high in relation to other states, but it is uneven from school to school.
5. Students and, to a degree, staff in Maine secondary schools view educational experiences as irrelevant or disengaging for many students.
6. Maine students feel disengaged from serious decisions about their own education, about school life, and about their futures; many parents share these feelings.
7. The highest percentage of graduates in Maine's history is accepted at higher education institutions, but their rate of completion is no better than the national average and many have little confidence in the value of higher education.
8. Maine high schools serve diffuse purposes and struggle to succeed at them all.

Summarizing the commission's findings, *Promising Futures* reported: "students and educators, in general, described Maine secondary schools that are academically focused but rarely exciting or challenging, social but strangely impersonal and sometimes hostile, orderly but ill-suited for learning, predictable but lacking application to life" (p. 3). While these observations did not describe every Maine secondary student, staff member, or school, they profiled important challenges facing the state's system in general and, in some part, each school across the state.

At the center of this diagnosis was recognition of the impersonal quality of the learning experience. Although our high schools average 440 students each, they are structured and often run as if their enrollments were five times that size. They are facing growing diversity among their students yet seem paralyzed by the uniformity and inflexibility of their curricula, schedules and policies, and teaching practices. Maine's high schools are taking in adolescents with widely varying learning styles, histories, cultural and social backgrounds, and future aspirations—and the variations are expanding. But our practices are handcuffing teachers, counselors, administrators, parents, and students themselves from devising educational paths that are at once academically ambitious and personally relevant and engaging. The result is too much apathy, too many inequities in both opportunities to learn and to succeed, and too many students who, although they graduate, have not benefited intellectually and developmentally from their high school years.

The commission's membership (including two students, seven teachers, three principals, three superintendents, a state teacher association leader, and three university personnel) spent long hours evaluating the implications of these current realities. For this diverse group, starting with a data-gathering task engaged every person in learning the statewide secondary picture together and leveled differences in background, age, and status. The description of current realities established a basis on which to build a collective view of a more desirable future.

As we read widely about secondary reform, our understanding of how others believed adolescents could and should be taught gradually took form. Ted and Nancy Sizer spent a day with the commission, and the Northeast and Islands Regional Educational Lab at Brown University offered ample access to new concepts and models. Using an iterative process, the commission constructed a set of Core Principles to guide the development of Maine's secondary schools.

Core Principles for Secondary Educational Practice in Maine

Successful secondary educational experiences require:

1. A safe, respectful, and caring environment that ensures that every student can attend fully to her or his central mission: learning.

2. Adults to hold high universal expectations of all students (incorporating the Maine Learning Results) and to provide a variety of pathways for students as they strive to meet these expectations.

3. Frequent assessment of student learning and use of these assessments by students, teachers, and parents so that all can share responsibility for planning and carrying out learning activities.

4. Teaching and procedures that honor and build upon the unique contributions and needs of each learner so that all students will make full use of their opportunities to learn.

5. Staff, parents, and especially students to be engaged democratically in decisions about learning and the conduct of the school so they learn civic responsibility and skills and so that respect and equity are ensured among all members of the school community.

6. Internal coherence among school mission, goals, actions, and outcomes so that the efforts of students, staff, and community result in the fulfillment of mission and goals.

These six principles reflect the strong belief that secondary schools can and must offer Maine's youth an education that is as personally relevant and caring as the education we often associate with elementary and middle schools. Every student must feel significant and believe that adults and the school as a whole care about him or her both personally and academically. A school expresses this care through high expectations and multiple pathways for learning, by providing clear goals and learning opportunities, and by offering frequent, constructive feedback. Further, students are given responsibility for their learning, their behavior, and their participation in the society of the school.

In short, the commission concluded that our high schools needed to be given back to educators, students, and parents, and these essential partners needed support as they created new environments that placed learning and teaching at the center. Policies, procedures, district preferences, and past practices were to play second fiddle to the pathways of each student's learning journey.

Promising Futures presents fifteen Core Practices that commission members judged essential to the functioning of a successful school (see Appendix). Eight of these practices address teaching and learning, and seven present preferred schoolwide structures and patterns of behavior, culture, and policy. They are described and illustrated in *Promising Futures* in an effort to give Maine secondary schools concrete ways to start thinking and planning about their own practices.

SPREADING THE SEEDS

The Commission on Secondary Education completed its work in July of 1998. In our final meetings that spring, we talked long and hard about the approach we should take to have maximum impact on practice throughout the state. Here, we faced the "personalization policy" oxymoron: how were we, a statewide group, to encourage personalization when the success of such an effort relies so heavily upon the commitment, sensitivity, and efficacy on the part of every teacher and every student in our high schools? Certainly, a report that called for new mandates and required practices would not do. Nor would a call to arms that fundamentally insults educators, parents, and students by questioning their intelligence, commitment, and aspirations. We came to the conclusion that our approach must, in fact, do just the opposite: it must honor the good intentions of educators, students, and family and invite them into the arduous but exciting work of reinventing secondary learning and teaching.

We wrote in the Executive Summary to *Promising Futures*: "[this document] is not a menu of mandates. Instead, it is intended to stimulate discussion and action in every district in Maine so that every one of our teenagers will leave school prepared for his or her own promising future" (p. 1). Put simply, our report was the result of our listening to Mainers, so it would represent back to them the major themes in what we had learned. The commissioner of education had created the commission to seek ways to improve learning for every Maine student; our work did not carry the force of law or regulation, and we did not want it to. We concluded that a public invitation to engage in conversation about the needs of adolescents and the best practices necessary to meet those needs would have far greater mileage than the alternatives we have become so accustomed to.

In keeping with this invitational approach, we planned a statewide convocation to unveil the essence of *Promising Futures* and to engage participants in discussion around it and some examples of exemplary practice. We invited all 155 high schools, semiprivate academies, and vocational schools to send teams. Supported by the LAB at Brown and the Maine Center for Educational Services, the Maine Department of Education thus kicked off its statewide effort to personalize secondary learning in September of 1998. Following the convocation, a copy of *Promising Futures* was mailed to every secondary educator, every central office, every school board chairperson, and every legislator and policy leader in the state.

The coordination of the commission's follow-through activities was guided by this approach. Commissioner Albanese chose to embed this work not in an established office or role in the department but in a new entity entitled the Center for Inquiry on Secondary Education (CISE). CISE's unusual title, while it created some uncertainty, gave the first two staff members considerable freedom to reach out to schools and groups throughout the state. Gordon Donaldson, on leave from the University of Maine, joined with Susan Hackett Johnson, newly hired Comprehensive School Reform Demonstration (CSRD) project coordinator, to structure the beginning stages of the center. Two department staff, Connie Manter and Karen Rumery, both of whom had served on the commission, also allotted time to the effort. These four individuals formed a team whose purpose was to plan and implement the dissemination of the findings of *Promising Futures* and to offer support and professional development opportunities to those schools that chose to take on the challenges facing secondary schools.

During its first year of operation, 1998–99, the CISE devoted much of its time to:

- Hosting regional forums to discuss *Promising Futures* and its implications for schools and communities.
- Developing an information flow between the Maine Department of Education and schools through the creation of the first statewide newsletter, *Pursuing Promising Futures*, and a website devoted to secondary schools.
- Creating a process for secondary schools to apply for Comprehensive School Reform Demonstration (CSRD) grants.
- Nurturing working relationships with a variety of existing profes-

sional organizations representing teachers, principals, superintendents, university faculty, and policy makers.

- Creating two summer academies for school teams where exposure
  to the Core Practices and planning for their own improvement
  would be the primary focus.

In its second year, the work of CISE expanded with the increased
support of the Department of Education and the hiring of two per diem
consultants: Pamela Fisher, former cochair of the commission, and
George Marnik, a member of the commission. Both had worked extensively in Maine secondary schools as teachers and principals. Key to
the continued success of the CISE team was their ability to work
together in planning a more intensive statewide approach and to call on
each other's strengths in implementing that plan in an effective manner. Their varied experiences throughout the state and the contacts they
had developed over the years helped to open doors so that the conversation could begin as school personnel wrestled with the meaning and
implications of the Core Principles and Practices.

Over the first two years of its existence, the CISE developed a multi-
faceted approach shaped to meet the unique needs of schools, professional organizations, and geographic regions of the state. This
approach reflects the theme of personalization that runs through *Promising Futures* itself. If CISE was to succeed in its efforts with adults, it
would have to recognize that schools, and the people who work in
them, are at different points along a continuum of readiness for such
fundamental rethinking, reculturing, and reorganization. The staff
would have to overcome the "one best practice" thinking that often
pervades education and work with individuals in a way that they found
meaningful to themselves and the issues they were facing in their
schools. Unless these efforts were viewed as personally relevant to
their learning and growth, the possibility of significant change would
diminish greatly.

STRATEGIES FOR ENCOURAGING
PERSONALIZATION IN EVERY MAINE
SECONDARY SCHOOL

Several strategies were developed and implemented during the first two
years of CISE. First, our commitment to an invitational approach to

schools and districts meant that we would meet interested educators and citizens in their schools, not in Augusta, the state capital, or only at state-level meetings. So our effort became field-based, placing CISE staff and sometimes the commissioner himself in schools and at local and regional meetings, workshops, and conferences. Staff needed to be multiskilled, credible, and willing to travel.

Staff have been called upon to function in many roles: as consultants to principals, teacher leaders, and district superintendents; presenters at professional development activities; facilitators of faculty discussions and study groups; providers of information; and linkers of resources among schools. The invitational approach meant that our central obligation was to be responsive to the needs of those working most closely with students as they took on the challenges raised in *Promising Futures*. Two members of our center who are employed by the Department of Education as Regional Educational Support Team facilitators kept the network of regional REST facilitators abreast of the services available from CISE.

A keystone to these efforts has been a series of intensive, weeklong, residential Summer Academies offered in different regions of the state. The academies were open to teams of teachers, principals, and others whose high school and/or vocational center were interested in learning more about *Promising Futures* and its implications for their school. More specifically, the goals of the academies were to:

1. Provide exposure to the Core Principles and Practices through workshops conducted by practitioners who had successfully implemented such efforts in their schools.
2. Develop an action plan that addressed a current challenge faced by the faculty of the participating school.
3. Facilitate the process of working in school-based teams of educators through the assistance of a school coach.

Over the course of these academies, connections evolved and became increasingly evident among participants, resource people, presenters, school coaches, and staff. The academies were successful in creating an atmosphere were conversation among those working in the field to put the recommendations of the commission into practice provided the impetus for school teams to push their own thinking and planning forward. Midwinter academy reunions provide an opportunity to reconnect and reaffirm the efforts taking place in schools. The power inherent in such relationships, we think, transfers to colleagues and students back in the schools of academy participants.

A third strategy has been the state's commitment of federal Comprehensive School Reform Demonstration funds to secondary school improvement. In 1998, Maine sought and received permission from U.S. Education Secretary Riley to devote its entire CSRD program to the support of *Promising Futures* (a decision which recognized *Promising Futures* as the state's own "model" for comprehensive school improvement). This commitment fuels the center's effort to improve practice school by school and to develop demonstration sites and resources that others can call upon. All schools chosen to receive CSRD funds are required to address Core Practices 6, 7, 9, and 10, focusing on the development of common learning goals and Personalized Learning Plans for students; the articulation of learning standards, activities, and assessment procedures to students and parents; the creation of instructional teams for students and teachers; and making instructional and learning needs drive the use of time, space, and schedules (see Appendix). In 1999, eleven schools were chosen from among thirty applicants (or roughly 20 percent of all Maine secondary schools) to begin work toward these goals.

A more recent development in the work of the CISE is the advancement of a public agenda for secondary school improvement. The center formed a representative, statewide advisory council to help encourage and link statewide efforts at professional development, school improvement, and policy revision associated with secondary schools. CISE staff has served on the commissioner's statewide advisory committee on the implementation of the Maine Learning Results. Staff have, as well, helped to draft legislation and regulations that pertain to high school graduation requirements and have contributed to a major statewide initiative focused on "ethical and responsible student behavior." While pulling the CISE staff away from direct service with schools and educators, such broader involvement helps to impact our schools and communities by setting a statewide expectation for all Maine secondary schools.

IMPACTS: INITIAL EVIDENCE THAT SCHOOLS ARE WORKING TO PERSONALIZE LEARNING

Now, in the third year since *Promising Futures* was mailed to every secondary educator in Maine, we can point to some evidence that it has taken hold and that the CISE's strategies are bearing fruit. It is too early to definitively know if Maine youth are, in fact, experiencing stronger relationships with faculty, writing and using Personalized Learning Plans and portfolios, and following their own learning trajectories guided by these plans and by the adults around them. However, if the state can sustain its investment in CISE and if districts and schools can continue to make secondary education reform a priority, we expect a number of these initiatives to pay off. We report here some of the early evidence that makes us hopeful.

The *Promising Futures* effort has raised a consciousness in Maine secondary schools and boardrooms regarding the need for a more personalized approach to secondary learning. Conversations at professional meetings, discussions at high school faculty meetings, and school improvement planning sessions are now peppered with references to *Promising Futures* and the fifteen Core Practices. Most encouraging is the response from secondary school teachers, many of whom have said, essentially: "it's about time we really looked at the learning process and diversified our teaching and programs to meet the needs of the kids we're missing." *Promising Futures* has been, for them and for many principals, a reason to believe that their schools can improve.

Increasingly, advertisements for principals and teachers carry the qualification, "Must be familiar with *Promising Futures*," indicating that superintendents and school boards are opting for a secondary program that attends to differences among students. Newspapers and school newsletters carry stories and features that focus on the impacts of the report on changing practices in their local schools. In the first public stance of a statewide organization, the Maine Principals' Association at its November 2000 Fall Conference unanimously adopted a resolution endorsing *Promising Futures* "as an excellent opportunity to improve current structures and practices through serious reflection."

Indeed, the frequent mentioning of *Promising Futures* in public and professional gatherings—and sightings of the document itself—give us reason to believe that a movement has begun throughout Maine that, if sustained, could make a palpable difference in how and what future youth learn.

A second impact of the center's work is appearing in the eleven CSRD schools. For example, Penquis Valley High School has instituted grade-level faculty teams in the ninth and tenth grades that are cross-disciplinary. They meet daily, often with individual students, and have devised a structure for each student to develop and use a Personalized Learning Plan. These are the focus of student-led conferences at which parents or guardians and teachers are present. To accommodate these changes, the school administration has altered the master schedule and stepped up professional development efforts to assist all teachers and address multiple learning styles through diversifying their teaching styles. Similar efforts are underway in the other CSRD sites and will soon be occurring in a dozen more schools when the second round of funding is initiated.

Another CSRD school, Poland Regional High School, opened its doors in September 1999 and is the first new high school built in Maine in twenty-five years. It is modeled on the principles of the Coalition of Essential Schools and is committed to a core curriculum for all students within the context of a personalized learning environment. An essential element of the school is their daily roundtable meetings. The goals of these meetings are to foster connections between teachers and students, develop a student's plan for academic and personal success, and involve students in the decision-making and governance process of creating a new high school. Parents will also be a part of the roundtable format over the course of the school year during three student-led conferences that focus on an individual's Personalized Learning Plan and progress in meeting annual goals.

Perhaps more heartening are the efforts undertaken in schools without additional grant money or where grant awards were not initially targeted at *Promising Futures* as they were in the CSRD schools. In one case, four high schools in the Bangor area, under the rubric of the Penobscot River Educational Partnership, spent a year together studying needs and options for improvement. They each elected to pursue the goal of personalization: advisor/advisee programs, Personalized Learning Plans, and greater attention to student planning in the context of their thinking about their postsecondary futures. Leadership teams in each of these schools are advancing specific strategies for school restructuring and reculturing with this broad goal in mind.

Individual schools in diverse parts of the state are pursuing their own ways to make learning more meaningful for students. The Liberty School, a small, private high school in Blue Hill, has created a Community Council to foster its mission of operating as a Democratic Learning Community, and students and parents serve on several other committees that govern the life and curriculum of the school. Students also meet regularly in advisory groups where they focus on their own academic and social growth, as well as contribute to the daily maintenance of the school through a work component. A genuine sense of collaboration between students and teachers pervades this small school.

By contrast, one of the larger schools in Maine, Mt. Blue High School and the Foster Technology Center, has sent a large team of faculty members to the CISE Summer Academies. The school identified three major focus areas to guide their work: developing a greater sense of "connectedness" between staff, students and community; improving communication; and reexamining the school's academic program of study and requirements for graduation. Creating a more personal and caring environment for student learning is the thread that runs through these efforts. For this faculty struggling with many of the issues that face large schools, according to one member, "the *Promising Futures* work conducted by the Maine Commission on Secondary Education has provided an effective vehicle and roadmap for us to use as we continually look for ways to improve our educational program."

A STATEWIDE EFFORT CAN MAKE A DIFFERENCE

The success to date of our comprehensive approach to improving secondary schools through the personalization of student learning appears to stem from five factors. First, *Promising Futures* has generated strong advocacy for the Core Principles and Practices within schools. Bolstered by the work of CISE staff, some state leaders, and some university faculty, the document and its propositions have resonated with frontline educators. It has given many people the language and the courage to promote recommendations in their own schools for more responsive and more learner-centered practices. The inclusion of students, teachers, and principals on the commission and our willingness to listen to the real concerns of students and educators in the state as we developed *Promising Futures* are largely responsible for creating this level of agreement and advocacy.

Second, Maine has avoided the dangers associated with broad mandates and structural approaches while asserting that the personalization of learning must occur in all secondary education institutions—our 118 public high schools, our eleven private schools that essentially serve public clientele, our twenty-six secondary vocational schools, and our private and alternative schools. We have emphasized voluntary, local participation in this statewide effort while insisting on the need for change and the personalized nature of that change. Key to the success of this approach is the understanding that educators, students, and parents will identify those practices that best address the unique needs of their own communities. While CISE has generated a strong following for basic principles of personalization, the journey toward their realization in every school in Maine will be as varied as the communities these schools serve.

Third, Maine's approach has required that state-level promoters listen sincerely to the frustrations, challenges, and beliefs of teachers, principals, superintendents, and parents—even when they appear to contradict the philosophy and vision of *Promising Futures*. If trust is to be built, individuals must be engaged in a genuine conversation about their students' learning and their own practices, for it is through these conversations that they can seek and find their own best solutions. CISE staff have approached local schools ready to both explain and advocate for the vision embedded in *Promising Futures*, but they visited those schools also as learners, ready to listen and talk with others to identify how CISE and the state can support and facilitate each school in the monumental effort to succeed with every student.

Fourth, the state has served as a convener of people concerned about secondary education and as a facilitator of thinking and planning for improvement. CISE has initiated workshops and established Summer Academies to give interested adults and students opportunities to inquire into their own learning and teaching practices and to explore alternatives to them. High schools are noted for their sense of isolation and the resilience of their structures and cultures. Bringing people together who share a common purpose is perhaps the single, most visible step that can be taken to begin to value people and to create a culture that supports greater personalization in schools. We have learned that educators who themselves feel depersonalized by their environments face extraordinary odds in personalizing the learning and the school experiences of their students.

Finally, *Promising Futures* has met with success because students lie so clearly at the heart of the document and the efforts of CISE. *Promising Futures* describes Maine kids and explores the challenges they face as learners and as young adults emerging into an uncertain and changing world. It is filled with the words of these youth and invites adults to think hard about how their current practices and attitudes affect what and how these adolescents are learning and growing. Without preaching, it has encouraged Mainers to apply the Core Principles and Practices in the document as a yardstick in their own schools, professional organizations, state agencies, and school boards. It has helped them examine the ways in which their beliefs are voiced and enacted.

From this has come in some schools and communities a greater will to personalize the learning experiences of youth and decisions to change teaching, learning, and leadership practices to make personalization a reality. In many respects, Maine's experience has mirrored the advice offered by Nel Noddings:

Too many of us think that we can improve education merely by designing a better curriculum, finding and implementing a better form of instruction, or instituting a better form of classroom management. These things won't work. . . . We need to give up the notion of an ideal of the educated person and replace it with a multiplicity of models designed to accommodate the multiple capacities and interests of students. We need to recognize multiple identities. (Noddings, 1992)

The *Promising Futures* effort is growing into a movement throughout Maine. It is a movement that licenses educators and citizens to discuss the difficult issues that often divide schools and communities. Will we care equally for every high school student? Will we ensure equal opportunity to learn and equal success in learning to each child and her or his family? Will we apply equally the high standards for learning outlined in the Maine Learning Results? The state, in endorsing *Promising Futures* efforts, has said, "No longer can we, nor are we willing, to allow our secondary schools to be characterized as cold, uncaring institutions. They must educate every student to high standards and care for each student's future success. Only then will every one of our youth have the promising future we owe him and her."

RESOURCES

Noddings, N. (1992). "The Challenge to Care in Schools: An Alternative Approach to Education." In *Advances in Contemporary Educational Thought*, Vol. 8. New York: Teachers College Press.

Promising Futures: A Call to Improve Learning for Maine's Secondary Students. (1998). Augusta ME: Maine Department of Education.

Public Agenda. (1997). *What American Teenagers Really Think about Their Schools*. New York: Author.

APPENDIX

Summary of Core Practices: Maine Commission on Secondary Education

A. Core Practices for Learning and Teaching:
    1. Every student is respected and valued by adults and by fellow students.
    2. Every teacher tailors learning experiences to the learner's needs, interests, and future goals.
    3. Every teacher challenges learners both to master the fundamentals of the disciplines and to integrate skills and concepts across the disciplines to address relevant issues and problems.
    4. Every student learns in collaborative groups of students with diverse learning styles, skills, ages, personal backgrounds, and career goals.
    5. Every student makes informed choices about education and participation in school life and takes responsibility for the consequences of those choices.

6. Every student employs a Personalized Learning Plan to target individual as well as common learning goals and to specify learning activities that will lead to the attainment of those goals.

7. Every teacher makes learning standards, activities, and assessment procedures known to students and parents and ensures the coherence among them.

8. Every student who receives the secondary school diploma has demonstrated, through performance exhibitions, knowledge, and skills at a level deemed by the school and by the state to be sufficient to begin adult life.

B. Core School Practices to Support Learning:

9. Students and teachers belong to teams that provide each student continuous personal and academic attention and a supportive environment for learning and growth.

10. Learning governs the allocation of time, space, facilities, and services.

11. Every teacher has sufficient time and resources to learn, to plan, and to confer with individual students, colleagues, and families.

12. Every staff member understands adolescent learning needs, possesses diverse skills, and is a constructive model for youth.

13. Every school has a comprehensive professional development system in which every staff member has a professional development plan to guide improvement.

14. Staff, students, and parents are involved democratically in significant decisions effecting student learning.

15. Active leadership by principals and others inspires and mobilizes staff, students, and parents to work toward the fulfillment of the school's mission and, within it, their own learning and life goals.

For copies of *Promising Futures* or to inquire about Maine's secondary reform effort, please contact the Center for Inquiry on Secondary Education, Maine Department of Education, 23 State House Station, Augusta, ME 04220; (207) 624-6600.

CHAPTER 16

Focused Thinking

Aiming School Accreditation toward Improving Learning

PAMELA GRAY-BENNETT
New England Association of Schools and Colleges

INTRODUCTION

The year 2000 carried with it a lot of hoopla: celebrations, new millennium resolutions, anxiety that changes made wouldn't be right, wouldn't work. The same things were felt in accreditation in New England. The year 2000 brought with it celebrated and profound changes in the accreditation process of the Commission on Public Secondary Schools (CPSS), changes that the region's secondary schools felt as a quiet revolution of the purpose of schools and the purpose of learning, teaching, and leading. Those intimately involved were worried that it might be too much change undertaken too quickly, that the changes wouldn't be right and might not work. Revolutions occur when a group takes responsibility for significant and quick change because there is no alternative and what exists doesn't work and may even be detrimental. That's just what happened in New England. It happened very quietly, but in response to increasing noise.

The grumbling had started in the early 1990s. The Commission on Public Secondary Schools, one of five commissions in the New England Association of Schools and Colleges, the region's accrediting body, began a decade-long period of introspection and redefinition of the standards and process for accrediting public secondary schools, a talking-out-loud reexamination that reflected a growing understanding that the traditional accreditation process and priorities had to change in order to stay vital and relevant to schools. The changes inevitably led to a focus on personalization in terms of the unique needs of students and the unique needs of the teachers and leaders in schools.

The talking and the grumbling were preceded by plodding, appropriate, and unfocused changes that evolved over time and were grounded in several seminal shifts in thinking in the mid- and late 1980s. They involved (1) an adjustment to the standards, (2) a change in the information schools reported to the commission, and (3) a broadening of my own knowledge as the commission director of school evaluation and accountability systems.

BEGINNING CHANGES IN THE STANDARDS—THE 1980s

From their initial establishment in the 1960s, the Standards of Membership were about the things that went into schools and supported their functioning. Today's term would be "inputs": books, guidance services, library resources, facilities, staffing levels, broad processes to create the curriculum, records, and financial support. They had titles such as Philosophy and Objectives, Program of Studies, Administration, Records, School Facilities, Educational Media Services—Library and Audiovisual, and School Atmosphere. The academic and cultural focus was limited to three standards:

- Standard on Philosophy and Objectives: "The school shall have a clearly stated educational philosophy which shall be supported by definitely stated objectives designed to meet the needs of the students and community served."
- Standard on Program of Studies: "The school shall have a carefully planned program of studies and activities consistent with its stated philosophy and objectives."
- Standard on School Atmosphere: "The school shall have an appropriate intellectual atmosphere which indicates that an effective educational program prevails."

Any changes in the standards from 1968–1985 were relatively minor, involving such things as changes in titles from "Guidance Services" to "Student Services," "Philosophy and Objectives" to "Philosophy," and "Educational Media Services—Library and Audio-visual" to "Educational Media Services."

But in 1985 a bold step was taken to require that schools meet a new standard entitled Pupil Performance/Educational Results. The standard read:

> There shall be a systematic and continuous evaluation of progress in achieving the goals of the school. The level of pupil performance in all courses and activities shall be commensurate with the abilities of the students and the expectations of the school and community.

For the first time there was agreement in the New England educational community served by the commission that discussion of the results of schooling warranted a separate standard and that schools should be held accountable for achieving articulated school goals, which at the time were typically in the form of objectives about what the adults in the school would do and provide.

There was also imbedded in the new standard a clear suggestion that there should be different expectations for different students because students had differing abilities. Though weakly stated and ultimately weakly monitored by the commission, commitment to and accountability for school goals entered the accreditation scene in the 1980s and set the stage for accountability for a different kind of school goals in the late 1990s and the year 2000. The concept of having different expectations for different students was the 1980s version of personalization. Though discriminatory by today's standards, the statement was significant because it was the first to reflect learning goals for kids.

The introduction of this standard was reported to have caused great consternation not only on the part of schools undergoing a self-study in preparation for a comprehensive decennial evaluation, but also on the part of team chairs. Gary Baker, who provided training to team chairs regarding the new standard which was to go into effect in 1985, commented, "The general reaction was that the team chairs thought it was more bureaucracy, more red tape, just another example of a new educational fad that would go its way and create more work, but would not really be necessary." Member schools and chairs didn't know what the standard meant. There was tacit agreement, however, that it was appropriate that an accrediting agency look at the results of education, even if it was achievement of school-specific goals regarding what educators would do and provide for students.

By 1988, at the time of a scheduled review of the Standards for Accreditation, the commission voted another significant standards shift. This time its standard on "Curriculum" was changed to "Curriculum and Instruction." Such a change reflected general acceptance that the accreditation process should not only look at what is taught (curriculum), but also how it's taught (instruction). The new standard read:

> The curriculum, including student activities, shall be designed to fulfill the philosophy and goals of the school and shall be diversified and balanced. There shall be evidence of coordination within and between subject areas and between grade levels. Instruction shall be consistent with the school's philosophy and goals and shall be supported by research on teaching and learning. Data from the assessment of educational progress shall be used on an ongoing basis to improve curriculum and instruction.

The changes in the Standards for Accreditation in the 1980s likely seem quite tame when seen through a lens today. The region's accrediting association never viewed itself as having the responsibility for spearheading change, but rather just doing what the membership wanted and perhaps pushing schools in safe ways. In retrospect the changes were reflective of the understanding of practitioners of what they should be looking at or talking about with regard to school improvement.

In spite of these alterations, nothing significant changed in the content of evaluation reports or in the action of the commission around instruction or assessment, but the seeds were there.

CHANGES IN THE COMMISSION MONITORING OF SCHOOL IMPROVEMENT IN MEMBER SCHOOLS

Parallel to the inquiry and changes that were effected regarding the standards was the beginning of commission questioning of how it monitored schools' efforts to address identified recommendations in decennial evaluation reports.

Previously, schools had provided an update to the commission on their progress at completing recommendation from evaluation reports by indicating in a copy of the report the status of each recommendation (e.g., the number "1" meant it was Completed, "2" meant it was In Progress, "3" carry through was Planned for the Future, "4" Rejected meant the school challenged the validity of the recommendation, and "5" indicated that the school had taken No Action).

In the late 1980s, commission members expressed concern that the reports schools were submitting were inadequate because they contained insufficient information. The commission determined that without explanatory information regarding what had been done to address a recommendation, it couldn't make a reasonable judgment about the appropriate next step for the school's improvement. As a result, the commission began a process of asking for explanatory information about the status of progress. This action opened a Pandora's box, because once schools started to explain how they had resolved identified problems, the commission became involved in judging the quality of the resolution of problems, in effect the adequacy and effectiveness of resolutions.

This was the beginning of a different role for the commission. This expanded role went beyond judging a school's adherence to qualitative standards to judging a school's follow-up through the qualitative assessment of progress. This was a first step toward rigorous, local, case-specific monitoring of schools, in effect, case-specific personalization of the uniqueness of school growth and improvement.

Further, commission staff examination of decennial evaluation reports revealed that teams and team chairs needed to better explain the "Perceptions" section of evaluation reports that introduced the ensuing commendations and recommendations. CPSS evaluation reports had had a "Perceptions" section for many years. These perceptions represented the thinking of the team. Unfortunately, the quality and depth of observations of the teams as expressed in "Perceptions" varied widely. As a commission staff member I felt strongly that the explanations of problems simply were not clear or sufficiently developed. This identification of a problem eventually led to the provision of training programs for team chairs and to adjustments in training materials. The training of chairs to push teams to elaborate on the implications of their observations as they related to strengths or needs meant the establishment of a qualitative standard for evaluation reports. Reports had to be more in depth and more personalized so that they would be more useful to the evaluated school and more useful to the commission.

The shift in the monitoring of schools and in the quality of reports written about schools is significant because it reflects a change in the commission's view of its role. Rather than continuing just to do the safe things like push for changes in resources, buildings, books, and libraries, the commission decided that it must push hard for quality change, that it must get involved and make judgments about the adequacy of school practices and school improvement efforts, and that it must have significant information from the team about the school to really understand the school's strengths and needs. These changes reflected the commission's assumption that accreditation had to "stand for something" not just in terms of meeting the standards at the point of the decennial evaluation, but also throughout the decennial cycle. It marked a commitment to involvement with the school, working with the school, and giving feedback to the school. In effect, it was the beginning of significant personalization of the relationship between the school and the commission. This assumption of a new role was a significant precursor of the extension of quality assessment to the follow-up process in the 1990s.

IMPACT OF THE PRIORITIES EXPRESSED THROUGH OTHER SCHOOL ACCOUNTABILITY SYSTEMS

In the educational community during the early 1990s, school quality review and the Coalition of Essential Schools were gaining attention. David Green's work in upstate New York, southern Maine, and Illinois focused on what teachers were actually doing in their classrooms and how teaching and learning happened. As well, Ted Sizer's clear focus on getting at reform through a professional dialogue about teaching and learning, the use of critical friends, and shadowing students, a methodology he used in writing *Horace's Compromise,* made sense to me in my new position as director of the commission because it pointed to working with teachers to reform schools instead of working with systems. In effect, Sizer was saying that if the focus is on learning, then the teaching will quickly change, and the systems will then follow. The aptness of such inquiry and priorities was consistent with what I believed should be the emphasis in accountability systems that are seeking to reform schools.

At the same time there was a growing societal movement toward criticism of schools and educators. While Washington, D.C., developed Opportunity to Learn Standards which briefly made the news and then disappeared, state departments of education were increasingly arguing that the answer wasn't in "inputs"—those things they perceived were the subject of accreditation review and even Opportunity to Learn Standards—but rather in student performance, "outputs." The broader educational community's talk and the political talk were about what students were learning, not what educators were doing or providing. In fact, looking at what teachers do to assess the adequacy of a school was considered not only misguided, but also evasive and illegitimate. The pendulum had clearly swung from the far side of "outputs" to the far side of "inputs." Outputs were viewed as the singularly legitimate way to evaluate the quality of schooling.

By 1996 two things were apparent to me: (1) the new Standards for Accreditation, scheduled for a routine five-year review in 1997 and taking effect in 2000, had to focus on teaching and learning, and (2) the only way that I could ensure a focus on teaching and learning in the standards was if there was an inescapable reason to do so. The compelling reason I identified would be in the form of a commission mission statement. The problem was that there was no mission statement and there had never been one. So, in 1995 in response to a recommendation of a small, exploratory evaluation of the CPSS accreditation process, the commission's Leadership Council formed a committee to articulate a mission for the commission. In 1996 the commission approved the mission, then called a statement of purpose, which reads as follows:

> CPSS and its membership serve the public interest by requiring that accredited schools maximize learning for all students by meeting identified standards.

At the same time I actively sought help rethinking the work of visiting teams. Through a referral from Bob McCarthy, a leader in the Coalition of Essential Schools, I met Tom Wilson of Brown University, who had recently published a book entitled *Reaching for a Better Standard: English School Inspection and the Dilemma of Accountability for American Public Schools.*

Wilson's work showed that school accountability in England focused on teacher practices in the classroom. This focus paralleled that of David Greene and School Quality Review. Although I had initiated considerable work both on the standards for accreditation and the self-study process, what I had never really examined was the fundamental work of visiting teams. Wilson was the perfect person to help the commission tackle that work.

That's not to say that there hadn't been any tinkering with team process over the years. As a result of the commission's vote in 1993 to eliminate program review, the schedule of team meetings, the focus of team writing, and the subsequent team reports changed because the team's job was solely to assess the extent to which the schools met the standards, not to engage in departmental program review.

What had never fundamentally changed or even been challenged was the process by which teams worked, perhaps because it was never thought to have problems. As a result, it had continued as it had always been: a schedule of activities that included observations of parts of classes, meetings with librarians, guidance counselors, administrators, self-study committees, parents, etc. The reports resulting from such visits had begun to talk a bit more about instruction and assessment, but not much for the simple reason that the standards themselves didn't talk much about instruction and assessment. The body of 150 team chairs and assistants who led CPSS visits had approached school evaluation in the same fundamental way since the 1960s. In fact, they clearly liked knowing how to do the visits, and they didn't really want them to change.

I had a different idea. I wanted someone to look at the team visit so that I could be sure that it focused much more on teaching and learning, to counteract what I felt was legitimate criticism of the accreditation process: that team reports focused on everything *but* teaching and learning. Tom Wilson and I worked collaboratively to obtain funding for a proposed project that would examine the CPSS team visit, sponsored by the Regional Laboratory at Brown University. Wilson was an expert in school accountability systems. His book about English school inspection emphasized that practitioner judgment must be valued because such judgment provides the most effective feedback to schools about teaching and learning and offers the most useful information for school improvement. He was anxious to study American school accreditation in light of his work with English school inspection.

The LAB at Brown decided to make a considerable commitment to CPSS, one that expanded Wilson's study of the team visit by helping to support the commission's scheduled examination of its Standards for Accreditation as well as a subsequent adjustment to the self-study process.

Never before had the commission sought outside involvement. The truth is that never before did anyone think outside assistance was needed. But as the director of the commission, I felt strongly that accreditation as it was practiced was vulnerable to potentially severe and justifiable criticism and to withdrawal of membership. Accreditation costs schools money, it takes time, and it takes resources. Schools had to be guaranteed value added and a significant return on their dollar. Accreditation as practiced in the 1980s and early 1990s wasn't, to my mind, worth the expense and effort. It had to change. I also strongly believed that if the accreditation process were substantive, there would be no problem sustaining the membership.

Over a period of several months, representative member school administrators and commission members met to rewrite the standards. It was clear that this time tinkering with the standards wouldn't do. Rather, the standards had to be turned on their heads, totally rethought in light of the commission's mission focus on teaching and learning.

The committee charged with the task was led by Bob Mackin, a commission member, principal of Souhegan High School in Amherst, New Hampshire, and nationally recognized leader in school reform and personalization. The committee began by developing a scheme (see figure 16.1) to illustrate their thinking.

Input and feedback were sought from such noted educators as Linda Darling-Hammond from Columbia University's Teachers College,

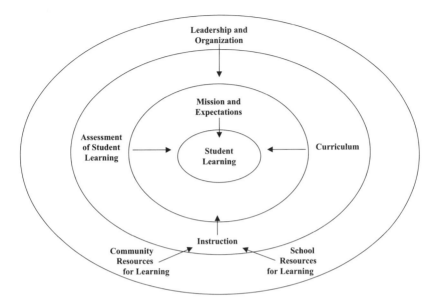

Figure 16.1.   A schematic of the commission standards.

Deborah Meier from the Mission Hill Pilot School in Boston, Fred Newman of the University of Wisconsin, and Richard Elmore of Harvard University. NASSP's *Breaking Ranks* was studied, and its various concepts were incorporated into the standards. Questionnaires were sent to member schools seeking practitioner input. A draft of the standards was sent out to member schools calling for feedback. Regional meetings were held to discuss the draft standards. The committee ultimately settled on seven new Standards for Accreditation, focused on Teaching and Learning and the Support of Teaching and Learning.

THE END RESULTS: ACCREDITATION STANDARDS FOCUSED ON PERSONALIZED LEARNING

The Standards for Accreditation that were created had a primary focus on the systems, processes, practices, and priorities of teachers around student learning, more specifically, learning that is engaging, personal, equitable, in-depth, and focused on growth. There were four teaching and learning standards: Mission and Expectations for Student Learning, Curriculum, Instruction, and Assessment of Student Learning. Another three standards focused on the support of teaching and learning: Leadership and Organization, School Resources for Learning, and Community Resources for Learning.

The standard on Mission and Expectations required that schools commit to schoolwide learning goals that apply to all students. This notion of committing to essential learning was strongly advocated in NASSP's *Breaking Ranks*. At first blush the idea seemed not so radical. After all, schools had for years routinely promised to commit to things in their philosophy statement. What was different was that the commission was saying that the commitment could no longer be about what teachers would do and provide. Rather, it had to be about the learning that was expected of *all* students by the unique educational community served by the school. Further, there had to be agreement on the meaning or definition of each schoolwide learning goal that constituted this schoolwide common core of learning, and on the level of accomplishment that was targeted for all students for such learning. In fact, the standard on Mission and Expectations for Student Learning required specifically:

> There shall be a separate document developed by the faculty that defines the school's academic expectations for student learning in specific, measurable ways, describes specific levels of performance, and indicates which level is the indicator of successful accomplishment.

The commission's 700-school membership had approved the standard, but probably didn't fully understand what they had gotten themselves into.

For schools in New England it turned out to be a radical idea. High schools have no difficulty promising that certain things are taught, for example, problem solving, writing, higher-order thinking. The notion of everyone agreeing that such learning concepts should be included in the curriculum was one thing. Having to agree on what was meant by such terms and what were the characteristics of "good enough" learning that was expected of every student in the school was quite another thing.

The reason such a commitment to essential learning is radical is that it challenges the commonly held notion of the purpose of a school. In New England, most high schools practice a purpose of delivering knowledge. This purpose is frequently encouraged by state accountability and school evaluation systems that focus on explicit, often innumerable, learning goals and learning experiences by discipline. Such a discipline-specific state focus encourages fragmentation and isolation of departments.

The commission's new standard on Mission and Expectations for Student Learning required, instead, that teachers, in effect, be hired to help students achieve the school's learning goals through the vehicle of their own subject area. Instead of subject area knowledge being the end, it was to be the means. The new standard on Mission required that teachers work together and share responsibility for ensuring that students achieve the school's fundamental learning goals.

A commitment to the achievement of essential learning also challenged the belief in the rightness of the long-held belief in the bell curve. If the goal of the school were for all students to achieve at a high level, accepting student performance at the range of levels illustrated in a bell curve would mean that it was acceptable for the vast majority of students not to achieve at a targeted high level. The commitment that all students will achieve core learning goals means that the school will not take "no" for an answer. It means that the job of the school is to know where students are in their knowing and to use such information to adjust what is taught and how it's taught, to help ensure that students achieve at the level desired by the school for the core learning goals articulated by the school community as reflecting community-valued learning.

The degree to which this commitment was to be made was further spelled out in the standard on Curriculum:

From the document that defines the school's academic expectations, each curriculum area shall identify those expectations for student learning for which it is responsible and shall have clearly articulated learning standards in support of such expectations.

The curriculum plan shall ensure that all students have sufficient opportunity to practice and achieve each of the school's academic expectations for student learning.

This new standard called for schools to be explicit regarding exactly which disciplines and courses were responsible for teaching the specific learning goals in the mission. Departments and courses were being asked to take "dibs" on specific school learning goals. Requiring this meant that the curriculum had to be personalized in the sense that it had to be tailored to community-supported and shared learning goals. Previously, departments could get away with promising that somewhere, in this or that course, school learning goals were addressed or covered in some vague way. Now the standard said the school had to know exactly where such learning was being addressed through the curriculum and instruction. Such identification had to be explicit.

The requirement for equity of opportunity also forced member schools to be able to prove that, no matter what configuration of courses students took, the school could guarantee that every student in the school—not just the academically advanced, college-bound, or AP students—would get sufficient practice developing the learning skills that the educational community valued. This commitment to providing students with equitable learning opportunities requires building a curriculum based on learning goals, not on Carnegie units. It requires that the school personalize its educational program so that it is aligned with and reflects the personal—that is, local—learning goals of the community, the school's private common core of learning. This is a radical notion for all but a few schools in the six New England states.

The new standard on Assessment of Student Learning also called for schools to be accountable for knowing exactly how well students are achieving the learning goals to which the school had committed itself. This was expressed in indicators that read:

The administration and faculty shall use agreed upon levels of performance, indicators of successful accomplishment and other data, to assess the progress of students in achieving the school's stated academic expectations for student learning and regularly report the findings to the public.

The administration and faculty shall use assessment data to determine student success in meeting the school's stated civic and social expectations and regularly report the findings to the public.

For member schools this was another radical notion. Once again, it was one thing to say a school had a strong commitment to specific learning goals and a plan to ensure that there would be sufficient learning experiences for all students in support of such goals. It was quite another to say that a school would actually commit to knowing where each student in the school was in the achievement of such learning goals. The commission required that schools use agreed-upon levels of accomplishment to assess the extent to which students had achieved school learning goals. Further, the standard required that schools approach the determination of such achievement through both formative and summative assessments.

Summative assessment was something most schools understood. It was evident through the use of standardized tests, final exams, and other assignments. Such vehicles for assessing learning are the *sine qua non* of most schools. Assessment—testing—is something done at the end of the teaching. It's the place where success in learning has traditionally been determined.

The standard on assessment acknowledged this purpose, but downplayed it in favor of requiring schools to check learning as it was happening through formative assessments so that curriculum and instruction could be adjusted to better meet students' learning needs, to assess student growth over time, and to help inform students regarding their learning progress. This new emphasis changed the primary purpose of assessment to one that valued the personalized knowing of what kids know.

Embedded in the concept was a challenge to the typical teacher's notion of the purpose of teaching. It placed the teacher as coach or advisor, the teacher as the one whose job it is to check learning. This requirement would have teachers transform themselves into gaugers of student learning with a compensatory purpose, sensors of learners with the responsibility to adapt what's taught and how it's taught so that students could better achieve the desired learning goals of the course and of the school.

The requirement that schools take as their purpose the one-on-one achievement of learning by all students in the school is the ultimate form of personalization. It puts the student in the center. It places the teacher in a secondary, supportive role. The shift might be likened to that of physician and patient. The physician's job is to get the patient as close as possible to the desired level of health. The goal of the physician isn't to give as much medicine as possible, but to give the right medicine and to monitor its effectiveness.

The standard on Assessment of Student Learning also pushed schools to assess and report student learning through a variety of vehicles. Schools are historically bad at demonstrating their own effectiveness. They don't show, or even know how to show, the community the learning that they assert is happening in their school. The requirement to show learning in ways other than through standardized test scores forces schools to think about the illustration and demonstration of learning to the unique public they serve. Most schools find such thinking foreign. Most don't want to put themselves out there to the public because it feels too risky and very personal. As a new requirement of the standards, the commission was in effect saying to schools that they have to take control of showing the community the learning that happens, that they cannot be victims of unfair, unrepresentative standardized test scores.

Other accreditation standards further pushed schools to focus on personalization. The standard on Instruction called for schools to develop a culture of inquiry, one where the quality of student works was talked about and where discussion of how teachers meet the individual needs of students is encouraged and supported. It called for teachers to meet regularly to discuss student work and instructional strategies for the purpose not only of revising curriculum, but also teaching practice. The standard explicitly called for instructional strategies to personalize instruction, to help students make connections across disciplines, to engage students as active, self-directed learners, to apply their knowledge and skills, and to involve all students in higher-order thinking.

Further, this accreditation standard called for instruction to be student-centered and engaging.

Initial accreditation reports based on the new standards revealed that the vast majority of schools in the region did not have such a culture; indeed, that they didn't know how to talk about student work. The traditional culture of high schools encourages and supports independence in the classroom, an independence that on the surface seems like the best of personalization. In fact, it's a distortion of personalization because it leads to teacher isolation and discourages the sharing of knowledge about individual students. The new standards asked for schools to place the needs of the students above the comfort and control of the teachers, an unknown and potentially threatening requirement for teachers and administrators who didn't really understand why such a change is important.

Another standard, School Resources for Learning, required schools to have an adult member of the school community who could personalize each student's educational experience. This indicator asked for schools to go beyond thinking of personalization as having a guidance counselor assigned to each student in the school to programs. Many high schools are too large and impersonal. Students get lost because of a lack of connection and a lack of caring. Many young people are disaffected. The explicit requirement that each student in the school have an advocate and a relationship with at least one caring adult was intended to ensure that all students receive consistent support in a new school culture that requires all students to reach high learning standards. The standard was again calling for teachers to rethink their roles away from being experts in their subject area to being experts in kids.

Finally, several of the standards called for professional development to focus on critical teaching and learning issues. They asked that schools provide time and opportunities for teachers to engage in intensive needs-based professional development as opposed to the traditional one-shot professional development workshop. The standards require that schools encourage personal engagement on the part of faculty in the personalized learning experiences of students and to gauge students' learning strengths and needs on an ongoing basis. A redesigned school cannot itself be student-centered and student-personalized unless teachers have the skills to redesign their own practice. The standards required that they receive the training and support to learn to change their practice.

So the stage was set. The commission had a mission that called for accreditation to focus on student learning. Through the efforts of Bob Mackin and the LAB at Brown, it now had standards on which it could hold schools accountable, standards that focused on student learning and the support of student learning in very specific ways. The standards spelled out the practices that should be evident in a school if it is to be appropriately focused on learning and the teaching, and has the resources that support and ensure a focus on learning.

THE ACCREDITATION PROCESS—A DIFFERENT KIND OF ACCOUNTABILITY SYSTEM

Changes in the standards were not the only changes prompted by the commission's involvement with the LAB at Brown. The self-study process also changed to one that looked at the personalized learning of the faculty regarding the personalized learning of students.

The Self-Study: Faculty Learning about Teaching and Learning

At a time when the public, federal government, and state departments of education were focusing on accountability systems about student achievement as determined by standardized tests, the Commission on Public Secondary Schools hunkered down and asserted that regional accreditation should be an accountability system that focused on what the adults in a school do that ensures an appropriate focus on student learning. In effect, the accreditation process became an examination of a certain type of "input"—systems, processes, and practices that keep the school focused on learning—about "output"—student knowing. "Input" and "output" became inextricably linked in the new accreditation process.

The self-study process was changed to require the school community to focus on the practices and priorities called for in the standards and to assess the extent to which those practices were in place. What differentiated the process from others was that it challenged the school to provide evidence to support its assertions about the existence of the practices in the standards, just as a decade earlier the commission had called for backup, explanatory information about progress addressing evaluation report recommendations in required follow-up reports.

Schools were asked not to complete questionnaires or write short answer responses, but to write thoughtful essays explaining the extent to which the practices in their schools reflected the practices called for in the seven standards. Although the number of self-study committees was greatly reduced, the challenge was greater because it called for schools to spend time judging their own effectiveness and proving their judgments. It called for schools to be reflective and to develop a cohesive view of their practice. Schools had never before been asked to prove, for example, that they focused more on depth rather than breadth, that students were engaged and challenged in their classes, that the school had a reflective culture where there was evidence of continuous discussion of the quality of teaching and learning, that teachers were current in their knowledge of best practice. Never before had they been asked to create a portfolio of representative student work. The accreditation self-study called for a different kind of introspection.

The self-study process had not changed substantively for thirty years. Schools were full of veteran faculty who had participated in a self-study process involving up to twenty committees for two and even three times. If the self-study process hadn't changed, veteran faculties would have been extremely resistant to undertaking another such self-study process. The requirement of seven self-study committees focusing on seven standards areas was different enough and interesting enough to engage largely veteran faculties, but it proved to be much more challenging than many initially thought.

Peer Review: Teams Learning about Teaching and Learning

The LAB at Brown's study on the team visit finally led to significant changes in the visit protocol, changes that shifted the focus of teams to shared conclusions about the school's relative strengths and needs and adherence to the Standards for Accreditation as well as more intense, personal team learning about the teaching and learning practices in the school. The first major change involved the practices of the team related to gathering information about the school. These practices included shadowing students, examining collected examples of student work, and interviewing teachers one-on-one.

While for years school evaluation systems such as School Quality Review included shadowing of students, this was a significant change: the work of accreditation visiting teams. Effective in 2000, all team members were required to shadow a student for half a day, not a length of time that was ideal, but one that provided significant information to the team. For most team members it was the first time they had engaged in such an activity. Its purpose was to force an understanding of the experience of students: the culture of the school, the degree to which students are engaged and challenged, the different instructional and assessment techniques used by the faculty, the adequacy of the facility and supplies, clarity of learning goals, interaction of teachers with students, etc. It invariably informed the team's personal understanding of the school.

Team members were also asked to examine collected examples of student work, a requirement that was approached by the teams with enthusiasm, but which was confusing. The majority of schools evaluated using the new standards and process had never even talked about student work, let alone gathered a "portfolio" of such work intended to represent the types of demonstrated learning in the school. The first group of schools evaluated frequently had school portfolios that were not user-friendly. Further, team members themselves came from schools where student work was rarely discussed. The result was that both the schools evaluated and the teams evaluating them were inexperienced in looking at and talking about student work. Although there was some confusion, schools and teams were beginning to think in terms of demonstrating the learning in their schools in ways far more school-personalized than through the results of standardized tests. Such new exhibitions reflected personal school statements about the learning that was valued.

Finally, a third significant change in the way that teams learned about the schools they were evaluating was through personal, one-on-one interviews with teachers. The visit schedule required that on the first day of the visit all team members interview two teachers, each for a half hour. During this interview teachers were to talk about what they teach, how they teach, and to discuss two examples of student work that represented how they ask students to demonstrate their learning and how teachers assess student learning. Again, this was a significant change for the evaluated school and for teams because it was about the personal instructional and assessment approaches used by the teachers in the school. For many team members and teachers alike, this was the first time they had talked about how they teach and assess learning.

The LAB's study did more than change the various sources of evidence and information to which the team had access. It also tightened and formalized the thinking of the team by requiring that all conclusions drawn by the team be agreed to by consensus. The notion of the need for consensus was not radical. Many team chairs would have said they had always, if somewhat informally, called for consensus in the crafting of "Perceptions" which introduced the team's stated commendations and recommendations with regard to adherence to the Standards for Accreditation. Tom Wilson's study of the effectiveness of teams stressed that requiring consensus ensured that every judgment, be it positive or constructively critical, would be right, that is, crafted perfectly to match the unique, personal, shared team belief about the quality of teaching and learning in the school. By reflecting the shared judgment of all team members, such conclusions would be unique and personal to the school. They would include as well the sources of evidence (e.g., self-study, teacher interviews, review of student work, meetings with students, direct observation, etc.) behind the judgment. This tightened requirement for unity of judgment was not as easy to implement in its purest form as teams first thought, but it was a sophisticated and appropriate change for teams, one that with practice would tighten the argument that team reports could no longer reflect the singular, biased judgment of individual team members.

The change in the visit protocol had a profound effect on teams and schools. Schools reported that they liked the structure and format of the site visit, stating that they marched the purpose of the visit and that the focus on teaching and learning was appropriate. Team leaders as well as school administrators particularly liked the student shadowing and the visits to classrooms for extended periods of time because they helped the team gain a clear sense of what goes on in classrooms. Teams reported that there was less isolation and pressure on individuals in the thinking and writing about the school. Team members worked together in a team effort to draw appropriate and useful conclusions. Teams clearly felt that the focus was more appropriately on teaching and learning and that the consensus requirements ensured that everyone on the team was of the same mind.

School Accreditation, Personalization, and Student Learning

Regional school accreditation has been around since the 1960s. Regional accrediting associations were the first to establish standards for practice. The accreditation standards and process always reflected the priorities and thinking of the educational community: They had to. After all, all regional accrediting associations are member-driven professional associations. The fact that the focus of accreditation of public secondary schools in New England shifted to student learning was as much a reflection of the realization of the leadership of the commission that accreditation couldn't remain competitive if it didn't change as it was a realization on the part of member schools that school improvement efforts must focus on student learning—if not because it should theoretically, then because the public demanded that such be the case.

The connection to personalized learning that developed was less than deliberate, but it clearly happened because educators' understanding of effective schooling is increasingly informed by the reality that personal is better. The standards to which the educational community holds itself accountable must by necessity get at the unique and personal nature of schools. Contrary to the trend by many state departments of education that all schools are alike and thus should all have the same goals, people in schools know that every school has a unique personality and culture, unique traditions, serves a unique community, and is peopled by students with unique needs. If schools are to work, then they must be built upon and celebrate their uniqueness. As such, all change must be based on personal, school-specific need.

In order for accreditation to work, it, too, must be personal. People make schools personal, and no schools are the same. In the 1980s the Commission on Public Secondary Schools recognized that if it was going to add value to a school it had to get into the quality and effectiveness of school improvement efforts. Once it changed its standards so that they focused on teaching and learning, it was inevitable that the commission had to focus on the quality and effectiveness of teaching and learning. Since all learning is personal, accreditation had to support personalized learning, and the learning had to be that of teachers, administrators, the school community, and students. In effect, the accreditation process had to ensure systemic change based on personalizing the school to the needs of students, and it had to change the character of high school learning for everyone, from students to teachers. Accreditation as well had to ensure that it encouraged schools to explore their own uniqueness and assert an independent pathway to school improvement by focusing on the effectiveness of instruction and learning as they uniquely play out in the school.

Accreditation is to schools as personalization is to students. Just as adolescents balk at being treated as members of a category, schools balk at being treated as though they should be uniform. The standards movement manifested in state standardized testing imposes a single set of performance expectations on all schools. It has effectively captured the attention of schools, but it has failed to prompt educators to explore their uniqueness and instead has deadened them. Accreditation in New England continues to be embraced because it asserts just the opposite: Schools need to be free to plot their own course. Further, the effectiveness of schools and of the teaching and learning that happen within them is not something that can be measured by the single indicator of a standardized test score. Schools are complicated and complex. The accreditation process in New England's secondary schools acknowledges that complexity.

The accreditation process is also fundamentally grounded in the belief that schools need to be treated as unique entities with responsibility for overseeing their own school improvement/learning process. Follow-up school improvement efforts must be based increasingly on agreed-upon needs for better practice for students, teachers, and administrators. The needs must continually be assessed based on data about practice and data about what students know on a day-to-day basis. The accreditation process has become a way to ensure that this happens through peer review and peer monitoring.

Accreditation standards support the personalized learning of students and teachers, and the accreditation process supports the personalized learning of the adults in the school. The accreditation process leads to personalized learning plans for schools, with the commission serving in the capacity of critical friends to whom the school is accountable. By insisting that all school improvement efforts be grounded in a focus on teaching and learning, the commission has forced schools to focus their reform efforts on teaching and learning. The accreditation process provides schools with a coherent view of change and a process to support it.

CHAPTER 17

Growing High School Reform

Systemic Change as Organic Adaptation

JOHN CLARKE

What is systemic change? Mechanical conceptions have dominated most discussions of the current school reform effort. In the language of mechanical systems, a control function at the higher levels of school organization requires new procedures at lower levels of organization that then realign themselves to fulfill new requirements and meet new expectations—improved student learning (Cohen, 1995). Mechanical systems obey mechanical laws, creating the illusion that changing one component in the system will change them all. As the chapters in this book have shown, changing the system of high school education requires simultaneous adaptation throughout the system, through mutual engagement among many people who share a belief in improved learning for all students.

While alluring in their simplicity, mechanical conceptions of school change run counter to the experience of most educators, who have learned to view all activity in school as deeply human, subject to the baffling complexity that permeates most human endeavors. By adhering to a mechanistic conception of systems while thinking about school change, we blind ourselves to the subtle processes that make improved learning a real possibility in the living human organisms called schools. A study of systemic change in five Vermont high schools suggests that change has to grow from seeds already planted in different high schools, fed by a constant flow of human energy interacting across all levels of school organization.

An organic conception of school change comes naturally to a rural state such as Vermont, where more than sixty separate school districts grow separately in mountain valleys lined up north to south like furrows in a cornfield. Each school and each district depends upon sustenance derived from the local environment. When nutrients flow naturally from the mountains to the valley schools, they thrive. When nutrients do not flow to the schools, they whither. A starving school may maintain its shape under these conditions, but it will also lose its color. It will fail to grow, declining into dormancy. Adaptation to changing conditions requires growth. Schools cannot improve student learning in a dormant state. The rate of energy flow between a school and its surrounding community determines a school's ability to grow. Growth occurs through the organized exchange of human energy.

Human energy is the key to school reform. While money is widely used to symbolize the nutrients schools need to grow, money simply buys time. Focused human energy is what school change requires. The statement is as true of first grade students weaving phonemes into meaningful words as it is true of a whole school district weaving separate projects into an action plan for districtwide reform. Phonemes do not make meaning. The projects do not make change. A school is less an aggregate of things than it is an ongoing interaction among many individuals, growing and changing in response to each other. It is the flow of human energy—human intelligence, you might say—that links small initiatives to a larger purpose, bringing flexible shape to the whole. A school's ability to reform its structure while it adapts its functions to fit new purposes depends on a steady flow of human energy. Mapping the flow of human energy during a period of high school reform can demonstrate how all components within the high school system can change as teaching and learning evolve in a high school.

ENERGY AND ORDER IN SCHOOL CHANGE

Educational research has not focused much attention on the flow of human energy during reform. In a research project exploring the work of problem-solving teams in school renewal, six Vermont educators developed the graphic in figure 17.1 to represent an organic conception of school renewal (Clarke, Sanborn, Aiken, Cornell, Goodman, & Hess, 1998). The tree at the center represents four levels of school organization growing under the bright sun of state and federal policy. Although legal requirements ensure the existence of all educating institutions, most of the energy for change, we came to believe, comes from those who are closest to the ground, teachers and students in classrooms. Most of the drive toward order, on the other hand, comes from central structures, district offices and state agencies developing policies and procedures to keep the school running. Growth during reform, we argued, does not result either from policy initiatives (top-down) or from classroom-based instructional innovation (bottom-up). Instead, growth results from the interaction of energy and order across all four levels of school organization. When all levels begin to interact around a shared vision of improved learning for young people, a high school begins to take on the character of a "learning organization" (Senge, 1990). When the levels of school organization interact continuously, changes initiated at one level of school organization shape responsive adaptations at connecting levels, creating patterns of self-organizing growth for the human energy flowing through the school.

We had developed this organic conception of school change to explain the relative success of problem-solving teams of teachers and administrators working on reform initiatives in Vermont high schools (Clarke et al., 1998). As we watched teams of professionals succeed in changing the circumstances of their own work, we fell increasingly under the influence of complexity theorists, observers in many fields who were trying to explain how self-organizing growth occurs in natural systems (Waldrop, 1992; Wheatley, 1999). In complexity theory, change does not occur in a neat linear sequence, as mechanical systems often do. Instead, change occurs as a whole organism or physical structure responds to complex changes occurring in its environment. "Though flexible, a self-organizing structure is no mere passive reactor to external fluctuations. As it matures and stabilizes, it becomes more efficient in its use of its resources, and better able to exist within its environment. It establishes a basic structure that supports the development of the system. This structure then facilitates an insulation from the environment that protects it from constant, reactive changes" (Wheatley, 1999, p. 92). While they appear contradictory, energy and order are complementary impulses in the process of organic growth.

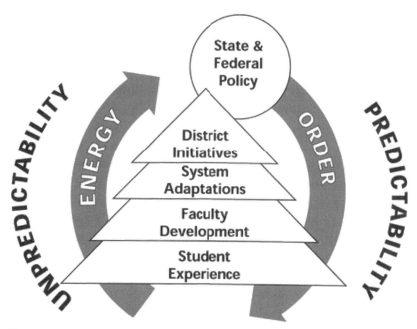

Figure 17.1.   One conception of systemic change (change tree).

To understand how school reform occurs, it becomes necessary to look at the whole structure at once. A researcher must develop a view of moving parts that remain connected throughout the period of study—essential components of a whole, living system. "One cannot understand the flow of innovations apart from the reform movements within which those innovations occur. . . . The idea of interdependence of the parts—the idea that changing a part affects many or all other related parts—is central to the concept of a system" (Morris, 1997, p. 24). To explore the intuitions that had emerged in our study of problem-solving teams, we set out to develop a moving picture of change in schools that were actively engaged in reform between 1992 and 1997. We discovered that we could "map" the events and interactions that constitute a local change initiative by interviewing the people whose energy supplied sustenance for those initiatives.

MAPPING THE FLOW OF HUMAN ENERGY

To map the process of school reform during a period of statewide reform, five interviewers began to explore the history of an instructional innovation that had influenced change in one in each of five Professional Development Schools associated with education programs at the University of Vermont (Clarke, Bossange, Erb, Gibson, Nelligan, & Spencer, 2001). Although the study focused on five high schools, the innovations themselves were unique to their schools:

- A cross-disciplinary investigation of Newton's laws carried out in a simulation of armed global aggression on the playing fields of a rural high school;
- The process of converting experiences in community-based learning to a plan for Personalized Learning Plans for all students at a city high school;
- The development of an imaging lab at a suburban high school, where students learn to create computer-animated graphics for local civic and business organizations;
- The development of an interdisciplinary global perspectives course at another suburban school in which students use sources from English and history to answer the question, "What does it mean to be Human?"
- A unit of study at a resource-poor rural high school in which students learn geography, geology, mathematics, and graphic design by completing a land-use plan for 100 acres of Vermont cut out at random from a topographic map of the state (Cornell & Clarke, 1998).

Each of these classroom innovations had become a prototype in its school for teaching and learning oriented to *The Vermont Framework of Standards and Learning Opportunities*, Vermont's guide to standards-based reform, developed from 1992 to 1997. Our interviews aimed to reveal how standards-based instruction emerged, took root, and grew to influence school reform during Vermont's most recent reform initiative.

As these innovations took shape, support emanated from five levels of school organization, described in figure 17.2. Beginning with the teachers and students in the classroom and then following leads from initial interviews into the organization at large, the interviewers set out to describe each innovation and record specific events that had influenced the innovation over six or more years, aiming to assemble a coherent explanation of the process by which a standards-based reform emerged and took root. When the interviews were complete, another researcher abstracted from the five narratives all the events that had played a role in the emergence of the innovation. He noted each event and the reported connections among events on parallel timelines for the five levels of school organization from 1992 to 1997:

1. *Policy development* at the state and federal levels;
2. *District initiatives* aimed at curriculum reform;
3. School-level adjustments in *systems and structures*;
4. *Faculty development* activities, group or individual;
5. Changes in the *student experience*: the classroom innovation itself.

Multiple connections among events during the innovation process thus formed a network reflecting the flow of human energy among the five levels of school organization. The maps revealed how human energy from the five levels of school organization interacted with each other from 1992 to 1997, forming five different patterns of change.

FIVE PATTERNS OF ENERGY FLOW

Figure 17.2 presents the pattern of energy flow in the five high schools, arranged in order from less systemic to more systemic, a ranking of the extent to which the five levels of school organization were interacting at the end of the study in 1997. The first school (A) followed a top-down pattern, using the policy drive from the state and federal levels to develop standards-based units of study for a few high school classrooms. In that high school, interactions among different levels of school organization were limited, engaging no more than two or three

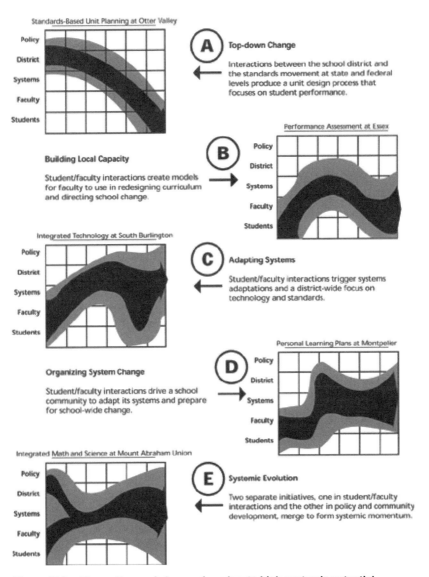

Figure 17.2.   Five patterns of change, from low to high systemic potential.

levels in any year. The initiative in School A ended when the unit design project ended and movement toward systemic change slowed. The next school (B) began to experiment with interdisciplinary courses when strong interactions between students and faculty in interdisciplinary classrooms pushed a strong program of faculty support into place. This bottom-up initiative never fully engaged district resources or the state policy initiative. Consequently, pressure toward systemic change declined in year 3 and the initiative was losing systemic momentum by 1997. Similarly, School C developed an "imaging lab" for students which grew rapidly to form energetic connections between four levels of organization in year 3, resulting in a districtwide technology curriculum. The absence of sustained interaction among all five levels in School C, however, prevented reform from spreading to other areas of curriculum in the school. Schools D and E both developed systemic momentum by 1997, in patterns that are distinctive to their culture and recent history. In both, events supporting reform were occurring simultaneously at all five levels of organization by 1997. Interaction among people at all five levels of organization was constant, allowing mutual accommodation to occur. Schools D and E are still engaged in developing personal education plans for all their students, based on Vermont's standards. After comparing the five maps, we concluded that systemic change depends upon high levels of energy exchange across all levels of school organization, self-organizing to actualize a shared vision of student learning within that school.

At lofty levels of abstraction, such conclusions offer little to educators working to improve learning for young people. The conclusion becomes useful only when we return to the human plane and remember that the energy required for school reform is human energy. We transmit energy to each other in our interactions, one interaction at a time. In the classroom, students interact with each other around projects— 100 acres cut from a topographic map, a new software animation packet, or the best way to express what it means to be human. At conferences and in-service days, teachers who share the same students form a partnership to link their community service requirements, co-teach fifty sophomores, or conduct "global armed aggression" on the soccer field. Administrators gather in conference rooms to fortify their courage for the new block schedule or to float the idea of merging academic departments. Policy makers gather a committee to draft new rules for teacher licensing or increased graduation requirements. To the extent that individuals pursue work separately while pursuing different visions for their common work, each interaction, even within a single organizational level, is fraught with the potential to fail.

Our study suggests that cross-boundary interaction is essential to systemic change in a high school. We found that system change becomes possible when individuals with different roles—students, teachers, school administrators, and policy makers—interact around a shared concern for student learning. The most powerful interactions in our maps occurred when the school community focused on instances of student learning, work completed by high school students to publicly demonstrate their accomplishment in relation to the standards. In a human organization, interactions across organizational lines weave the organization together, transferring energy and engendering a shared vision of purpose at the same time. In the schools in this study closest to "systemic momentum," interactions across organizational lines created a network for energy exchange that extended from the classroom to the boardroom. Only when communication is constant can innovation at one level of the organization force neighboring levels to adapt. When communication stops, innovation also stops, starved of energy required for growth.

From the perspective we developed in this study, we began to doubt that systemic change can be planned, designed, or implemented using the mechanics of systems management. Seeing the components of a school as separate entities simply reinforces the sense of isolation experienced by the people who learn and teach daily within their separate cells. Events that create interaction among students, teachers, administrators, and community members—with student learning as the focus—form the basis for further events and further invention. New innovations spring from the seeds of prior innovation. As innovations proliferate, school structures change their shape to allow further growth. As school structures adapt, they create the space for innovations that could not be imagined under earlier conditions. High schools grow toward reform when all the parts interact constantly, forming an organism flexible enough to adapt to the pace of change in the surrounding environment.

RESOURCES

Clarke, J. (1999). "Growing High School Reform: Planting the Seeds of Organic Change." *NASSP Bulletin 83* (606): 1–10.

Clarke, J., Bossange, J., Erb, C., Gibson, D., Nelligan, B., & Spencer, C. (2000). *Dynamics of Change in High School Teaching: A Study of Innovation in Five Vermont Professional Development Schools.* Providence, RI: Educational Lab for the Northeast and Regional Islands.

Clarke, J., Sanborn, S., Aiken, J., Cornell, N., Goodman, J., & Hess, K. (1998). *Real Questions, Real Answers: Focusing Teacher Leadership on School Improvement.* Alexandria, VA: ASCD Publications.

Cohen, D.K. (1995). "What Is the System in Systemic Reform?" *Educational Researcher 24* (9): 11–17.

Cornell, N., & Clarke, J. (1998). "The Cost of Quality: Designing a Standards-Based Unit of Study Project." *NASSP Bulletin.*

Morris, D. (1997). "Adrift in a Sea of Innovations: A Response to Alexander, Murphy, and Woods." *Educational Researcher 26* (4): 22–26.

Senge, P. (1990). *The Fifth Discipline: The Art & Practice of the Learning Organization.* New York: Currency Doubleday.

Waldrop, M. (1992). *Complexity: The Emerging Science at the Edge of Order and Chaos.* New York: Simon & Schuster.

Wang, M., Haertel, G., & Walberg, H. (1993). "Toward a Knowledge Base for School Learning." *Review of Educational Research, 63* (3): 249–94.

Wheatley, M.J. (1999). *Leadership and the New Science: Learning about Organization from an Orderly Universe.* San Francisco, CA: Berrett-Koehler.

CHAPTER 18

Conclusion: Gathering Momentum for High School Personalization

JOSEPH DIMARTINO, JUAN LOPEZ, and DENISE WOLK
Education Alliance at Brown University
ANNE MILLER
National Association of Secondary School Principals

There is mounting pressure from all sides to improve the quality of outcomes in our nation's high schools. More and more often our schools have been called upon to provide services they were not originally designed to provide. It is vital for schools to be able to change in order to provide the level of support needed by the new generations of students who attend them.

In *The Innovator's Dilemma: When New Technologies Cause Great Firms to Fail*, Clayton M. Christensen of the Harvard Business School details how businesses that are unaware of the shifting of consumer demands and changes in market climate tend to lose market share and, in many cases, go out of business. In a recent educational association meeting in St. Paul, Minnesota, sponsored by the Hubert Humphrey Institute and Hamline University on creating new urban schools (like the Met, charters, etc.), Christensen appeared via teleconference from Harvard. He said the same case should be made for our nation's high schools. If they can't be made to change, they cannot succeed in providing students with the world-class education that Americans expect. It is vital for schools to change to meet the needs of students on many interdependent levels.

The National Association of Secondary School Principals (NASSP) has been a valuable resource as well as a national voice for middle school and high school leaders as they strive to ensure the educational needs of our nation's youth are met.

That national voice was never clearer than in 1996, when NASSP and the Carnegie Foundation for the Advancement of Teaching issued *Breaking Ranks: Changing an American Institution.* The groundbreaking blueprint for action put forth more than eighty recommendations for restructuring the American high school in ways that will contribute to the academic success (and ultimately the life success) of our nation's young people.

Hailed as a call to action, *Breaking Ranks* helped launch a national dialogue on the effectiveness of our schools and the education they provide today's students. A product of that dialogue is the National Alliance on the American High School, a coalition of educational organizations and foundations established in the fall of 2000 to mobilize the resources, knowledge, and capacity of individuals and organizations to work together to shape policy, practice, and public engagement that fosters high academic achievement, closes the achievement gap, and promotes social and personal growth among all high school-age youth.

The alliance includes more than twenty-five organizations, including foundations; national membership organizations; educational institutes; universities; federal, state, and district education agencies; and high school reform model providers. In addition to creating a community of learners among organizations interested in high school-age youth, the goals of the group for the next three years include:

- Build the capacity of the alliance participants to initiate, sustain, and scale up high school and out-of-school programs that foster high academic achievement, close the achievement gap, and promote social and personal growth among all high school-age youth.
- Develop a common knowledge base on high school and out-of-school programs and policies that are designed to meet the academic and developmental needs of all high school-age youth.
- Inform and shape practice and policy at the local, state, and federal levels regarding the education of high school-age youth.
- Increase public awareness and engagement to support the development of effective high schools and out of school programs for high school-age youth.

The mission and goals of the National Alliance on the American High School and the fact that so many organizations are eager to be involved in its work are indicative of the increasing national pressure to improve our nation's high schools.

In the spring of 2001, the alliance commissioned a "mapping study" of high school reform efforts on the national level. Information gathered for the mapping project points out the danger of depersonalization.

When the federal Department of Education released "A Nation at Risk" in April 1983, it raised a bleak warning of "a rising tide of mediocrity" in our public schools. Although many efforts to reform schools sprang out of that report, there hasn't been much progress.

In the summer of 2000, Floyd M. Hammack, in a paper presented at the American Education Research Association, wrote: "The American comprehensive high school is at the crossroads, besieged on all sides both for what it does as well as for what it does not do. Hailed earlier as the embodiment of American ideals and aspirations, it is now seen as far too big, trying to do too many things and doing none of them well."

The dropout rates in major urban districts like Los Angeles, New York, and Chicago are more than 50 percent. According to the National Youth Employment Coalition, 15 million young people between the ages of 16 and 24 are out of school—almost as many as are in school.

Moreover, those youth who drop out are in many cases not entering the workforce. They're just "there." Jack Wuest from the Chicago Alternative Schools Network estimates that of the 53 percent of Chicago area youth who drop out of traditional high schools, more than 70 percent are just "hanging out." "Hanging out" tends to lead to high-risk behaviors like gang involvement, drug abuse, homelessness, teen pregnancy, and other rungs down the ladder to poverty and prison.

As daunting as these statistics are, there is hope. As researchers for the mapping project began to uncover strategies for reform that are working, one thing became increasingly clear as the picture began to emerge: personalizing the high school experience for students is the single most important thing that can be done to improve outcomes.

In *Democracy as Education*, Carl Glickman argues that the most important purpose of public schools is to teach "the young the knowledge, skills, and habits which enable them to lay more profound claim to the responsibilities and power of democratic citizenship."

He focuses on the students themselves and argues that democratic learning is:

- Students actively working with problems, ideas, materials, and people while learning skills and content
- Students having escalating degrees of choices, both as individuals and as groups, within the parameters provided by the teacher
- Students being responsible to their peers, teachers, parents, and school community to ensure that educational time is being used purposefully and productively
- Students sharing their learning with one another, with teachers, and with parents and other community members
- Students deciding how to make their learning a contribution to the community
- Students assuming escalating responsibilities for securing resources (of people and materials outside of the school) and for finding places where they can apply and further their learning
- Students demonstrating what they know and can do in public settings and receiving public feedback
- Students working and learning from one another, individually and in groups, at a pace that challenges all (Carl D. Glickman, *Democracy as Education*, U. of Ga., 1996)

The practices and principles in the following list are those most often found in successful nontraditional schools:

- Shared Mission: Successful schools almost always have a clear sense of goals and objectives that is widely shared by everyone associated with the school.
- High Expectations/High Standards: All teachers and students are expected to do well and succeed. Standards for student performance are clear and rigorous.
- Size/Scale: Students in small schools and small classes learn more, have fewer behavioral problems, and are generally better adjusted than students in large schools and large classes. Teachers also

report that they are happier and more effective in small schools and small classes.

- Qualified Teachers Working Together and Continuing Their Education: In successful schools, teachers work together, share ideas, and assume leadership responsibilities. Teachers have a voice and participate in decision-making. Staff development is an integral part of their daily work.

- Child-Centered Personalized Education: Good schools recognize the needs and talents of each and every student. Instruction and learning tend to build on student interests and knowledge. Students have a voice, and they participate in decision-making.

- Stimulating and Nourishing Learning Environment: The physical arrangement of a school and its ambience should encourage teamwork, enhance democratic values, and foster human relationships. Good schools reject homogeneous tracking. They often provide for peer mediation. They should be safe havens.

- Integrated Curriculum: Instead of teaching disconnected subjects, successful schools lead students to conduct in-depth investigations into real questions using all the skills and subject area knowledge necessary to complete the inquiry. The goal is higher-order thinking, not memorization.

- Time/Scheduling: The wise use of time and flexible scheduling designed to enhance teaching and learning is a major characteristic of many successful schools.

- Authentic Assessment: Because they are subject to requirements of their state and district, successful schools cannot avoid standardized testing, but their emphasis is on having students produce and exhibit real work.

- Real-World Learning: Many of these schools place their students in internships, mentoring relationships in the community, voluntary service programs. They understand that adolescents need genuine interaction and relationships with adults in order to develop values and good habits.

- Parental and Community Involvement: Successful schools encourage, perhaps even require, parents to participate in their children's education. And partnerships with community organizations and agencies connect these schools to the real world.

Early in 2001, the Carnegie Corporation of New York announced a new initiative for high school reform. In that announcement, Carnegie stressed the need for major change in urban secondary education:

> There is a growing acknowledgement across the country that young people today need high-quality education more than they ever have before. Success in the knowledge-based economy requires mastery of high school level literacy and mathematics, the ability to solve problems, work as a member of a team, and use technology. Real wages for high school graduates are declining and the increasing wage gap between those with and without post-secondary education places high school education at the crossroads of income inequality. High schools today must give all students the option of post-secondary education.

If we are serious about getting all students to achieve at high levels, we must seriously examine the needs of each student in our schools. To think that we can reach all without significant personalization of learning is failing to completely address the task. In the first five chapters of this book we presented real-world instances of schools that were implementing personalized learning in different and interesting ways that is allowing those schools to meet the needs of *each* of its students. Through Elliot Washor's description and Priscilla Santana's autobiography we see how personalizing learning as at the Met school can radically change for better the life of a student. Elizabeth Cushman-Branjes describes the development of student profiles at East Side Community High School and how they provide a clearer look at the abilities and accomplishments of individual students than norm-referenced achievement measures. David Gibson and Anne Friedrichs, explain how organizing school development activities to support Personalized Learning Plans at Montpelier High School has led to improving individual student achievement. John Clarke uses changes at five Vermont high schools to explain how high schools must develop practices that allow each student to realize personal aspirations and activate personal talents. And, Edorah Frazer, a high school teacher, uses her experience at three different high schools to discuss the effect that designing personalized learning programs has on both students and teachers in the high school classroom.

The Carnegie report continues:

> Today's students also need schools that give them experiences and knowledge that will build the civic competencies of tolerance, intergroup communications, conflict resolution and engagement in public life they need to assume the responsibilities of democratic citizenship in a diverse country. Unfortunately, our system of high school education is not designed to meet this challenge.

We agree with the Carnegie premise that our systems of high school generally are not designed to meet this challenge, and we have presented instances where schools and other organizations addressing the needs of adolescents have in fact addressed these issues responsibly and well. Pam Fisher, a seasoned observer of teachers, describes a high school system that engages all students in democratic learning. Patti Smith and Karin Schaefer describe the growth students experience by participating in a variety of innovative service projects. And, Adria Steinberg, Jane Milley, and Marty Liebowitz describe how community engagement can propel high school students toward learning through real-world experiences.

More from the Carnegie report:

> The structures of high school that have traditionally sorted students into college prep, vocational, and general education tracks now have increasingly severe consequences for most students, restricting their futures. Although most cities have a few magnet high schools and promising small schools or alternative schools, there is strong evidence that in all cities the overwhelming majority of students attend large, impersonal schools that are not organized to respond effectively to the diversity of skill levels, and particularly the reading and math problems, of entering students.
>
> These schools do not help students gain the competencies needed either for post-secondary education or entry into the knowledge-based work force. In these schools, teachers are assigned large numbers of students and are pressed to produce higher levels of student achievement

without the opportunity to get to know their students or to form a professional community focused on teaching and learning. These schools fail to engage young people, leaving many students bored, disconnected, and seeing no purpose in their education. Often these schools lose substantial numbers of students, particularly at the 9th grade. They graduate fewer than half of their entering 9th graders in four years, and less than a quarter of students are reaching the levels of achievement they will need for post-secondary education and workplace success.

Again, we have presented specific examples of how systems can be aligned behind personalized learning that is leading them to meet the needs of each student. Tom Billings, a veteran teacher and teacher educator, describes how a teacher education program embedded in the changing high school experience can bring new energy to professional development.

John Clarke, Joe DiMartino, Patti Smith, and Edorah Frazer, after shadowing students through a day at seven different high schools, describe components to consider while planning to personalize high school learning and to exploit the dynamics of tension between individual aspirations and the school structure. Bob Mackin, a principal who has designed and managed high schools that support personalized learning, describes high school systems that engage young adults. Mary Ann Lachat shows how schools can build capacity to effectively use data on multiple indicators of student performance to support equity, accountability, and program improvement. Hal Hayden shows how school communities can organize themselves to pursue the vision of a *Breaking Ranks* high school by activating the tension between aspiration and actuality in a high school faculty.

Of course, to be effective, change must go beyond the school to the larger systems necessary to support change. So, we have presented a number of cases where courageous innovators have moved the larger systems to become strong supporters of personalized learning. Andrew Seager and Cynthia Jorgensen describe the organizational dynamics that supported the evolution of high school education from the factory model to practices that fit the information age in three separate high schools. Gordon Donaldson and George Marnik explain the state of Maine's effort to support personalization in a long-term initiative for all students in the state. Pamela Gray-Bennett explains how a regional accreditation process has put high school reform on a cycle of professional self-examination and program adaptation to benefit students and educators alike. And, John Clarke uses a study of personalization at five Vermont high schools to show that systemic change depends on simultaneous adaptation of practice at all levels of high school organization.

As we have seen in *Personalized Learning: Preparing High School Students to Create Their Futures*, there are schools that are making significant progress in creating an environment that fosters these practices and principles and are achieving real results. We have seen proof that schools can and do create environments that engage and enrich the lives of all students, and that by doing so, schools can and do achieve the higher levels of knowledge in this information age. By using the tools and practices described herein, individual teachers, schools, districts, and states can and are building a new system where every young person is a valued member of an interdependent team of learning and teaching. We're not saying that it is easy. In fact, it is difficult knowing where to begin and how to proceed, but every journey begins with a first step, and creating personalized learning environments is the surest step to success.

Dr. A. Thomas Billings is a graduate of Salem State College (B.A. in history and M.A. in American studies). He received a C.A.G.S. in education administration from Northeastern University and an Ed.D. in educational leadership from Nova Southeastern University. At present, he is a tenured associate professor of education at Salem State College (Salem, MA). He has three wonderful children and has been married for twenty-seven years to his "college sweetheart," Sheila Farren Billings. On a personal note, she is Tom's inspiration. This year, after more than ten years of teaching at the elementary school level (mostly kindergarten), Sheila has taken on the challenge of becoming a high school teacher. Her greatest strength is her personalized teaching style. If we all learned everything we really needed to know in kindergarten and if you really want to become a successful educator, then marry someone who has the soul of a kindergarten teacher. Tom did, and he dedicates his chapter in this book to her with heartfelt admiration, love, and respect. She is his best teacher.

John Clarke, Ed.D. has been treading the uneasy border between high school and college since 1966. He began teaching high school English in Massachusetts, but also worked with Upward Bound for both young students and Vietnam veterans until moving to Vermont in 1977. At the University of Vermont, he helped direct the Instructional Development Center, developed a learning support center for students at risk and developed continuing education programming for public school teachers. As a teacher of new teachers, John developed the first prototype in Vermont of a Professional Development School (1984), then helped redesign the secondary education M.Ed. at UVM to grow within a network of PDS partnerships, five of which currently support the school-based teacher preparation. In 1994, he received the Kroepse-Maurice Award for excellence in teaching from the University of Vermont.

John has taught critical thinking, learning theory, and curriculum design in the secondary education program at the University of Vermont and worked with high schools throughout the state on school reform. He has described a basic approach to critical thinking instruction in two books: *Patterns of Thinking* (Allyn & Bacon, 1990) and *Teaching Critical Thinking*, with Arthur Biddle (Prentice Hall, 1993). With more than thirty-five teachers and administrators in Vermont schools, he helped write *Field Guide to School Restructuring* (Holistic Education Press, 1994). With Russ Agne, he wrote *Interdisciplinary High School Teaching* (Allyn & Bacon, 1997). *Real Questions, Real Answers* (ASCD, 1997) describes a team approach to school improvement, led by teachers and school administrators. His writing also appears in *Phi Delta Kappan, NASSP Bulletin*, and other periodicals devoted to high school reform. He has worked as a researcher with the Secondary Initiative of the LAB at Brown University since 1995, publishing *Dynamics of Change in High School Teaching* with six other PDS site coordinators in Vermont, aiming to give teachers a voice in high school reform.

Elizabeth Cushman Brandjes trained as an educator during her undergraduate years at the University of Vermont where she found its progressive approach to education prepared her to teach in the alternative school setting when she first encountered it six years after graduation. Her work in traditional schools for the first five years of her career helped her understand what the education reform movement is reacting to and helped her realize how special schools like the East Side Community High School really are.

In 1996 she began furthering her education at Teachers College, Columbia University, where she completed a master's in education in English education in 1998. She found Teachers College to be the perfect place for learning how to "teach against the grain" and the faculty in the English Education Program, particularly Ruth Vinz, encouraged her to teach full-time while pursuing her master and doctorate degrees. The strong support for practitioner research espoused by the department has helped her to examine her practice closely and to realize that changing schools requires much more than top-down policies.

Cushman Brandjes' conviction is that the work of teachers and their students can provide the evidence needed to launch full-blown reform movements, and it is this belief that keeps her in the classroom. However, because she recognizes the need to train young teachers to become reflective practitioners who are also interested in reforming the system, she also teaches classes at Teachers College in the evenings. Her hope is to continue to be a part of both the secondary and higher education systems, recognizing that partnership between these arenas is key to improving the profession and the schools.

Joseph DiMartino is the director of the Student Centered Learning Program at the Education Alliance at Brown University. This area of work focuses on developing knowledge about, and assisting schools to achieve, personalized learning environments in high schools. He is passionately convinced that all learning is personal and that we will never get all students to achieve high standards unless we accept this fact. Joe's passion derives from a lifetime of working with and advocating for the educational opportunities for adolescents in a variety of settings. Whether on a playing field, classroom, or vocational placement, Joe has always strove to insure that individual youth have a voice in their education. He has utilized his role as parent, coach, mentor, and advocate to get to know hundreds of adolescents, and his passion for connecting with them continues.

Joe is first and foremost a parent. He has often affirmed that he has learned much more from his children, including the four that were adopted from outside the United States, than he could ever hope to teach them. His children are a diverse bunch, including two biological children, two Asians, and two Latin Americans. Because he is a parent to such a diverse group, he has witnessed firsthand the services gap that minority students have to contend with. He is convinced that the achievement gap is directly connected to the fact that minority children are not able to access the same quality of services as their white peers. Through the lens of their experiences he has devoted himself to promoting equity in education for all groups.

His experience as both a biological and adoptive parent has resulted in him being an unashamed promoter of adoption. He was founder of AGAND USA, Inc., a 501(c)3 corporation that has served as fund-raising entity for AGAND, an orphanage in Guatemala.

Gordon Donaldson came to his interest in high schools by teaching in them and serving as a principal for a high school and a regional vocational center. His teaching career began in Philadelphia in the late 1960s, where he discovered the sheer tonnage of the urban system and the impossibility of meaningful learning for all but the most privileged. He taught for a year at Charlestown High School in Boston, where the power of neighborhood schools for good and for ill evidenced itself. Following that, he and his wife taught on an offshore island in Maine. Gordon's assignments included being an English and social studies teacher for grades 7–9, physics, sociology, psychology, carpentry, athletic director/coach, and assistant principal. The K–12 school was home to ninety-five students. His public school employment rounded off with a seven-year stint as "supervising secondary principal" for a 7–12 junior–senior high and vocational center in Ellsworth, Maine.

The greatest lesson arising from this checkered career? The importance to adolescents of adults who will care for them, challenge them, provoke them to think and to write and to learn . . . and who are NOT their parents. The second greatest lesson? These relationships between educators and kids happen best in small institutional environments that can themselves respond to the pushes and pulls of adolescent minds, bodies, and souls.

Gordon's work in leadership development and school improvement has been guided by these lessons. It was no surprise, then, that Maine's Commission on Secondary Education (which he cochaired) turned out a report (*Promising Futures*, 1998) that placed these lessons at the center of its blueprint to reculture Maine's secondary schools.

Gordon can be found at the University of Maine in Orono (where he is professor of education), driving the back roads of Maine pushing for better schools and better leaders for them, and living on the coast. He is the author of eight books, the most recent of which is *Cultivating Leadership in Schools: Connecting People, Purpose, and Practice* (Teachers College Press, 2001).

Pamela Fisher cochaired Maine's Commission on Secondary Education in 1997; this commission published *Promising Futures: A Call to Improve Learning for Maine's Secondary Students*. *Promising Futures'* principles and practices capture the commission's passion for equity of opportunity for all Maine children to access knowledge. This report continues to receive national attention in the arena of systemic high school reform. The work of the commission resulted in the founding of Maine's Center for Inquiry on Secondary Education, which continues to support and guide secondary improvement throughout Maine.

Pamela was the principal of Noble High School during its alignment with the Coalition of Essential Schools. The school has been recognized throughout Maine and nationally for its successful work in high school reform. National Professional Resources recognized Noble in its video, entitled "The Crafting of America's Schools," narrated by Dr. Theodore Sizer.

Over the past several years, Pamela has lead a variety of seminars on high school reform and systemic change, and she consults regularly with groups interested in designing personalized learning environments for secondary students. Actively involved in educational policy in Maine, she is working with the Center for Inquiry to revise the state requirements for the high school diploma.

Pamela Fisher has a B.S. degree in chemistry from the University of New Hampshire, an M.S. in secondary education administration from the University of Southern Maine, and a C.A.S. in teaching, curriculum, and learning environments from Harvard University. She is currently the superintendent of the Acton School Department in Acton, Maine.

Edorah Frazer has developed her belief in personalized learning as a teacher and administrator in three innovative high schools: Thayer High School and Souhegan High School in New Hampshire, and the Gailer School in Vermont. All of these schools are members of the Coalition of Essential Schools, a national school reform network. As a member of the national school reform faculty, Edorah has coached Critical Friends Groups in schools and trained Critical Friends Group coaches nationally. She has consulted with schools across the country, supporting initiatives designed to increase personalized learning via team teaching, block scheduling, interdisciplinary curriculum, and advisory programs. She is currently working to create and support coherent, sustainable professional development systems for Vermont schools. She earned degrees from Wesleyan University and Antioch/ New England Graduate School, and is a doctoral candidate in educational leadership and policy studies at the University of Vermont. In addition to her professional activities, Edorah works with raptors and practices meditation and yoga.

Dr. Anne Friedrichs is personal learning plan coordinator for Montpelier public schools in Montpelier, VT. She grew into this work through thirty years in public education, teaching preschoolers to college graduates, designing programs from adult basic education to unlimited potential opportunities, and administrating at all levels. She particularly admires the powerful voice of learners as they take on their final year at each educational step: the four-year-old who independently takes the shovel to uncover the buried dinosaur or who climbs to the top of the jungle gym to shout, "I am!"; the fifth grader who mentors the first grader in reading or leads a schoolwide student council; the eighth grader who designs and creates a video introducing newcomers to the middle school; and the high school senior who organizes a school assembly addressing the topic of teenagers as victims of sexual violence. Her dissertation researched how one public high school focused their collective attention on preparing all students to voice their strengths, interests, and aspirations to enhance their own learning and inspire new academic truths.

Dr. David Gibson is senior associate with the National Institute for Community Innovations, concentrating on vision and project development, strategic planning, professional network building, national partners, and telecommunications in learning. He is also the professional development specialist with the Vermont Institute for Science, Mathematics, and Technology, concentrating on higher education reform and statewide professional development planning. His research and publications include work on complex systems analysis and modeling of education and the use of technology to personalize education for the success of all students.

Experienced in project and group development, Dr. Gibson helps plan and conduct planning processes with groups and will help groups articulate their goals and make plans for action. He helps manage dissemination strategies through national networks of preservice programs connected with the national partner organizations.

Recent original research involves the development of an application of complexity theory for combining qualitative and quantitative methods in educational research. The method uses the STELLA computer software to build testable simulation models of the change process in schools. Teaching experience is regularly updated with graduate program teaching. Recent courses include "Managing the Future," "Leadership and the Creative Imagination," "Developing Capacity for Action Planning," "Standards-Based Curriculum Development," and "Student-Centered Classroom Assessment."

Projects frequently call upon Gibson's experience in grant writing, communications, strategic planning, budgeting and control, program planning, staff training, consulting, collaborative problem solving, and technology. His knowledge bases include the change process, adult development, performance-based learning and assessment, and working within and building new policy environments.

Pamela Gray-Bennett recounts that she was a very young and very new teacher when she had her first experience serving on an accreditation team. It immediately made sense to her that schools should be looked at in their entirety so that the pieces all fit together with deliberateness and integrity. Nearly twenty years later, in response to an advertised opening at the New England Association of Schools and Colleges, she attempted to sell herself to the then director by telling him all the things that needed to change in the accreditation process. He hired her and gave her the freedom to effect those changes. By the time she assumed the directorship, her perspective had been broadened along with her assessment of what still needed to change. She could feel that many schools just weren't working for kids or, for that matter, for teachers and administrators. The world was changing, but schools were insisting on the same deadly, boring approach to education. It was also terrifyingly apparent to her as the leader of a key educational commission that the accreditation process wasn't helping to transform schools into places where the atmosphere is charged with the excitement of learning; and where kids, teachers, and administrators are engaged, instead of being disengaged and going through the motions of learning, teaching, and leading. Her chapter in this book is an explanation of the journey of change that she helped to make happen. Much of it was prompted by her own felt sense that if accreditation didn't begin and end with a focus on learning, it wouldn't continue to attract membership. The more she looked and learned about different accountability systems and best practices in effective schools, the more apparent it became to her that a focus on learning is grounded in the constant checking of where kids, teachers, and administrators are in their knowing and their growth. She hadn't thought about it or given it the name, but it was always, quite simply, about personalization.

Hal Hayden is presently employed by Brown University's Regional Educational Laboratory. He works with the new Principals' Leadership Network and is engaged in designing and conducting educational research in many areas associated with urban school reform.

Professional experiences include being the state director of special education for Kentucky, designing and implementing educational evaluation systems for the states of Maryland and Delaware, acting as a local director of special education in New Hampshire, being a principal of a school in northern Virginia, and teaching in Baltimore City and Northern Virginia.

Hal's educational background includes a Ph.D. in curriculum and instruction with an emphasis in organizational development from the University of Maryland and two master's degrees: one from the University of Maryland and the other from George Mason University.

Hal is married to Peggy and has a daughter, Katryna, who works at the University of Maryland. Hobbies include playing bridge, sailing, skiing, gardening, reading, and "just watching the birds eat."

Cynthia L. Jorgensen emphasizes that the intensity of her interest in school improvement and the passion she feels about equitable educational opportunity for all of our students derives from several early, formative experiences. She was raised in a small town on the high plains of South Dakota near a desolate, poverty-stricken Sioux Indian reservation. Her parents supported learning, and her mother was a teacher in one-room rural schools, a local school board president, and a civic activist who was a leader in integrating Native American children into "town" schools—not a popular role. She received an excellent education in that small town that led her to love school and prepared her to move on to a university far from home where the world and endless opportunities literally opened up for her.

Jorgensen notes that way too many students do not have positive school experiences, especially in high school, and do not receive the support they need to capitalize on their talents. Contributing what she can to help address these inequities is fundamental to her career as an educator. In her first job, as a college English teacher, she worked with high school graduates who were ill-prepared for further education and were facing limited options. Over time, as her concerns deepened, she worked at a state office of higher education to understand better what "the system" could do for young people. Later she worked with a national school reform center in Washington, DC, and at two state departments of education in the northeast because she had learned that she wanted to focus on K–12 schooling. Currently she is at the LAB at Brown University where the central mission is to advance their collective understandings about how to improve schools, promote equity for diverse learners, and support educators in strengthening teaching and learning. This is a mission that she has embraced.

Dr. Mary Ann Lachat is cofounder and president of the Center for Resource Management, Inc. (CRM), a professional services firm specializing in training, research, evaluation, and technology services for districts and schools. She has more than thirty years of experience with school reform initiatives at national, state, and local levels. Her work has consistently focused on practices that improve student learning, and her monograph, *Learner Based Accountability: Making Schools Work for All Students* (Trinity College of Vermont, 1994), summarized research conducted in more than 150 schools on uses of data for school improvement. For the past three years she has provided technical assistance to numerous high schools as part of the *Breaking Rank*s project, a collaborative initiative of the National Association of Secondary Principals (NASSP), the Education Alliance at Brown University, and

CRM. She just completed *Data-Driven High School Reform: The Breaking Ranks Model* (Brown University, 2002), which describes how high schools are using data to support comprehensive school reform and the strategies and capacities that promote effective data use. She is the codesigner of the Socrates Data System, which provides districts and schools with unlimited capability to disaggregate data. Dr. Lachat has also written on equity issues in school reform and completed two publications for the Northeast and Islands Regional Educational Laboratory at Brown University: *Standards, Equity, and Cultural Diversity* (1999) and *What Policymakers and School Administrators Need to Know about Assessment Reform* (1999).

Marty Liebowitz began to focus on education reform in 1985 when, while working for the mayor's policy office in Boston, she saw education reform as a key to poverty reduction and community development. In that capacity she worked for four years on education reform policy issues in Boston. Since then, she worked for Expeditionary Learning Outward Bound, one of the New American Schools' design-based reform models. Since coming to Jobs for the Future, she has written numerous reports on effective practices for competency-based learning and assessment and a report on driving change in community colleges. Her current work focuses on policy and system changes in P–12 education, postsecondary education, and workforce development that will accelerate access to postsecondary education and create pathways to education and economic advancement through lifelong learning.

Dr. Juan S. Lopez has held various administrative and management positions in his 30-plus years as an educator. He currently is the director of communications for the Education Alliance/LAB at Brown University where he began his tenure as the director of dissemination and scaling up. During his five years at the alliance, Dr. Lopez has developed the LAB's state liaison system building it into an extraordinarily successful component of the LAB's outreach efforts to all levels of constituents in the Northeast region.

Prior to coming to the alliance, Dr. Lopez held a variety of instructional and management positions including assistant superintendent for the Bridgeport public schools, one of the Northeastern region's largest and most complex urban school districts. He also was superintendent of the vocational-technical school system for the state of Connecticut. As a native Spanish speaker, Dr. Lopez is able to successfully communicate directly with the growing number of Hispanic school leaders and teachers in the Northeast and the islands of Puerto Rico and U.S. Virgin Islands, which is the LAB's service area.

Robert Mackin ("Dr. Bob") has served as both a middle school and high school principal over a twenty-three-year period. Each of his principalships has led to national recognition for his schools. Fox Lane Middle School in Bedford, NY, was selected as one of the first "blue ribbon" schools of excellence (1984). Fox Lane High School, under Bob's direction, became one of the first members of the Coalition of Essential Schools. In 1991 Bob became the founding principal of Souhegan High School, which has emerged as a national model for school innovation and reform. Souhegan was selected as the outstanding high school in Hew Hampshire in 1994 and as a *Redbook* magazine "Best School" in 1996.

Dr. Mackin was chosen as 1995 New Hampshire Principal of the Year and was runner-up for the National High School Principal of the Year award in 1996. He is a member of the national school reform faculty (formerly of the Annenberg Institute of School Reform at Brown University) and recently served as director of Breaking Ranks in the Ocean State at Brown University. He currently serves as president of LEAD New England, an educational consulting firm that supports high school redesign throughout New England. He has been a workshop leader and keynote speaker nationally for more than twenty-five years.

In 1998, as a member of the Commission on Public Secondary Schools of NEASC, he led the rewriting of accreditation standards in New England, which, in turn, have affected significant reform in the region's high schools. His most recent publication dealing with personalization of high schools ("Hey Dr. Bob, Can We Talk?") appeared in the *NASSP Bulletin* in December of 1996. A book about Souhegan High School, coauthored with Peggy Silva and entitled *New Standards for Mind and Heart: Creating the Good High School*, will be published in March 2002 by Teachers College Press.

Dr. Mackin grew up and graduated from high school in Norwalk,

Connecticut. He received his B.A. in politics, cum laude, from Princeton University; his M.A. in education from Stanford University; and his Ed.D. in administration and school reform from the University of Massachusetts, Amherst. He presently resides in New Hampshire with his wife Eileen, a practicing visual artist and an arts-in-education specialist who works with teachers in using the arts to support learning in the academic subject areas.

George Marnik has worked in secondary schools as a teacher and principal in Pennsylvania, New Jersey, and Maine for most of his career in public education. He served as a member of the Maine Commission on Secondary Schools, which published the report *Promising Futures* in 1998. This document guides much of the school reform work currently taking place in Maine high schools. Professor Marnik continues this connection as a "school coach" with schools engaged in the process of school improvement. During the last several years he has become increasingly involved in leadership development work with teachers and principals throughout the state. He is currently a facilitator with the Maine School Leadership Network and an assistant professor in educational leadership at the University of Maine.

Dr. Anne Miller was recently selected to be the executive director for the Association of School Business Officials International (ASBO). Before joining ASBO, she spent several years with the National Association of Secondary School Principals (NASSP) where she served as executive director of their foundation as well as director of development and strategic alliances. She is also the cofounder of the National Alliance on the American High School and served as their first chairperson.

Dr. Miller also held positions with the Eastman Kodak Company for twelve years. She served as their director of corporate education initiatives for worldwide employee training, and as the CEO's advisor on K–12 education policy issues and programs. She also was director of education solutions and services, a group that developed and marketed image-based technology solutions to improve teaching and learning. Prior to joining Kodak, Miller was a teacher in K–12 schools and at the University of Kansas and the University of Missouri.

Dr. Miller holds bachelors' and masters' degrees from the University of Michigan and a Ph.D. in education from the University of Illinois.

Jane Milley, Ph.D.: While much of her professional career has been in higher education, she has been interested and concerned about the quality of K–12 education and the preparation of teachers since the mid-1970s. In 1991, while provost of one of the campuses in the State University of New York system, education reform swept through the state. She diverted a great deal of her attention to developing partnerships between the university and the local school systems, and simultaneously reorganized the university to develop a school of education that would focus on education reform and quality teacher preparation. As she became more knowledgeable about the K–12 national reform agenda, Teach America emerged on the agenda of the American Association of Schools and Colleges. Her team's work with the local community, the Private Industry Council, and the unfolding of professional schools of development was recognized at the national level, and the team participated in two national summer institutes with other national leaders. Since that time she has continued to deepen her knowledge and involvement in K–12 reform with excursions out of higher education to direct a business/education partnership, to actively participate in the Holmes Partnership, and then to join Jobs for the Future. Her current work focuses on developing a more integrated system of education, with well-planned and coordinated transitions from high school to postsecondary education resulting in progressive educational attainment and credentials for all learners. At the same time she remains concerned that education be connected to learner interests and abilities as well as opportunities to apply learning in a "real" world context.

Karin Schaefer is a visual artist who lives and works in New York City. She exhibits in New York and has an upcoming exhibition in the Barbican Center in London. In addition to directing Side by Side, she has worked in a variety of capacities to bring the arts to a diverse population of children and adults. Experience in New York includes artist's residency at the Isamu Noguchi Garden Museum, arts and literacy consultant for the Partnership for After School Education (PASE), art director for the Rheedlen Foundation, art director for Borax Films and

Cicala Filmworks, and kindergarten teacher at the Brooklyn Waldorf Kindergarten.

Andrew Seager: An enduring passion in his life has been to understand the dynamics of change and seek to support purposeful change within individuals, in organizations, and at a larger scale. Working with high schools and attending to the needs of their students has been a recurring theme for him within that more expansive topic area.

Mr. Seager's first job after college was as assistant director of an Upward Bound program that served students and high schools in the most rural parts of Maine. Later, when he returned to the United States after years of working for rural change in Africa, he became codirector of an alternative high school. The population the high school served was once again primarily those who were least economically advantaged. This project gave him time to return to the theme of change and continuity in high schools. He continues to be engaged by evolving questions about high schools because he finds it so difficult to make sense of his own high school career. The alternative high school project helped sharpen some of those questions such as, What is the relationship between change and learning? and, Why are high schools so difficult to change? Emphasizing that high schools seem to be semi-independent organizations but are locked into larger educational, community, and political systems that influence them and sometimes hold them hostage, he asks, How do we help those who work in them full-time interact more fruitfully with their environment to bring about change? Recognizing that students are those who have to do the work of learning, he asks the question, How can their multiple perspectives and concerns be integrated into the daily work of high schools? In seeking answers, his own learning goes on.

Patti Smith, Ed.D. is the assistant director of student centered learning at the Education Alliance at Brown University, where she is involved with personalizing the learning experience for high school students by assisting districts and schools with implementing the *Breaking Ranks* model for high school reform. She is the executive director of Side by Side Youth Leadership Program, a service-learning program working with college-age students to teach them leadership skills through mentoring and community living. The program is located at Sunbridge College in NY. She has been a school designer for Expeditionary Learning Outward Bound and has taught kindergarten, middle school, and postsecondary students. She is the author of *More Lifeways*, a book on family life in the 1900s, and of *Taking a Risk in Education: Waldorf-Inspired Public Schools* and *Urban Waldorf: A Day in the Life of an Urban Public School*, both documentary films about education renewal.

Adria Steinberg's introduction to high school reform came in 1962 when, as a senior in a Washington, DC, high school, she joined other students from across the city to form High School Students for a Better Education. In the nearly forty years since, the passion to improve high school has led her into the projects that have shaped her career: founding and leading an alternative high school; writing and editing *The Harvard Education Letter*; working with the National Coalition of Advocates for Students on Our Children at Risk; revamping a vocational education program at an urban high school, which she then wrote about in *Real Learning, Real Work* (Routledge Press, 1997) and *City-Works* (New Press, 1999); doing research, policy, and professional development work relating to school-to-work and other forms of personal and community connected learning at Jobs for the Future, where she coauthored a book, *Schooling for the Real World* (Jossey-Bass, 1999); and numerous publications on project-based learning, work-based learning, and the redesign of comprehensive high schools, including *Knowing and Doing: Connecting Learning and Work* (published by the Northeast and Islands Regional Educational Laboratory at Brown University) and *Reinventing High School* (published with the U.S. Department of Education's New American High Schools initiative).

In her current work at Jobs for the Future, she is directing a multiyear initiative called From the Margins to the Mainstream, the goal of which is to translate into policies and lasting institutional arrangements the practices of personal and engaged learning so evident in a growing number of small schools, as well as in arts, youth, and community development programs that young people gravitate toward in their discretionary hours.

Elliot Washor is coprincipal of the Metropolitan Regional Career and Technical Center. He has been involved in school reform for more than twenty years as a teacher, administrator, and video producer. He has taught all levels from kindergarten through college, in urban and rural settings, across all disciplines. He has served as a consultant to schools throughout the United States and Europe. At Thayer High School, his professional development programs won an Innovations in State and Local Government Award from the Ford Foundation and the Kennedy School of Government at Harvard.

Elliot has a M.A. in education from Harvard University. He is also codirector of the Big Picture Company along with Dennis Littkey.

Martha Williams is cofounder, vice president, and director of the Center for Resource Management, Inc. (CRM), a professional services firm specializing in training, research, evaluation, and technology services for schools and school districts. She has been a key developer of CRM services that focus on improving student achievement, and has developed practical hands-on resources that support school reform. Ms. Williams designs CRM services related to helping schools and districts use data for accountability, program evaluation, and improvement, including database development, data integration, disaggregation, and analysis. She directs the CRM software development team and oversees the delivery of products and services associated with the Socrates Data System, a complete decision support system that integrates data from multiple sources and provides districts and schools with virtually unlimited capability to disaggregate data. She has designed and led numerous professional development programs focused on using data for continuous improvement, served as the director of several state and national projects, and provided technical assistance to numerous school improvement initiatives. Ms. Williams has served as a consultant, trainer, and evaluator for a wide variety of programs and initiatives that focus on improving student outcomes, and has made numerous presentations at state, regional, and national conferences.

Denise Wolk served as managing editor on this project after spending much of her career working in the world outside of school reform. In the summer of 2001, she worked as a researcher/writer for a mapping project to inform the National Forum on the American High School by researching the various reforms occurring in high schools and assisted in compiling a report to inform the forum's work. Wolk also provided extensive fact checking and editorial services for Dr. David Kessler's book *A Question of Intent,* chronicling his role as commissioner of the FDA during the tobacco wars of the 1990s.

Having completed the mapping project and this book, Wolk found herself drawn into the world of high school reform and has joined the staff of the Education Alliance to try to make an impact in the lives of all high school students. She lives in a small town on the eastern shore of Narragansett Bay in Rhode Island and is married to Emmy award-winning filmmaker Cal Wolk. She has a son, Dylan, and a daughter, Ashley, who are the lights of her life, and to whom she dedicates her work.